The Cattlemen

by

W. R. McAfee

DAVIS MOUNTAIN PRESS

Portions of this book have appeared in *The Cattleman* magazine.

Published by Davis Mountain Press, P.O. Box 2107, Alvin, Texas 77512

Library of Congress Catalog Card Number: 89-90310
ISBN Number: 0-9623394-1-5

Printed in the U.S.A.

For My Sons

Russ, Joel, and Danny

Table of Contents

                                                                    Page

Introduction .... i-viii

Part I

As Roy Told It 1

Part II

As Others Remembered Them......................... 99

Part III

As I Knew Them..................................... 193

The Interviews 243

Part IV

Historical Pictures................................. 246

Index... 261

Acknowledgements

I wish to extend my thanks to the following people for their help and encouragement while working on **The Cattlemen**: Mrs. Dorothy Reid, Fort Davis, Texas; Jack Scannell, Midland, Texas; Pat Mulloy, Fort Davis, Texas; Lou Reid, Alpine, Texas; J. W. and Betty Reid, Silverton, Texas; Josie McCutcheon, Hunt, Texas; D. D. and Marjorie Patteson, Hunt, Texas; Mrs. Rena Duncan, Fort Davis, Texas; Allison Ryan, Marfa, Texas; and C. K. Smith, Marfa, Texas.

INTRODUCTION

There was a time when the word cowboy meant something entirely different than it does today, a time long before the dime store novels and the flickering talkies, before the electronic cyclops, before the Hanks and Waylons and Willies and Jerry Jeffs. That time was long before my father's or my era; and belonged, really, to the old ones who made the word. They're all gone now, though.

To understand what the word cowboy really meant, you would have had to have known the superb and incomparable skills—save those of the Steppes horsemen—of the hacienda vaquero who worked and died for the privilege of feeding himself and his family. Or you would have had to have been mustered out of a Civil War army to drift west, looking for work, finally finding it horseback up trails named Chisolm and Loving and Goodnight, working for cattlemen still carrying the lead or scars, pushing bush-mean Longhorn cattle—five million by one count—ahead of you; survivors, too, in a pitiless environment that usually allowed only one mistake. You and a few thousand like you would have gone up those trails at different times earning thirty-odd dollars a month frying your brains astride a horse that would as soon kick them out as pack you; would have had to wash down flour-heavy chuck wagon food with scalding black coffee whole-bean broiled; would have had to endure choking dust and boils and chilling rains that left you shivering uncontrollably in the saddle; arriving finally at some clapboard shacktown to blow several months wages beginning with a ten-dollar bath and a new suit of clothes and ending with a multiday drunk and gambling orgy with, if you were lucky, a woman who wasn't infected.

Perhaps if you were perceptive or wanted something a little different, you would have begun setting aside some of your money at the end of those drives. Mostly, though, you would have left those towns with only your headache and new clothes, often soiled or ripped from street fighting; would have left flat broke with parts of your anatomy wrapped in kerosene-soaked rags. Or maybe you wouldn't have left at all, having been dumped in a shallow grave somewhere for calling a cardsharp's hand or a dandy out over a woman, or having had your skull crushed by thugs or thieves infesting those early boomtowns, robbing you as you lay crumpled or heaving in an alley or asleep on the prairie just beyond the town, feeling up to the end you were somehow invincible after surviving those months on the trail.

You wouldn't have known this kind had always been with the doers, would still be following the easy money of the young or whiskied during the gold rushes and the First War's tent cities; would follow Texas' oil boom and World War II's army towns, complete with the same cheap buildings and cardsharps and painted ladies and now, bath massages. It will be the same tomorrow, perhaps, when star travelers return.

Barbed wire ended the trails during the late 1800's, but the early traditions and skills remained intact for several years. A few people, myself included, were lucky enough to have known some of the men who used these skills. Today I doubt there are five hundred left who do. These you won't find in week-night dance halls or punching at bloody bags in chic country discos or sitting in some whitewashed rodeo chute. Fact is, it's doubtful you could find them at all since they and theirs mostly live quietly and to themselves like those before them; its doubtful, really, you could recognize a real cowboy. That's how the meaning of the word got changed, you see, because few people know what a cowboy is—or even was—anymore. My interest with the word, then, centers on the men who deserve the title.

I was fortunate enough to have worked with and known two such men—Wade and Roy Reid—brothers who were born during the 1880's, too late to make the long drives, but still early enough to learn firsthand the trade and skills of the open range from those who'd followed the big herds. Being young when I first met them, I didn't understand fully what they were about.

Their ranch was located in the Barrilla Mountains about thirty miles northeast of Fort Davis, Texas, and didn't even have electricity, as we know it, until the Sixties. Up until then they used their own generator, drank their own well water, ate their own beef. They were completely self-sufficient. A pair of Levis was all one of them bought one year during the Depression. They told of people offering to work for food during those times. They also allowed themselves an ancient radio hooked to an old battery for early morning livestock reports and an occasional evening baseball game. The last time they took it to town for repairs they discovered no one made the radio, or its tubes, any longer. So, they broke down and bought a new one, and later a television, shortly after the REA got around to running them a line during the Sixties. They both enjoyed the TV until they died.

I first entered their world about six months after World War II started, born in a little house-hospital in Alpine, Texas. Some say you don't remember things when you're an infant; but I know that's not true because my father, who was working for them at the time, and my mother bundled me up and took me back to that ranch when I was just a week or two old. In the mornings they would get me up and lay me in a crib while they had breakfast or sit me on the porch with them in the evenings; and I tell you my body and soul and senses absorbed the sights, the sounds, and the smells of that ranch and those mountains, beginning when I was just a few weeks old. In the forty-odd years or so since, there has hardly been a day I do not recall the Davis

Mountains or those memories formed there as an infant, a child, a young man. The mountains gave me something—I can't define it—that I still call on and retreat to mentally from time to time. Living in what passes for a civilized world now, I've yet to shake a bedrock desire to return, not so much for the people—for most I knew are gone—but to the place.

★   ★   ★

All of this has little to do with the word cowboy, which I'd started out to discuss. Myself, I never pretended to be one, even though I rode a bronc or two and chunked a few loops. I knew better than to apply the term cowboy to myself, and would not let anyone else apply it either; scoff at those who try to apply it to themselves today. I had no real abilities or talent in terms of the rides or loops the old ones made or used. None of us did. Oh, I could do things about as good as most kids my age who'd been on ranches, but in the real sense I never earned my living with them, and neither did the others. It was, rather, a novelty I'd fallen into, could relate to and have fun with from time to time. What skills I had only enabled me to ride along and observe the people for whom the skills had real meaning, and to whom the word cowboy, then later cattleman, really belonged.

Roy was deft with the rope, could throw all the loops. Wade was the better rider. Both were in a class by themselves. They made their livings horseback early in their lives, using cowboy wages to put together a ranch—the Eleven Bar (11)—and a name for themselves as cattlemen; did it with work so hard it would have driven lesser men away had they even contemplated such an undertaking; succeeded in the shadow of giant ranches long-since history with enough cattle and land to support themselves for the next sixty years; succeeded patiently and right.

Neither were greedy and always seemed to enjoy what

they had. When they were past fifty, they thought they might be getting on "up there"; so, they invited my father to come to the ranch to work and perhaps take over in a few years. That's how I first wound up on their porch in the evenings—sleeping, absorbing, watching the fireflies or listening to the horses in the corral snorting at some boogery twilight shadow. They both lived and worked on nearly three more decades, however, and needed no one other than some occasional help at shipping time and, I liked to think, myself during my teenage summers. They complemented one another and knew what they were about. Cowboys. Cattlemen. They never dwelt on it or talked too much about it. The real ones never did.

No, the word cowboy has shifted—I'm not sure when—from what it originally meant, which was earning a living from the back of a horse to a rodeo chute and eight or ten seconds in a tight-fitting shirt and a pair of bright chaps and stylish hat before a screaming crowd. From there the country music crowd and the rurals grabbed it and for the longest time it was appropriate slander when applied to someone by someone from either the East or West Coast. One of the better rodeoers, after walking around a southwest coliseum between events at an annual stock show and observing the big store-bought buckles and hats and Skoal cans and back-pocketed Lone Stars—the whole kicker au naturel—said he thought about going home and putting on a baseball cap and tennis shoes.

From there the word snuck up on its critics in the cities and suddenly the hat and boots and Levis were by God voguish after Travolta and Town and Country made cowboy "in" at—yassah—long last. Some even tried living by a code they didn't understand and wouldn't have known what to do if someone violated it. The point being the word now is far removed—don't let your babies grow up to be cowboys—from the men who made their living horseback; who had to know how to rope and tie and doctor a cow with worms in rough country by themselves; who could get on and off a mean horse in the middle of nowhere; who could ride all day without water and little to eat; who could help a cow deliver a breech calf and fix a windmill or fence; and who, for more than a decade, slept on the ground in canvas-covered bedrolls stretched alongside a little wooden feed shack beneath a huge bluff, cowboying for other ranchers, all the while putting together their own herd and ranch.

Wade and Roy Reid did these things, and I consider myself privileged to have caught just the tail end of their lives. Their struggle to build a ranch from scratch never left them bitter or hard, and they willingly shared their time and place with family and friends. They were gentlemen in the truest sense—not without fault or tempers—but gentlemen who were unfailingly courteous to men and women alike, and on whose word you could depend. Somehow, in between the droughts and Depression and screwworms and recessions, they managed to serve on their Production Credit Association's board and chair their county's Democratic Party. Beau McCutcheon, a neighboring rancher, remembered:

"During early elections, we always voted a few hundred yards west of the old Limpia Post Office there on those little flats next to the windmill across the road from Bennett's Limpia House. It was on Willis' land, and we always just set up a tent to vote in. Wade Reid was always election judge during the early years. Each year on Election Day, old man Lewis would come riding in to vote; and he'd get a ballot and rub his eyes and say, 'Aw hell, durned if I didn't go off 'n leave my glasses at home. Wade, could you help me with this ballot?' And Wade, knowing he couldn't read or write too well, would ask him how he wanted to vote, and would vote him the way he said every year."

★   ★   ★

It was the blurred picture of the black bear, though, that eventually led me to record some of their life. I found the picture in an old box one night at their ranch house. The bear was lying on the ground, obviously dead, with a rope around its neck. Wade and Roy were recognizable, standing beside lathered horses. Two women were sitting on horses, also looking at the bear.

I took the picture upstairs and asked Roy where they'd killed it. Roy was trying to listen to a baseball game on his old radio and mumbled something about Wade's killing it "out on top" so I showed it to Wade and asked him what he'd shot it with. The conversation, as best I recall, went something like this:

"I didn't shoot it."

"Well, how did you kill it?"

"With rocks."

"With rocks?"

"Yeah, we chased him along, and I finally got a rope on him and was able to pull him into a mesquite bush. When I did, I just stepped off and went to chunking rocks at him."

"By yourself?"

"By myself."

He went back to reading. Roy, I found out later, had caught up with the bear first, but each time he put a loop on him, the bear would "reach up and kick that loop off with a hind foot and never miss a stride. Damnedest thing you ever saw." Eventually Roy would have to pull his horse up lame, and Wade would close the gap, manage a loop over the bear's head and forepaw, and pull him tight into the big mesquite bush. Later years, during an interview, Wade summed up the Davis Mountain ranchers' philosophy about bears:

"When I was growing up, there was a lot of lobos in the Panhandle as well as the Davis Mountains. They was mean and destructive on livestock, so people went to work killing 'em out. But what a lot of people don't know to this day was that black bears was a lot more destructive than either the wolf or panther. Those damn bears would slap a baby calf with a front paw and kill it for no good reason. They'd do the same to an old cow's flank, and the cow would wind up with worms and die if you didn't get to her and get her doctored. And bears was awful bad about wading into a bunch of sheep and just killing the whole lot of 'em."

This book is about Wade and Roy Reid and about their ranch, the Eleven Bar. It was compiled from interviews with both men, and from those who knew them best.

To my knowledge, Wade and Roy Reid had no enemies and no debts when they died. They were, in my opinion, cattlemen the likes of which we will never see again.

W. R. McAfee
Alvin, Texas

Wade Reid, at far right with his rope still around the neck of the black bear he roped and killed with rocks. Bears were numerous in the Davis Mountains during the early part of the Twentieth Century. At far left is Florence "Happy" Reid, first wife of Wade Reid. Roy Reid is second from left. Jimmie Tom Bell, Happy Reid's niece, is third from left. Below: The group with the bear loaded aboard a horse. Wade Reid is at left. Circa 1920's

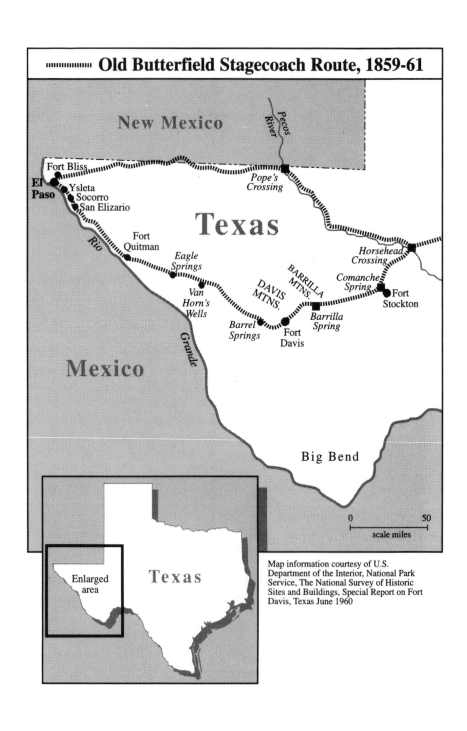

Old Butterfield Stagecoach Route, 1859-61

New Mexico

Pecos River

Texas

Fort Bliss

El Paso

Ysleta
Socorro
San Elizario

Pope's Crossing

Fort Quitman

Rio

Eagle Springs

Van Horn's Wells

DAVIS MTNS.

BARRILLA MTNS.

Horsehead Crossing

Comanche Spring

Fort Stockton

Barrel Springs

Fort Davis

Barrilla Spring

Grande

Mexico

Big Bend

0   50
scale miles

Enlarged area

Texas

Texas

Map information courtesy of U.S. Department of the Interior, National Park Service, The National Survey of Historic Sites and Buildings, Special Report on Fort Davis, Texas June 1960

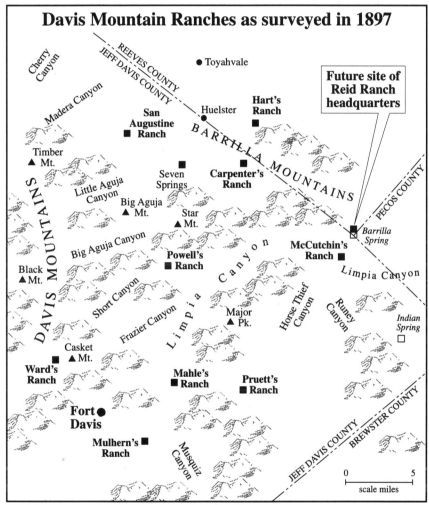

Davis Mountain Ranches as surveyed in 1897

Cherry Canyon

REEVES COUNTY
JEFF DAVIS COUNTY

● Toyahvale

Madera Canyon

San Augustine ■ Ranch

Huelster ●

Hart's Ranch ■

Future site of Reid Ranch headquarters

BARRILLA MOUNTAINS

Timber ▲ Mt.

Little Aguja Canyon

Seven Springs ■

Carpenter's Ranch ■

Big Aguja ▲ Mt.

Star ▲ Mt.

PECOS COUNTY

DAVIS MOUNTAINS

Big Aguja Canyon

Powell's ■ Ranch

Canyon

McCutchin's Ranch ■

Barrilla Spring ⊠

Black ▲ Mt.

Short Canyon

Limpia Canyon

Limpia Canyon

Frazier Canyon

Major ▲ Pk.

Horse Thief Canyon

Runey Canyon

Indian Spring □

Casket ▲ Mt.

Ward's Ranch ■

Mahle's ■ Ranch

Pruett's ■ Ranch

Fort ● Davis

Mulhern's ■ Ranch

Musquiz Canyon

JEFF DAVIS COUNTY
BREWSTER COUNTY

0   5
scale miles

Map information courtesy of Texas State Archives; U.S. Geological Survey, Texas Fort Davis Sheet, March 1897

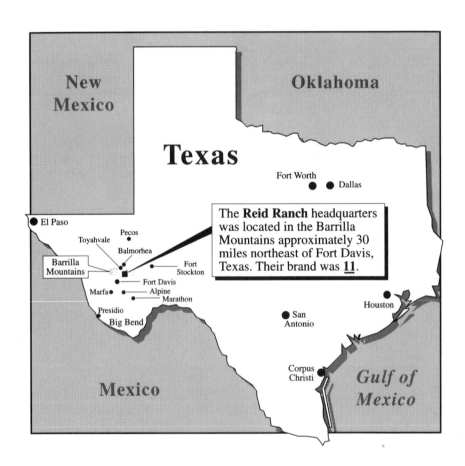

The **Reid Ranch** headquarters was located in the Barrilla Mountains approximately 30 miles northeast of Fort Davis, Texas. Their brand was **11**.

The Cattlemen

"...*Fella asked me one time what my philosophy of life was. I told him it was a belief in a Supreme Being. I say that because of the number of times in my life when just a few seconds—one way or the other—would have been all for me. Whenever I found myself in one of these situations, I always called on Him, and He was there. I never knew a time He wasn't. Those times helped me, or I wouldn't be here. That's been the thing I've always relied on, always remembered. The Creator, the Being who created the whole thing, He's always with you to go on through. That's the way I've always lived. I've never looked back or questioned that.*"

Wade Reid, 1971

Part I

As Roy Told It

Limpia Canyon. Circa 1905-1910.

1

Our Mama's father and his brother were in the Confederate cavalry during the Civil War. Our uncle was wounded once in the arm. They mostly liberated horses from the Union. Horses were a lot easier to hit than men during a battle, so they always went down first. This kept both sides needing horses for their cavalries and after a couple of years of war, there was a real shortage. Our grandfather said they seldom took horses from Southerners because they needed them to help grow food. He told us about a trap they laid for twenty-five Union cavalrymen. They could see them coming in the distance, so they scattered and hid among the trees and brush. When the Union soldiers rode into the trap, our grandfather and his outfit steps out and tells them to throw up their hands and dismount. All the old boys put up their hands, but just sat there staring at our grandfather and his unit. Finally one of these fellows tells them in broken English they can't dismount because they was tied on the horses. It turned out the Union men were Germans. When the North run short of men, they began recruiting in Europe and these German boys signed up. Couldn't but one of them speak a word of English, and they'd never been on a horse in their life. North said it didn't matter, that they needed cavalry, and to get on their horses and go to the front. So they'd just tied one another on their horses and headed out. Our grandfather said after they took all their guns and equipment and horses and headed back toward Southern lines, these old German boys just fell in behind and followed them on foot.

Our grandfather's commander finally had to surrender, so he called the unit together—seventy-two men in all—and thanked them for their service and told them they were all free to go home. Our grandfather and uncle swung aboard their horses and headed towards Texas. When they got there, he sent word to our grandmother in Tennessee to bring their three children—one of whom was our mother—on to Fort Worth as soon as the railroad was finished. When they got there, they settled north of Fort Worth. That's where our father George Reid met and married our mother.

George Reid was born in Kentucky. His family had moved to Illinois sometime afterward, and they'd come to Texas with a wagon train right after the Civil War ended. They settled north of Fort Worth, too. He and mother had a small place in Wise County. Four of us kids were born there—Bob, the oldest, in 1885, me in 1886, Wade in 1888, and Sid in 1890.

Now George was a carpenter by trade, and he was working along at different jobs when he heard about the state offering land in the Panhandle. So he rode out into the Texas Panhandle, found some land he liked in Swisher and Brisco counties between Silverton and Tulia on Rock Creek and filed on three sections. I think the land cost him a dollar an acre. The state required ten percent down, and I think they carried his note at three percent. Some of that land is still in our family today.

They said it was hard to get people out into the Panhandle at first. The state started out by offering hundred and sixty acre leases to anyone who would improve it. But there was still a lot of unused land in the state in the late 1800's—several million acres—and few people were willing to take it up. So another law was passed making it possible for big ranches to lease all the land they wanted for three cents an acre a year just to give the state some income. The state also began deeding land to anyone who'd done work for them. A great part of the Panhandle country—two or three million acres—was deeded to a group of men who'd agreed to build the state a capitol. The land wasn't worth much at the time, but these old boys figured it would be someday. Their ranch became the XIT.

Anyhow, this was how a lot of the big Panhandle ranches

got started. Charles Goodnight had already ridden in there and went to leasing land and ranching along the Palo Duro Canyon. He saw the canyon had good water and grass, and he went to crossbreeding Longhorns with beef cattle until he had him a good herd built up. He got an old boy named John Adair, an Irishman, to put up most of the money for the operation. Their outfit was the JA, named after Adair. By the time we got there, most everyone was shipping their cattle out of Amarillo because they had two rail lines there. They just trailed the cattle cross-country to the shipping point.

One unusual thing about the cattle business right after the Civil War was the U. S. didn't have any money. The South was completely broke and the North had very little. What money there was for the cattle industry came from England, Scotland, and France. Truth is, most of the big ranches started with money from European investors, and most of the Panhandle cattle money came from Scotland and Germany. Colonel Slaughter didn't have a great deal of money when he started his place. He borrowed most of it at first, then after several years he was able to operate on his own. It took all of those early ranchers a good long while to build up their capital. Goodnight and Adair used European money, too. Adair never thought of the Panhandle as home. He figured that country as just a place to make a living. After Adair died, his wife come to the U.S. and moved into the JA headquarters, fixed it up, and took great pleasure in living there.

Now Goodnight's cattle grazed that Caprock country—all up and down the Palo Duro—and watered there at the Tule Creek. There wasn't much surface water then. The big ranches had what surface water there was pretty well tied up. Dry spells hurt everyone then, too. There was lots of water underneath, but nobody knew about it at the time.

Sometime around 1890 the state passed a law that allowed a person to file on a section of land for a dollar an acre at three percent interest. That got people coming to the Panhandle to file on the land. Some would work for one rancher, then another, trying to save enough for the down payment to file on a section or two.

Anyhow, after our daddy filed on his land, he started moving our belongings to the Panhandle in 1890. He loaded a wagon down with his farm tools and rounded up his animals. He had two pigs, a half-dozen hens, a rooster, seven cows, a bull yearling, and four horses. Two of those horses were Fatima work-horses, and the other two were saddle horses. He hired an old boy to drive the wagon, and he drove the cows. One cow had a calf on the way, so he just built a box on the back of the wagon and sat the calf in it. He said the calf hung its head out and bawled all the way. When he got there, he sent this old boy on to Amarillo to get wood to build our house with. George told him he would meet him back there on a certain date, then he come back to get the family. Now he hadn't had a shave or haircut since he left. When he got to the house and hollered at us kids to come there, we took off running in the other direction. Bunch of little old kids barely walking. We didn't even recognize him.

When Mama regained her strength after Sid was born, we left Wise County and traveled as far as our Grandfather Hutchison's place in Young County. He had a home in Farmer, northeast of Brad, Texas. We saw two Indians being taken to court in Graham. Later, we boarded an immigrant train to Amarillo. Along the way, about thirty or forty Comanches rode up beside our car. They told us they were some of Quanah Parker's old Comanches, but they weren't bothering anyone then.

Mama took her Bible with her when we left for the Panhandle. It was the only thing she had to read the first three or four years we were out there. We got our mail twice a year and there wasn't any newspapers. About the only people we saw were cowboys coming through. Some of them would be on the dodge, some would be riding for the big

6

outfits, and some would just be looking for work or a meal. A few of these old cowboys would be trying to homestead like us. They'd file on the land hoping to hold onto something that would amount to something. About all these cow punchers ever had was a bedroll and saddle and a couple horses. They'd dig them a little half dugout in the breaks there up under the cap rock and use cedarwood and sod for their roof. Later, when the Fort Worth-Kansas Railroad started hauling lumber into the Panhandle, everyone went to building shacks or wood houses. Most of the lumber came out of Amarillo because the cap rock was a hard place to get over and through with a heavy wagonload.

Our daddy saw right off he'd have to have something to feed his cows to get them through those Panhandle winters. He got hold of some oat seed and planted about sixty acres, made a good crop, then tried some corn his daddy had brought from Illinois. His dad had worked for a big corn grower in Illinois. Trouble was they needed water to grow it. So, they went to work digging a well.

Grandpa Reid dug our first well with a pick and shovel and struck water at about fifty feet. Once they had water, it made everything more livable and crops a whole lot easier to grow. Right after that an old fellow who'd drilled a well or two using horses down around Fort Reardon come along digging wells for Panhandle homesteaders who could afford them. The horse circled and provided the power to drill the wells. Truth is, wasn't too much money out there then. Everyone just pitched in and helped one another when someone needed something. If an old boy lived thirty or forty miles away and needed help, why you went and helped him. Wasn't anyone around to enforce the law then either. Everyone just looked after themselves.

About the only fence in our part of the Panhandle when we got there was the JA drift fence that Goodnight and Adair had built. Our place was located on the south side of that fence. Beyond us, on the south, there was nothing but

7

open range. No grocery stores, no post offices, nothing. The fence had been built for a purpose. During the winters when those hard Panhandle blizzards hit, Goodnight's cattle would come up out of the Palo Duro and head south, drifting with the wind. By spring, they'd be several hundred miles away. So Goodnight and Adair decided to build a drift fence across the canyon to stop them. Trouble was, no one in the U.S. manufactured the kind of barbed wire they wanted for such a fence. So Adair went back to England, bought enough wire for a fifty mile, five-strand drift fence, and they went to work on it. They put it in seven miles south of the Tule Creek. It had five strands with a cedar post every thirty feet and two steel stays in between. The two center wires were smooth so the cattle wouldn't cut themselves. Antelope drifted over the fence in blizzards, but cattle would drift into the fence and wall up in a little wad. Sometimes they would generate enough heat to keep from freezing to death until the blizzard blew over. Some of them just froze to death in piles, though.

Now when they put the fence in at the JA, they pushed all the wild horses to the south side of it. Those horses had been used to coming from the running water in Yellow House Canyon and going on into the Tule, but the drift fence cut them off from the Tule. Those mustangs were some pretty good blooded horses that had come out of Spaniard stock. They had been brought up into that Santa Fe country. The Indians had run a bunch of them off into the Palo Duro. There was one stud that ran with a bunch of mares. He was a big, coal black horse about fifteen to sixteen hands with a tail that drug the ground. You could tell he had good blood in him from somewhere. When the ranchers went to gather up those wild horses, they'd get a bunch of cowboys who knew the country. A couple of these old boys would fall out down through there behind those mustangs. They'd run them in relays with fresh saddle horses at each stop. Funny thing was, they couldn't catch the older mustangs, even in relays.

But the colts and the younger horses would get winded and finally an old boy would get a rope on one and they'd take the horse to town and sell it.

Fella by the name of Gardner caught one of those filly colts and come by and sold her to our daddy for five dollars. She was black with brown markings. About every other colt she had was as gentle as they come, but the ones in between was as mean and hard to break as you could imagine. We brought some of that mare's descendants with us when we come to the Davis Mountains. Those mustangs weren't much to look at, but you couldn't wear one of them out.

Now the ranchers and the settlers around us decided they had to get rid of this black stallion because he'd kill their horses if he come across one on his range. They tried catching him and couldn't. So they shot him.

I saw once how far a horse could go in a day when I was just a kid there in the Panhandle. Our daddy was carpentering at the time, and he'd gone where the work was. Fact is, he didn't stay much atall when we was little, so mostly it was Mama and us kids out there by ourselves.

Anyhow, one Fall night just about sundown, an old boy come along afoot—it was seldom you ever saw anyone afoot in that country—and he walked up to our door and asked to stay the night. Well, Mama told him we only had a little two-room shack and there wasn't much room. The old boy saw that, so he asked if he could just sit by the fire all night and come daybreak, he would leave. Mama looked him over good and decided what he said was true and that he wouldn't do us harm, so she told him, "All right, come on in." He tried to refuse supper, but she fixed him something and made him eat it. Anyhow, he sat there nodding by the stove all night and kept a little fire going in it to keep warm. Next morning when daybreak come, he stood up, finished the coffee Mama had give him, thanked her for the night, walked out our door, and headed south down a cattle trail that come by our place. It was one of those trails they'd used to move cattle north,

9

and was well marked. We found out later this old boy followed the trail south into the Quitaque Breaks, then cut off and went to a little dugout there where a man was holding his little girl. She was about four years old. This man had evidently kidnapped the old boy's daughter for him in Dallas and had brought her to the dugout. The old boy was going there to pick her up and take her on to Denver, and did.

Well, the next night, just about sundown, a ranger rode up to our gate with a colt buckled on and a Winchester stuck in his saddle, asking if he could stay the night. He looked tired, so Mama tells him he can sleep up in the loft and we'll all sleep down below. He told us where he'd left from that morning and had ridden straight across to us. We figured it to be around eighty miles from our place. Anyhow, he was riding a big, long legged dun horse. We took his horse down to our shed and cooled him off and watered him good. The next morning at breakfast he tells us he's after a man that had kidnapped a little girl, and he'd heard they come this way. Mama said, "Well, you're just about twenty-four hours late," and she described our other visitor.

The ranger thanked us, and we all went down to the shed with him. We saw his horse's ankles had swelled during the night, so us kids got a handful of Mama's swelling liniment and got down and went to working it into that old horse's ankles. Them times you didn't have a vet, and you made your own liniment. Anyhow, we worked those ankles good and loose, gave the ranger a little bottle of our liniment, and sent him on his way. We heard later the ranger tracked this guy aways, but lost the trail where he'd turned into the Quitaque. The fella he was after went to Mexico after he dropped his daughter in Denver. Later years that same ranger retired and bought a little place there about three miles from us.

Early Panhandle settlers nearly always kept a milk cow around—milk was one of their staples—but milk cows wasn't much for beef. The Longhorn was still around then, but it wasn't a milker, and it took a Longhorn four, five, six years sometimes to make a decent beef. Lots of the early ranchers would gather up a herd of those five- and six-year-old cattle and head them north during the early summer, letting them graze along the way. By the time they got where they was headed, those old Longhorns would be fat and decent beef. The problem was waiting on the Longhorns to mature. So some of the ranchers tried the Durham cattle, but they weren't hardy enough. Then they tried crossing the Durham with the Longhorn, but they lost the milk again and still had to wait on the calves to mature. Finally they tried the Hereford and found out they gave enough milk to raise a hardy calf fast. They didn't have to wait several years for the carcass to mature, either. The Hereford caught on fast as a breed in the Panhandle and West Texas. Course, the first Herefords weren't anything like what we got now in either beef or milk production. I think an old boy by the name of Ikard brought the first Herefords to Texas sometime during the 1870's.

Panhandle ranchers had plenty of grass before 1900. They couldn't overstock the range because there was so much of it, and there wasn't enough water to go around. They relied on natural lakes, rivers, creeks, and springs to water their cattle. This naturally kept them from overgrazing their ranges. Later, when the windmills caught on, the ranchers added more stock.

About every three years during the late 1800's and early 1900's, they'd have a money panic. These panics began in 1896, continued on through the Spanish-American War, and on into 1913 until Wilson took office. Money market people would pull their money out of banks and other lending outfits, leaving both depositors and creditors high and dry. These manipulators would be trying to drive interest up and values down. Besides having to put up with droughts and blizzards and the like, money panics was something else early ranchers and homesteaders had to contend with. People trying to get a start depended on the local banks.

Wilson ended the money panic when he went in though. He got credit banks established and took the money market away from Wall Street and put it into Federal Reserve banks. Up to that time, the money markets on Wall Street controlled all the national banks. By taking the money off Wall Street, banks were free to go to the Federal Reserve and negotiate for money without fear of having it called in every two or three years.

2

Before we got to the Panhandle, Mackenzie had crippled the Comanches' ability to make war on the ranchers and settlers when he killed most of their horses up on the Tule in '74. Back then, you just didn't do anything afoot in the Panhandle. That boneyard was about six miles from our Panhandle house and about eighteen miles from where he fought the Comanches in Palo Duro Canyon. The cowboys always called the "bones" Mackenzie's battleground then, but it was really Mackenzie's boneyard. Those bones, and all the buffalo bones, stayed until 1883.

As kids, we'd gather buffalo horns and pile them in our yard. They was our cattle, you see, and about the only thing we had to play with. We'd get them horns strung out on trail drives, headed for market. An old buffalo hunter told us they killed, skinned, and stacked the hides around the clock. That's why they was killing the buffalo—for the hides. Then they'd haul them to a rail head at places like Colorado City and ship them. Our granddaddy told us buffalo were all over the plains before there was a market for the hides, but twenty-four months later you had to look to find one.

The buffalo were good for the Indians, you see, but not the white man. The meat was black and coarse and about all the buffalo hunters ever ate was the hump, which was tender, and the tongue, which they dried and ate. Goodnight used to barbecue a buffalo every once in a while there around Amarillo, but compared to beef, they really weren't good to eat. About the best wild meat I ever ate was elk and quail, and I tried them all—bear, antelope, deer. Pheasant and grouse was good, too.

Anyhow, a market opened up for the buffalo bones in the 1880's. They found out you could make fertilizer and other things out of them. Those old bone hunters hit the prairie with side-boarded wagons filled to the brim. They hauled bones by the tons to Wichita Falls and places and sold them for seven dollars a load. Dealers shipped them somewhere in Ohio where they were converted to fertilizer.

Our grandfather told of the bone hunter who stumbled upon Mackenzie's boneyard near our house. Said his eyes like to have crossed. He loaded up a wagon, put a sign up declaring the rest of the bones his, and headed for Wichita Falls. When he returned, other bone hunters had cleaned him out. He said he would have killed them if he'd caught them.

The first drought I remember was in 1893. It never rained a drop. We had about sixty acres of good oats growing that year, and Mama's garden was in full bloom. Suddenly the sky darkened one afternoon and millions of grasshoppers covered the plains, eating everything. I never will forget their clicking. The grasshoppers were followed by more drought and a hard winter. By Spring, most everyone had left and forfeited their land back to the state. The only people left on the plains were the ranchers and a few families like us. It was 1894 before things got any better. The state got busy then and surveyed and organized the counties better so they could get mail brought in on horseback and, in general, began improving the land like they did everywhere else. It only took seventeen men to organize a county then once it was surveyed.

But they still had a hard time getting anyone to take up the land and pay taxes and interest on it right at first. Only the big ranchers took advantage of the land because they were the only ones who had any money after the grasshoppers and drought crippled the plains. I think the state was offering four sections of land for a dollar an acre at the time. Rule was you had to live on the land three years before claiming it. The big ranchers would tap a cowboy in their outfit or make a deal with a drifter to live—or squat—the required three years on four sections. They would pay the cowboy twenty or thirty dollars a month, plus a hundred dollars a section for the land at the end of the three years.

The squatter in turn deeded the land over to the rancher. There was some big ranches put together and kept together that way. And I don't ever recall anyone keeping a rancher's money or land at the end of those three years either because those old rascals would've put a bullet in anyone who tried. They was that way after fighting with thieves and Indians and Comancheros all them years.

George added to our frame house as the family grew. Eventually he and Mama had seven boys and a girl, Knox being the youngest, then Nig, Ted, Tola, Sid, Wade, myself, and Bob, the oldest. George left most of the farming to me and Wade and Bob. Bob hated farming. Being the oldest, he left home early and got a job on old man C. T. Word's ranch. He later lived with Grandpa after Grandma died. We raised feed, a few cows, some chickens, and a garden. Wade and I never liked farming either. That was one of the reasons the Davis Mountains appealed to us the first time we saw them. We knew no one could ever get a plow in the ground there.

We didn't have a school when we first got to the Panhandle, so the people got together and built a little one-roomer so kids like us could learn to read and write and figure enough to get by. Bob was nine, I was eight, and Wade was seven when the school was finished. It was about five miles from where we lived. George built us a little cart, put a board across it for us to sit on, and hooked us up to a gentle horse. That's how we all got to school.

The school building was about twelve to fifteen feet square. There was six of us little kids, ten married people, an unmarried girl about eighteen, and an older boy or two. That was our class. All of us learning to read and write and spell and figure. Every Friday our teacher would adjourn class right after dinner, walk up to his house about a half mile in back of the school, saddle his horse, and head out for some place about twelve miles or so the other side of Silverton. He'd stay until early Monday morning, then ride back over and start school again. As soon as the teacher was out of sight, we'd push everything against the wall. One of the older fellas would break out a French harp or some little instrument and we'd square dance. Big ones, little ones, we all danced with one another. That was about the only music we had out there. And the only church then was in Silverton. The preacher sometimes rode to our school and held services.

We went to school long hours and it was after dark when we got home in the evenings. Our schooling was concentrated during the four summer months. It was too cold to go in the winter, and a plains blizzard would freeze you to death in a minute if you got caught in one. You couldn't see ten feet in a blizzard snow. People would lose their sense of direction, wander off the road or trail, and out onto the plains where they froze.

When school was in session, we got up before daylight, milked, fed our cows and saddle horses—we all learned to ride as soon as we could walk—then ate. School started at nine because of the distance some people had to travel to get there, but we stayed late. Mother fixed us whatever we had—dried beef, vegetables, bread. We always ate it, regardless.

Our seats were one-by-twelve benches around the schoolroom wall. We held our slate between our knees and worked our lessons. None of the older boys gave the teacher a hard time because he kept a hardwood stick propped against his desk. And he didn't hesitate to put a knot on a kid's head if he gave him any trouble. The stick was a great attention-getter.

When some of our brothers got big enough to take over the homestead work, Wade and I saddled our horses one morning and pulled out for Silverton to see a couple of men named Tom Byrd and Banker John. We finished our business with Byrd and walked across the street to the bank. There was a depression and money panic on at the time, and we didn't have a dime to our name. I was old enough to sign a note, and I told Banker John that Wade and I wanted to buy a few steers.

He surprised us and said, "I've got a hundred head of steers out yonder I'll sell ya."

We told him we reckoned we'd go look at them. He said, "No need to do that. All you got to do is make me a note and pay it off when you sell your steers."

We told him if it was all the same to him, we'd go look at the steers. So we all rode out, looked the steers over, and asked him what he wanted for them. He said, "Well, I'll let you boys have them for twelve dollars apiece." They were sorry steers and weren't worth eight. We told him he wanted too much money for the steers. He said, "Oh, you don't have to have any money for 'em. You can just make me a note." We told him a note didn't matter because we'd still have to pay for the steers. He said, "You don't think you want 'em at all?" We said, "No, they're not good enough." And he said, "All right. Let's go back to town." So we rode along behind his buckboard, and when we got to the bank, he said, "Come on in."

We tied our saddle horses at the hitching rail outside and went in. He looked at us and said, "You want to buy a hundred head of steers?" And we said, "That's right." He said, "All right. I'll let you have the money. I'm not going to make no note or nothing. Here's a checkbook. You go out and buy your steers. When you get back, let me know and I'll come out and look 'em over, and we'll make a note for 'em then."

That's how Wade and I got started as partners in the cattle business. We just pulled out through the country with Banker John's checkbook, buying five or six steers as we went. We'd throw them together at night, roll out our bedrolls, and move on slow the next morning, letting them steers graze and gain weight until we had our hundred head.

Back then two people could make a verbal contract by one of them saying, "I'll buy your calves at so many cents a pound." Nothing was written. He just made the statement he'd buy the calves at a price. If the other man accepted and wanted a little forfeit money on the calves, the buyer gave him a check and stated when he would receive the calves. And by God he either received them on that date or sent word why he couldn't. And the other man delivered the calves. Now a lot has been written about deals being made on a man's word, but the motivating factor behind all that and a man keeping his word then was this—if an old boy come along and said he'd do something, and didn't, he knew someone would come looking for him. And when they found him, he run a damn good risk of winding up with a bullet in him. You always concluded your deals with a handshake, but that was a formality. It was the side arm and saddle rifle that made a man's word as good as his bond at first. Later, when things got more civilized, most of the ranchers I knew carried this concept over and operated on their word, at least among themselves, right on up through the Forties and Fifties. Old Joe Espy in Fort Davis was like that. When he told you there was something he would do, he done it. You could depend on him. Everything has changed now. You go to put a bunch of calves on a wheat field somewhere, and you better by God have a lawyer draw up the contract.

We had maybe nine dollars a head in those steers when we got back to Silverton. Banker John come out there at the edge of town, looked those steers over and said, "Looks like you bought yourself a good bunch of steers. I'll give you twelve dollars a head for 'em." We told him we didn't think he understood. That we wanted to sell them, not give them away. He just laughed and said, "Well, let's go make a note for what you spent, and I'll sign it." George happened by the bank while we was there and said, "John, you want me to sign those boys' note?" And Banker John said, "No, I don't need your name on this note."

We leased a couple sections alongside some open range north of Rock Creek and put our steers on it. That winter was cold and hard, and we stayed in the saddle a lot, moving them to keep them from dying. Wade got off to break water ice one morning during a storm and both his feet got soaked. When he finally got back to the house, he was almost froze in the saddle. We had to pop his feet loose from the stirrups. It was several weeks before he could use them at all. Then, just as he got to where he could walk, rheumatism drew his toes up under the balls of his feet, pain set in, and he found himself crippled the rest of his life. That's how come he always walked so funny.

We kept them steers from freezing that winter and let them graze the open range until along in March when an old boy come along and offered us thirty dollars apiece for them. We sold them on the spot, paid off our note at ten percent and that was the beginning.

3

By 1909 Wade and I were running quite a few cattle in the Panhandle. We'd made a little money off that bunch of steers Banker John had helped us buy, and we'd put it right back into cattle. We'd run the cattle on land we leased from the state by paying the taxes on it. Given the Panhandle's history of money panics and droughts and bad winters and grasshoppers during the latter part of the 1800's, there was patented land available that people had just walked off from. A person could use it if they paid the taxes. As a result, we always had a place to run our cattle and had managed to put some money in the bank. But a few green years had brought people back to the Panhandle and it was filling up fast. That's when we decided to come south to see if we could find some good land to buy.

We ran across an old boy wanting to sell a good saddle horse, a wagon, and two runaway mules. We made him an offer and he took it. We left a brother in charge of the cattle and headed south. Fella by the name of Barney Stark asked if he could ride along with us. We told him to throw his stuff in the wagon.

We were a couple of weeks coming the first time we come down, what with our two runaway mules and wagon and all. We came through Lubbock, which was just a small railroad spur at the time, and on through Brownfield, Seminole and Schafter Lake, into New Mexico and down that old Cargyle Draw country and on into Monahans and Pecos. We spent a night with an old man who had six sections of land west of Monahans. He was a friend of George's who'd come from the plains, filed on the land, and become discouraged. He asked us where we were headed and why. We told him we were looking for land, and he offered us his six sections. We looked it over, decided it wasn't worth our hard-earned money, and moved on. Later it became part of the Permian Basin. We always laughed about that.

When we left the Panhandle, we said we were going south until we found some land that couldn't be plowed. Soon as we hit the Davis Mountains, we knew we'd found it. The grass was good and there were springs everywhere. All the draws and creeks ran freshwater. I think if we could have made the kind of land we wanted, it would have been just like the Davis Mountains.

Long years later I went back to the Panhandle to visit my brother working the old homestead place, and he had one of them old plains plows sitting there in his yard. He points to it and says, "I don't know what I'm going to do with the damn thing." I says, "Give it to a museum. I don't want it 'cause them things were one of the reasons I left this country in the first place."

Anyhow, our first night in the Davis Mountains we stayed at the Jeff Ranch with the McCutcheons. Willis McCutcheon was one of the earliest ranchers in the northeastern Davis Mountains. He was the oldest of a family of thirteen and had left home and begun ranching for himself near Victoria, Texas sometime during the 1870's. He kept hearing about some Texas mountains with good grass farther west, though. So one day he and his brother William, the second oldest, and a younger brother named Jeff, saddled up and rode west until they found the Davis Mountains. The country was all open then with most of the Apaches in northern Mexico and the Comanches confined up north. About the only people there were a few renegade Indians, a handful of ranchers, a squatter or two, and some Mexicans. Wasn't much law then to speak of either. They said a Mexican could kill a Mexican in a fight and they'd let him make a run for Mexico. They knew a relative of the murdered man would eventually hunt him up to settle accounts. If a Mexican killed a white man, though, they'd do everything they could to catch and try him before he got to the border, because once he got into Mexico, they knew they'd never find him. And if a white man killed a white man, they'd usually try him in El Paso if they caught him.

They said the country was brush free then, too, and the grama grass was so thick you couldn't see the ground. Willis said you could ride out across the flat between Alpine and Marfa, or between Marfa and Fort Davis, and never see erosion. He said it was because either the Indians or lightning burned the brush, weeds, and other trash back every year. About the only plants that really had time to grow and seed each season was the grama grasses—probably the finest anywhere at the time. Hell, you hear a lot about grass fires every year. They used to burn that Star Mountain country off on purpose early of a Spring or late winter. Beau McCutcheon would sometimes ride along and pitch a match out there and just let it burn. This kept new grass coming and the brush burnt back. After they quit letting people do that, the brush took over.

Anyhow, Willis and William and Jeff came to the Davis Mountains, liked what they saw, and immediately claimed a lot of the good land north of Fort Davis sometime during the 1870's. They went back and trailed their cattle from Victoria, built a nice house, and were doing good near as anyone could tell. Jeff took sick shortly afterward and died. No one is sure what he had. They named the Jeff Ranch after him. Then William was killed by a man in a dispute over some burros. The man was an early freighter who used burro trains to pack freight into the Davis Mountains and Big Bend. Now the McCutcheons didn't mind the freighters passing through their country, but they objected to them turning burros loose on their land. Burros multiplied fast, ate lots of grass, and competed with cattle for forage in the winter. A lot of the early ranchers shot wild burros where they found them so they wouldn't multiply. Anyhow, this man had turned a large number of his freight burros loose to graze there about where Limpia Creek turns east. He'd spread his bedroll and was taking a siesta when William happened upon the burros. William pulled his Winchester and started shooting burros. The shooting woke the man up who sees his burros dropping, so he grabs his rifle and shoots William off his horse dead. The man was caught, tried, and sent to prison.

Anyhow, Christmas of 1882 Willis rode back to Taylor, Texas, where the rest of the McCutcheon family lived, and asked Bennett, another older brother, to go back with him. Beau and Jim, the two youngest brothers of the family, were there. At the time they were just two big-footed old boys who'd accumulated about thirty head of cattle, and about that many horses, and Willis says to them, "You boys want to farm the rest of your lives?" They said, "No." So Willis says, "Then if you want to ranch, you go to Taylor and buy everything you can afford in the way of supplies—wagon, riggin', mules, horseshoes, nails, and the like —and lease you a couple of box cars and ship your cattle and horses and yourselves—just get on there and ride with 'em—to Toyah, Texas. That's the end of the railroad. When you get there, unload everything and drive 'em due south 'till you hit a running stream of clear water."

So they did and when they got to Toyah, they unloaded and drove those cattle and horses right to the Aguja Canyon water. It was a big stream of springwater that run about half million gallons a day, and was located about eight miles due south of the Balmorhea State Park. The water was pure and cold and came from a hole a yard wide between two roots of a huge elm tree on the creek bank, some ten feet above the waterline. It just poured off into the creek below and into a big hole it had scooped out over the years.

Now most of the land was still virgin country when Beau and Jim got there in the early 1880's. About half of it belonged to the state, and the other half had never even been surveyed. Deal was, if you surveyed it, the state would let you have half of what you surveyed for fifty cents an acre and lease the other half to you. So Willis and Bennett hired them a surveyor and told him to get to surveying. Usually the surveyors just shot from scratch. They wound up with one section in Limpia Canyon with eight corners.

Beau and Jim did the same. They started surveying and buying land, first from individuals for twenty-five to fifty cents an acre, then from the state. They bought all the land where the present day Jeff Ranch is located, plus all the land south up Limpia Canyon to within ten miles of Fort Davis. And though the Jeff Ranch was their eastern boundary, they controlled grazing rights on land farther east to within ten miles of Fort Stockton. They also took in the Star Mountain country, and eventually built their west end headquarters on the north side of Star.

Now the McCutcheons bought all their supplies at the Union Trading Company in Fort Davis. The original building is still right there between the Limpia Hotel and the Fort Davis Bank. The Union handled everything a rancher needed—from horseshoe nails to feed—and gave him twelve months credit. When he delivered his calves in the Fall, he came in and paid his bill and took on supplies for another year. The Union Mercantile began as the old Keesey and Company Store in Fort Davis. Walter Miller and George Gann had gone together with Whit Keesey to work and run it. Then Joe Espy and a few of the other ranchers put some money behind the Union so the store could order in volume what the ranchers needed each year. That's when it became the Union Mercantile. Later Walter Miller's daughter, Audrey, married Tyrone Kelly who bought the Mercantile. After it was sold, it passed from the original founders.

Bennett McCutcheon and the Epsys bordered the Jeff Ranch to the south, with Bennett McCutcheon's land running up the east and west side of Limpia Canyon. During the Depression, Bennett had to let his ranch go when he couldn't repay an operating loan. Bennett kept the two sections of land there alongside Limpia Creek where he'd built his house, though. Later, the Epsys bought that portion of the ranch.

Now the Kingston Ranch bordered the McCutcheons west of Toyahvale, and Dick Riggs had some land there to the east. Further north of the McCutcheons were the Cowans whose land went on out into the flats, across the railroad and beyond. The Cowans had lots of land, but they couldn't run too many cows to the section on the flats. Fact is, you had to work those flats hard to get them to pay, even at fifty cents an acre. People back east thought just because the Cowans had a hundred sections of land out there they ought to be millionaires. What they didn't understand was you were lucky if you could run a dozen cows to the section in those flats. The Cowans worked hard every year just to keep their ranch together. Mr. Cowan built the railroad from Pecos to Toyahvale where a lot of the ranchers shipped from each Fall. He and a few others also put in the electric power plant and the mercantile in Pecos, and did a lot to develop the area. He owned the VH Ranch and was heavily invested, too, when the Depression hit.

The burnt house on the west side of the Fort Davis-Toyahvale road south of Toyahvale was Willis McCutcheon's homestead and headquarters house. It caught fire one day and burned when no one was there. Beau McCutcheon's homestead house was on the left two miles after you turned off the Fort Davis-Toyahvale road toward where the Boy Scout Ranch is today. It was called the 7-Ranch. Willis built in between the 7-Ranch and the Jeff. His ranch was called the 7-Springs Ranch.

Now during the late 1800's the McCutcheons probably controlled three or four hundred thousand acres outright and had at least that much leased for grazing purposes. Once they considered selling out to a buyer who gave them ten thousand dollars in earnest money. They started gathering and counting the cattle because they were going to get so much an acre plus so much per head. They stopped counting at twenty thousand head, having covered only a little over half of their country. After a brief conference, they all agreed to give the man his money back. They hadn't realized how many cattle they had. Old Lee Huff, who worked for Mr. Beau all his life, said they went on and continued the count, but ran out of time what with the work they had to do and all. They stopped counting at twenty-seven thousand head, and didn't really know how many were left.

When the state made it legal to homestead state-owned land, squatters started flocking to the Davis Mountains. To keep their ranches from being cut up, the McCutcheons went to the courthouses in Pecos and Fort Stockton and Fort Davis to find out exactly what state country they were using, and what needed to be squatted. Then they hired themselves some extra hands to squat their land, filed on it for them, and rode out across their country showing them where to live. At the end of the required time they paid each of them off and put the land back into the McCutcheon name. They said if they hadn't done that, squatters would have broken up all the big ranches—which was what the state was trying to do—and the country wouldn't have been fit for anybody.

They said there was one man named O'Dell who made his living during the period by going to courthouses and looking through the records until he found a section or half section with water on it that someone had missed. It would usually be right in the middle of some rancher's land. O'Dell would file on it then go out and squat it. There wasn't a darn thing the rancher could do. The rancher either paid through the nose for the water or paid O'Dell's price for the land. In the long run, it was cheaper to buy the land from O'Dell at the inflated price.

Another old man by the name of Lewis came out there from Midland and took up some good land with springs on it. He stayed a few years until it appreciated and until he had a couple of the bigger ranches wanting to buy him out. He finally sold his land and livestock. He was as proud as could be of his money, and no one could get him to put it in the bank. No sir, he just bought him a money belt and stuffed it in there, and it wasn't a week until he went up to Odessa to buy something. Some of those thugs that hung around the town knocked him in the head and took every cent he owned. He'd come there to the Davis Mountains by himself, finally married, then had his wife die in childbirth. A couple of his brothers came out there too, but they both died. That's the way the country was. You either came out there and got stronger, or you died.

Beau also had a cowboy who worked for him at the time. The cowboy was as honest as the day was long with Mr. Beau; wouldn't take a copper penny from him. But he'd been known to give things to Mr. Beau that Beau knew wasn't his. And Beau would always make good on it if he could find out where it came from.

Point is, the fella was also a top cowhand. Now Beau had a horse at his ranch they called the Gray Stud. He wasn't a stud really, but was just a great big old strong gray gelding. He was a top cow horse that would work all day and night. Word came out they had a herd that needed working over near Alpine one morning. The cowboy saddled the gray and left the Jeff Ranch one afternoon, rode the twenty-five miles cross-country to Alpine, helped cut a herd of several thousand steers, then rode back cross-country that night to the Jeff Ranch. He and the gray both looked a little drawn, but other than that they were both ready to go to work the next morning. They also used the gray to pull cattle out of bogholes during dry periods, too. The cattle would wade out into soft mud trying to get at water and get bogged down and couldn't move. If you didn't find them, they starved to death. Well sir, they said you could ride into a bog beside an old cow on that gray horse, and he'd lean over towards her so's you could just drop a rope on her and dally. Then he'd straighten up and come right on up out of there with the cow.

Old man Frank Heulster (Huelster, Hoelster; spelling

unknown) had a half-section of land over near Toyahvale there where he'd run the mail station for the stage. His three boys—Frank, Fritz, and Leo—all left home one day and came across to the Jeff Ranch and told Mr. Beau they were ready to go to work. About that time old man Heulster showed up and told them they'd all better get back over to their place. Frank rared back and said, "I'm twenty-one and I'm not going home." And he stayed right there and worked at that Jeff Ranch all his life until Mrs. Lee McCutcheon died. Then he went to San Angelo and married a woman he said he'd met through the mail. She quit him soon afterward, however, and married one of his brothers. Frank never did marry again. He stayed in San Angelo and worked at odd things and made enough money to live on. One day he said, "I think I've worked long enough and I'm just going to by-God retire." And he did. That was in 1968. He was eighty.

It was old man Heulster who'd run the stage coach stop at Barrilla Springs, then later at the Jeff Ranch head-quarters, and finally the mail station about five miles from the Toyahvale post office.

The stage route from Fort Davis came north down Limpia Canyon and split where Limpia Creek turned east towards Fort Stockton and the Barrilla Mountains. The route followed Limpia Creek to the Jeff Ranch headquarters, turned east just below the horse trap south of the house, and went on out through the Southside and English pastures.

★　　　★　　　★

From an interview with Jack Scannell[1]

The Overland's original stop was at the little spring at the mouth of Barrilla Canyon north of the Jeff Ranch head-quarters. They used it from 1851 to 1871. The stage didn't

---

[1] Jack Scannell, Professor of History, Midland College, Midland, Texas is the stepson of the late Wade Reid. When Journalist Bary Scobee came to the Davis Mountains to live about 1915, one of the first interviews he conducted was with Frank Heulster, Sr., operator of the Overland's Barrilla Mountain Station, and later the Toyahvale Mail Station. Scobee let Professor Scannell read the notes of his interview.

run during the Civil War. Wade and Roy's fence ran just above the spring. They often rode out by it to get to their mountain pastures. The first stage road ran west from Indian Springs along Limpia Creek, just south of Wade and Roy's house and parallel to their fence. Then it turned north up to Barrilla Springs along the Indian Springs fence there just east of the Jeff headquarters. The Barrilla station itself was just a two-room rock building with a big rock fence around it.

It was the worst place in the world for a stage stop in Indian country, so they moved the station and set it up right there at the Jeff Ranch headquarters in 1871. Frank Heulster, a German immigrant, was responsible for the move. When the stage line hired him, neither he nor his wife could speak a word of English. They'd come from Germany and landed at Galveston. A representative of the San Antonio-El Paso Stage Line, owned by Ben Ficklin after the Civil War, was in Galveston hiring operators for some of his stations. They offered old man Heulster a job and packed him off to run the Barrilla station. Now Heulster might not have known Indians or English, but he had good sense. He took one look at the station's location, lost a couple of mules to the Indians, and promptly decided that was one hell of a place for a stage station. His problem, besides its location, was that Barrilla Spring was outside the station's rock fence. The station itself was made out of rock and was encircled by this big rock fence about seven feet tall. Inside, and on each side of the gate, they'd built single rock rooms with thick roofs to live in. They kept the teams inside the fence between changes, but had to go about a hundred-fifty yards to water the animals in the spring. Every time Heulster left the fence and the rooms, he was exposed to Indian snipers. Even inside the rock fence, the Indians could shoot straight down into it. Before Heulster got there, Apaches had attacked the station and stolen fifty mules. Colonel Sewell sent his mounted infantry from Fort Davis to

29

chase them, but it was three days before they could get to Barrilla and pick up the trail. All they ever found were a couple of crippled animals the Indians abandoned.

It didn't take old man Heulster long to decide it was stupid to stay there until the Indians killed him and his wife. So in 1871, he went south two miles to the bank of Limpia Creek and hand-dug a well knowing there ought to be water there. There was and Heulster built a new Barrilla stage stop. That same hand-dug well still waters the Jeff Ranch today. During the drought of 1917, Wade and Roy carried water from that well to their shack when their well went dry. They'd put bands around barrels to hold them on the back of their old jitney and haul the water to their house.

Now the Army sometimes furnished the stage with armed protection from one fort to the next, but in what the Reids called their Northside there east of their house—almost all their east pastures, really—was an Indian campground. There were also two streams that ran through the Northside then. North Carrizo ran right along that little mesa east and into their English pasture, and South Carrizo ran south through the North and Southside traps, and on into Limpia Creek. North Carrizo wasn't really a creek, though. It was an irrigation ditch the Indians had dug from South Carrizo Creek to water their cornfields on the flats there between the two mesas. They were mostly Apaches. Comanches were always passing through—going and coming on forays into Mexico—but they never stayed.

Anyhow, the Apaches would pick up the stage and chase it into the Barrilla station. Army escorts and old man Heulster fought a two-day battle there at the Barrilla stage stop one time until the Indians lost interest. Heulster had built an adobe wall around the Barrilla stop about eight feet high and a couple feet thick, complete with European parapets. That's how they held the Apaches off. One man was killed on the stagecoach and they buried him inside the walls because they couldn't get out. You could see the grave there for years and years just west of the Jeff house. It was about ten or twelve feet from old Frank's well. But the Indians never took the station, and Heulster and his wife lived inside the fence, never venturing out or opening the gates until they could see the stage. As the stage drew close, they'd throw the gates open and the stage and horses would slide to a halt inside the corrals. If Indians were after it, they'd pull up aways out. Once, an Apache slipped up from Limpia Creek, vaulted over the stage wall, sprinted across the enclosure, skirted up the opposite wall, and disappeared. Everyone was so surprised they didn't have time to shoot. They waited for the attack the rest of the day, but it never came. The stage line was closed down in 1883 when the Southern Pacific was completed.

4

There was, at one time, a small Limpia post office on Willis McCutcheon's land where Limpia Creek turned east away from the Fort Davis-Toyahvale road. You could also buy a few groceries there, and there was a big warehouse out back with horseshoes and other ranch supplies. Willis had married a girl from Houston whose brother had bad health, so they brought him out there and let him put in that little post office and store and all, hoping he would get better and it would help him out. It did. They closed it after awhile and went to trading at the Union in Fort Davis.

How Horsethief Canyon and Frazier Canyon got their names there on the Jeff Ranch is also kind of unusual. Two young cowhands working north of Fort Stockton got mad at their foreman one July Fourth after he told them they couldn't go to town to celebrate. An old man who worked at the ranch saw how mad they were and talked them into helping him steal some good horses from the ranch to sell in old Mexico. Evidently the two cowhands thought it would be a good way to get even, so they helped the old man gather the horses and head south. Ranger Thalis Cook got word of the theft, and he and some deputies fell in behind the three, running them hard. When they crossed the Jeff Ranch, the ranger asked Beau McCutcheon and Bill Kingston for help. They caught up with the thieves and pinned them down in the rocks near what was to become Horsethief Canyon. They hollered at the young men to give themselves up, but they refused and were killed. The old man, Walt Frazier, was on a big, powerful horse when he made his break. He got through, and the ranger, Beau, Bill, and the deputies run him hard but never could gain any ground on him. He was just on a better horse. When he came to the canyon there on the west side of the Fort Davis-Toyah road, he turned and went up through it and that's where they quit the chase because everyone's horses was give out except his. Beau and the rest of them just started calling it Frazier Canyon and the other one Horsethief Canyon after that. That's how they got their names. Horses were expensive then, and you had to have good ones to survive financially on a ranch. Consequently, horse stealing was a serious offense. The McCutcheons raised all of their own horses.

Anyhow, Frazier rode on until he came to the Texas-Pacific Railroad where he caught a west-bound freight. Later, they caught him and sent him to prison for five or six years. I'm not sure about the names of the two young men who were killed. Their family ranched somewhere near Abilene. Both were given a proper burial in Fort Davis. I know Judge Weatherby said a prayer over them.

Anyway, after we spent that first night at the Jeff Ranch with the McCutcheons, we pulled out up Limpia Canyon the next morning, then up Musquiz and on over to Alpine where we sold our team of mules.

Now we'd broke those mules just like they used to break stagecoach mules, which was by harnessing them up and letting them by-God run flat out for two or three miles, resting them for a few minutes, then letting them run again. You ran them like that until they were broke or tired. Coming south off those plains, there weren't any fences and the country was fairly flat, so we'd tie those mules to harness and let them run until they'd get enough. Time we got to Alpine they'd had enough, too, and was good and tired. Anyhow, an old boy running the dairy there in Alpine saw our mules—they was good-looking animals—and said he wanted them. So we sold them to him. He put them up to rest for a day or two, then hitched them up to his milk wagon one morning. I think he finally got them stopped somewhere down around Marathon. Someone told us those mules kept Alpine out of milk for a week.

Ross Miller's daddy was a real estate agent there in Alpine, and we told him we was looking for some land. He said old man Stillwell was trying to sell four sections with a shack and tank full of water on it south of there, just east of the Chisos Mountains. He said it had a nice big creek—Tornillo Creek—running right through it. We found out later the creek was as dry then as it is today except when it flashfloods. We rode down to Marathon and saw they were hauling ore there out of old Mexico and shipping it. There was a pretty good wagon road south, and we decided to use it to get to the Stillwell place. We stopped at old man McIntyre's store in Marathon for supplies before we left. He said, "Well, you better buy some oats to feed your animals 'cause there ain't a damn thing 'tween here 'n the river."

We bought oats and headed south for a couple of days until we come to a dirt tank. It was the first water we'd seen since we left Marathon, so we stopped, unhooked our horses, and staked them on the dam which was covered in grass. We were sitting there about three o'clock in the afternoon, letting the horses graze, when old man Jim Stroud rides up. He asked us where we was headed and when we told him, he says, "Well, ain't no use you boys going down there to look at the thing. I've got to gather some steers, so you just hook up and come on up to the ranch house, and I'll put you to work." We said okay and rode to his headquarters which was located about two miles into the Rosillos Mountains near a big spring.

The next morning old man Jim and the three of us left his ranch and he showed us his country. We wound up at the Stillwell place. The shack was built out of river canes, filled and padded and covered with dirt. A good rain would have washed the mud on top of whoever was inside. There was a tank and a little windmill not pumping water enough for a nest of yellow jackets. We agreed the place didn't look like it was worth the five hundred dollars, so we rode out and covered Stroud's country east of the Chisos and west of Tornillo Creek. There were wild burros in herds of thirty or so throughout the Chisos. Stroud told us about the cowboy who'd come down there to corral a bunch of those burros to

34

sell. All he did was run a horse to death on the desert floor. We also met old man Burnham who was living in the Chisos then.

The next morning Stroud put a few supplies in his wagon and we crossed over into what he called the Big Bluff country east of the Rosillos to work some cattle. But before we got far we come upon a big steer two panthers had killed the night before. Old man Stroud said, "We'd better go get the dogs right now 'cause them is two we have to get."

So we went back, gathered up his dogs, and picked up their trail. They bayed about noon at a cave up the side of a bluff. The opening was about twenty foot from the top with a narrow trail down to it. We rode above the cave and Wade got off and took out his old six shooter. I hooked my rope around his chest and eased him down in front of the cave opening with my horse. He couldn't see anything. The dogs was going crazy and Barney was fooling around an opening he'd found on top the bluff. When he dropped a rock into the opening, it scared the panthers. The male come up out of Barney's hole and like to have scared him to death. Stroud had his 30-06 saddle gun out. When the panther jumped toward a rock, he nailed him right back of the shoulder. Meanwhile, the female headed toward the mouth of the cave where Wade was dangling on my rope. He started kicking and hollering and shooting, and she come out right by him and took off down the mountain, the dogs tumbling after her. Wade hadn't hit nothing. I pulled him up and we measured the male at eleven feet, two inches from nose to tail tip. He was a big, heavy old cat. We asked Wade how come he didn't hit the other one, and he said it was a little difficult to concentrate when you're hanging at the end of a twenty-foot rope with a full-grown panther coming at you.

The dogs bayed the female again in Devil's Canyon, a box canyon about a mile long with sheer rock walls on three sides. She couldn't get out unless she came by us and the only way we could get down was to lower someone on a rope again. Wade said he believed he'd let Barney down this time. The dogs were running up and down the canyon sides above another cave so we let Barney down, and he eased up to its opening with his pistol ready and here she come right by him. He emptied his gun at her, too, but didn't hit anything. Stroud was standing up on the canyon rim, though, and made a long shot down and into the canyon and killed her. Afterward, Barney said he thought he understood what was wrong with Wade's aim.

We went on and gathered about five hundred Mexican steers for Stroud. He'd sold them to Gage, and we trailed and bedded them to the Gage Ranch. Once there we pushed them in Gage's corrals and chutes and branded them. They were too many and too big to throw and brand.

Stroud paid us off and Gage hired us for about thirty days for his roundup. He had about eight other men working for him and was branding as he went. We threw the day's gather into a herd, put the irons in the fire, and started to work. Quick as you'd look up there'd be someone there with a calf on the end of a rope. We'd work maybe fifty head a day, then move on to a new range, gathering and working as we went, day after day. Gage had a big ranch. Nobody even thought about working eight hours, and we told time by the sun. You got up at five o'clock, ate breakfast, saddled your horse, and tried to get to the backside of where you were to start the gather by daylight. At sunup you'd start back with what cows you found. We'd throw the cattle together and start with the branding. Usually we'd finish about sundown, eat, take the remuda to the holding trap, and get back to the wagon about ten-thirty at night, just in time to throw our bedrolls off the wagon and fall into them.

Gage had about eighty horses in his remuda, all broke to stand in a rope corral. After breakfast the roundup crew formed a rope corral about sixty feet square. You pitched one end of your rope to the man next to you until a rope corral formed, everyone holding the ends of two thirty-foot ropes. Each man had about eight horses assigned to him. You'd call the name of the horse you was suppose to ride and the wagon boss roped him, led him to you, and held your ropes while you put your bridle or hackamore on him. Then you held your horse and ropes until each man had a mount. When everyone had a horse, the wrangler took the remuda, and you folded your rope and saddled.

Pat Murphey was the main man at Gage's and old man Cal Feldman, a long tall old boy, was the wagon boss. Pat Blye, a black bronc rider who worked for Gage, was as good a rider as any I ever saw. He lived there in Alpine. Old man Blye, who lived in Alpine, was one of the Big Bend's first settlers.

We finished working for Gage and returned to Alpine with our wagon. Barney caught a train there and headed back to the Panhandle. We bought six head of broke horses with the money we'd made, hitched a couple up to our wagon and rode across to Fort Davis where Harold King was having a big dance in his garage. It was the first garage between El Paso and Del Rio. Later, Keesey Miller owned it. We tethered the horses and camped out south of town. There weren't no houses to speak of, and the old fort was about the only thing on the north end.

We pulled out down Limpia Canyon for Toyahvale the next morning and were two days getting there. Limpia ran clear water all the way. We rode on and met a fella with twenty head of green broncs and traded him our wagon and a team of horses for the broncs. We also swapped him a gentle horse for a pack mule. Then we started north again, riding them broncs as we went. This was when Wade got his neck broke. He crawled on one of them high pitching horses one morning, and they bucked up under a low telegraph line. The wire caught Wade just under the chin. It made a half-moon burn on his throat, jerked his neck back, and almost tore him out of the saddle. Somehow he stayed on and when the horse turned and started back towards the line again, Wade was down in the saddle where he could dodge it and

37

rode that old bronc down. Wade's neck was awful sore for a few days, but we didn't know he'd broke it. He never could turn his head and look behind him after that. He always had to turn all the way around to see behind.

When we came through Pecos, it had wood sidewalks, a mercantile, courthouse square, big alkali holes in their streets, and the railroad, which had come through there about 1882. A mule pulling a milk wagon down main street there sidestepped one of these holes, but the wagon fell in and turned over. Story was Sal Meyer was driving one of the first cars in that country from Fort Stockton to Pecos when he drove off in one of them holes. Bill Ikens came along with a buckboard and team of mules. Sal stopped him and said, "I want you to pull me out of here." Ikens says, "Tell you what I'll do. I'll pull you out of there for five dollars." Sal says, "I won't pay you no five dollars." Ikens says, "Well, good day," and rode off.

We rode through Pyote and on to Odessa which only had a few buildings. From Odessa we headed north, tethering the pack mule, fixing supper, and stretching out for the night. We kept our frying pan, coffeepot, salt, water, coffee, and beans packed on the mule. Wherever we tethered the mule, the broncs would stay right with him. We ate each morning before daylight, caught the pack mule and a gentle horse, roped us a bronc, topped him off, and headed north again. We did that all the way to the Panhandle. It took us two weeks to get there. We didn't cross a fence and damn few roads. We had the horses broke when we got there and didn't have no trouble selling them. That was the Fall of 1909.

Wade's arthritis got worse after we got back to the Panhandle, and his feet begin to hurt him all the time. It was getting cold, and Wade said he didn't want to fight another Panhandle winter hurting like he was. We had several sections of the Price land leased and some stock on it, and I told him I'd stay and look after our stock if he wanted to go back down and look for some land. We had about three thousand in the bank and a good bunch of cows, calves, and steers grazing. You just couldn't leave livestock then without taking a loss from blackleg, screwworms, or blizzards.

Wade took his saddle and bedroll, pitched them on a southbound train, and headed for Alpine. When he hit town, he bought himself a horse, found out Mr. Beau McCutcheon was needing riders, and headed cross-country to his headquarters northwest of Fort Davis. He got there, hired on and became good friends with "Mr. Beau," as everyone called him. Wade also started putting together our place while he was working for Mr. Beau.

Now while Wade and I were working for Gage, he'd offered us the same kind of deal he'd been offering other cowboys—thirty dollars a month to work for him while we squatted the land he was leasing from the state. At the end of three years, he would pay us a one-thousand-dollar bonus—"bonus us" it was called—and we would deed the land over to him. We told him if we filed on any land, we'd prefer to pay our own expenses, but we would work for him for thirty a month until we made enough money to carry us through. He said we couldn't file on any land he was using, and he expected us to come back and take him up on his offer. Right then we determined to find our own land in the Davis Mountains.

One of the first men Wade approached was a man named Miller who'd homesteaded a big section with a spring on it about two miles northeast of the Jeff Ranch headquarters. He said he'd sell it to Wade. The Miller spring and the grazing rights around it was what caused the Dick Riggs-Jim McCutcheon shooting.

Riggs was grazing some land there north and east of us. He and three brothers—Dick was the oldest, then Raneck, Monroe, and Tom—had left Kimball County to settle on the northeast side of the Barrilla Mountains in 1885, north of the Jeff Ranch. Monroe outlived them all. Annie Riggs, who'd married another Riggs, Barney, owned and ran a hotel east of the courthouse in Fort Stockton. I think Annie lived there until she died. I stayed at the hotel in my younger days. It's a museum now.

Monroe said they were headed for Arizona when they got to the Salt Lake there on the Pecos River and camped one night. Dick could see the Davis Mountains in the distance, so he told Monroe to sack up some jerky and bread and coffee and ride over there and see who was in the mountains.

When he got over there around the big spring in Balmorhea, they found the Saragosa Cattle Company grazing the Toyah Creek and the flats. No one was on the north side of the mountains except a few old settlers like old man Beard who had a little spring up there.

When Monroe got back and told his brothers what he'd found, they all broke camp, forgot about Arizona, and headed for the Davis Mountains where they started leasing land.

So Jim McCutcheon ranched on the south side of the Barrilla Mountains and the Riggs ran cattle north and east of him. In between was the Fonville and Lockhausen claims—two squatters—and the Miller section on the south side of the Barrillas. There was a man named Frank Rodgers who had two or three sections near the Miller Spring. Dick Riggs had leased those sections, too.

Miller lived in a tent at the spring. It was one of those old droughty years in 1906, and Jim McCutcheon had come by and said he'd give Miller a hundred dollars for that year's lease for the water and grazing rights around the spring. Miller said okay, but Jim didn't have his checkbook so he didn't leave him a check.

A couple of days later Dick Riggs shows up at old man Miller's and offers him a check for two hundred dollars a year for the grazing and watering rights, and Miller accepts that too. Dick returned and began rounding up steers to put on the land he'd leased. Jim came to the roundup there at the Carrizo. He saw they were cutting these steers out, so he asked Dick Riggs what he was going to do with them.

They were both sitting on their horses, side by side, when Jim asked him the question. Dick replied he was going to turn them loose over at the Miller Springs. Now both those men had mean tempers, and they didn't make a man Jim McCutcheon was afraid of. Words were exchanged. Jim took a big switch he was using for a quirt and went to whipping Dick Riggs over the head with it. Dick drew his pistol and shot and broke Jim's whipping arm. The bullet knocked Jim off his horse, but not out. So Jim reaches over with his good arm to try to pull his pistol out of his belt, and Riggs shoots him in that arm, too. The angle that Riggs was shooting from, though, caused the bullet to pass through Jim's arm and enter his stomach.

When he saw what he'd done, Dick spun his horse and headed for Alpine to give up to the ranger there.

There was a bunch of riders there who saw the whole thing, including Dick's brother, Monroe Riggs. Old man Stuckler, who was also at the roundup and who had a deputy's commission, saw what happened and hollered, "I deputize everybody on this roundup to catch that man." Monroe fell off his horse with his Winchester and said, "I'll kill the first man that starts after him." No one moved.

The ranger took Dick on to El Paso where he was charged. Eventually he come clear because both men had been wearing guns. Just about everyone carried a six-gun then. That's why you didn't have many serious arguments or written contracts. Everyone just did what they said they'd do. I think, too, maybe old man Miller figured they could both water there.

They loaded Jim aboard his horse and took him to the U-Ranch headquarters. One rider went to Pecos to get Dr. Jim Camp, the family doctor. The doctor drove his horse and buggy all the way out there and operated on Jim on the kitchen table at the U-Ranch headquarters. The table stayed there at the U-Ranch until the Sixties, but the ranch started

41

changing hands and someone moved it or sold it. If the shooting had taken place today, Jim would have lived. As it was, he died there on the kitchen table that September with Doc Camp trying to save him.

Now several of the McCutcheon riders were going to go over and kill Dick Riggs, but Mr. Beau stopped them; said there'd been enough killing, and that Jim didn't have any business whipping Dick over the head anyway. In fact, he reminded them that Dick and Jim was both friendly enough with one another, and it was their tempers that caused the killing. Later on, they had to remind Mr. Beau of his advice.

On the north side of Star Mountain, where the Scout Ranch is today, there was a fella who had a little old box canyon on his place with a six- or seven-strand barbed wire fence across its entrance, complete with gate. He'd go steal calves and put them in there until they were weaned. You couldn't hear them calves bawling down in the canyon, and as soon as they stopped and were eating on their own, he'd mark and brand them and turn them loose on his range.

Mr. Beau kept missing calves and noticing heavy bagged cows and no calf carcasses around. He began putting two and two together and found out this man was stealing his cattle. The day he found out about it he come back to his house, saddled him a fresh horse, rigged up his saddle scabbard, got his saddle gun, and headed up the canyon to kill him. That simple.

Now Jim and William had already been shot, and Jeff had died early out there, so as soon as the family found out where Mr. Beau was going, they stopped him and talked him out of it. Everyone was afraid both of them would die up there in that canyon. They would have, too, because Mr. Beau would have kept on coming until he either shot the man or was killed himself. Thieves just weren't tolerated then. Word got back to this rancher that Mr. Beau had started up there to kill him, and Mr. Beau never lost another calf.

Anyhow, Wade bought that section with the spring on it

from old man Miller a few years later. We eventually built our house right there near the spring beneath the bluff. Then Wade got to know John Fonville who was living in a little shack at the mouth of what we called Fonville Canyon. He was just south of the U-fence there in the mountains. Wade talked him into selling his three sections to us, and that's when he wired me to come down and take a look at the land. He was waiting for me with a horse when I got off the train. We rode the Fonville sections out the next morning. Both of us saw those mountains were covered with good grama grass, so we paid Fonville fifteen hundred dollars for his squatting rights, plus a dollar twenty-five an acre. We also made the state out a check for a dollar to a dollar fifty an acre, depending upon the section. The whole thing cost us about three dollars and fifty cents an acre.

Then we rode cross-country to Pecos, registered the land in our names, got a copy of the deed, and rode back to Alpine. I gave Wade my horse and caught the train back to the Panhandle.

5

When Mr. Beau found out we'd bought the land, he says to Wade, "Now you boys can't make a livin' on that land. Besides that, I wanted to buy it. I'll give you fifty cents an acre profit if you want to sell it." Wade told him he didn't want to sell it.

A few months later Wade bought another mountain section on the northwest corner of the ranch which we called the Rincon. Then he bid on a good canyon section from a man named Lockhausen who'd squatted three sections west of Fonville. It had good strong springs up high near its head. The springs—Headwater we called them—were higher than the Fonville country to the east. Wade told me later he was already thinking of a way to get that spring water to the Fonville and into our mountains. We went ahead and borrowed the money and paid for the Lockhausen country. It cost us about three dollars an acre.

By now the bigger ranchers had got word Wade was buying some of the high country and the springs there in the Barrillas, and a bidding dispute started. They offered old Lockhausen a little more money, but he'd already give Wade his word and shook hands and that was that. Then they tried to argue with the state, but we'd already filed. We got the canyon and called it Lockhausen Canyon. It was ours and everyone accepted that. This gave us about five sections or so of good mountain pasture. Mr. Beau told Wade, "Well, you boys seem determined to make a go of it out here."

Then Wade met old man English who had a section in the mountains just south of Lockhausen Canyon and a couple sections east of the Miller spring in the flats, which we leased. English was about seventy when Wade met him. He had a home in Alpine, but he stayed out there and batched most of the time. He always came by the Miller squat with his dog going up to check his west end cattle and the spring there where they watered. He told Wade one day he wanted to sell him the two sections in the flats. I was working in New Mexico when Wade wired me he was going to buy it. I wired him back to go ahead and file on whatever else he could to connect our flats with our mountain sections.

Wade did, and we called these sections the North and Southside pastures there east of the house. Then we were able to lease another section east of the North and Southside from Willis McCutcheon. Anyhow, we wound up with the horse trap there around the house, which wasn't quite a full section; a small half section bull trap we used in the winter that went east beneath the bluff behind the house; and the three sections we'd bought and leased in the flats.

The flats and mountains connected where our pasture dropped into Barrilla Canyon near Barrilla Springs. To get to our mountain pastures, you had to cut across the Jeff Ranch where Barrilla Canyon opened onto the flats or circle east into the U-country and back up toward the Fonville Canyon. Our Barrilla pasture connected the ranch, but just barely. We had to take what land we could to get to put our place together, you see, and were damn glad to have it.

I stayed in the Panhandle, worked for the Word's at the Frying Pan, and looked after our cattle at the Price place while Wade was working for the McCutcheons. Ever once in awhile I'd find a good cow or two and ship them down to Wade. Then Wade would buy a good cow or two, and that's how we started building our herd. I got my draft notice about then, but Jim Dinwiddie, Frank Culp, and myself got a six-month deferment so we could sell our livestock. They'd raised my lease on me in the Panhandle to twenty-five cents an acre, and I'd already decided not to pay it, knowing I was going to have to go to the Army. So I sold our stock, deposited our money in Alpine, and rode out to our little two-room squat shack we'd built right near the Miller spring.

We didn't have a house or anything to live in during the first years we were out there. We just camped right there on the little hill below the big bluff and slept on the ground for

45

several years. Finally we built us a little wooden shack where we kept our food and feed. Unless it rained, we slept outside and did our cooking inside. We also had about forty head of two-year-old heifers grazing our mountains that were doing mighty good.

There wasn't anybody there at the squat when I got there. Wade was taking hot baths at Hot Wells in Presidio County for his rheumatism. He was in pain most of the time about then. Anyhow, I checked our heifers and rode back into town. That's when I found out Bob, our oldest brother, had bought three hundred two-year-old steers from Lee Caldwell. He'd drawn a check on our account in Alpine—we had him on it then—and bought the steers with the money I'd made off our Panhandle cattle. Then he'd shipped them up to the Santa Fe Ranch in New Mexico to graze. I hoped he was taking care of them because we kept almost all our money in cattle in the beginning.

Anyhow, as luck would have it, I ran into Bob who'd rode cross-country from New Mexico to our place, hoping to catch me or Wade. He'd dehorned and turned his steers loose to graze some of the mountain country there in New Mexico and had gone to work for the Solias Cattle, Land, and Livestock Company. Everyone called the outfit the "Sly" Livestock Company. But he'd gotten so busy he couldn't get back to take care of the steers. He said the damned screwworms and grizzlies was eating them up, so we both rode back to New Mexico to try and salvage what we could.

Now the Sly Livestock Company, which was run by the Reynolds brothers out of Las Vegas, New Mexico, had gone in with Bob on the Santa Fe's lease and put about two thousand head up there with him. But the grass played out during the summer of 1916, so we took these steers on up to Rancho de Taos in New Mexico. The first snow that September in Taos was roof deep and caught everyone off guard. We managed to get about seven hundred head out of

46

those mountains, but the rest had to fend for themselves. Old man Gusterol, who lived at Taos—a Jewish fella who'd come out there with a pack on his back—said he'd been there three years and that snow was by far the deepest he'd ever seen. I visited with the old man a lot. He had a lot of property.

I told Bob I didn't have long before I had to leave for the Army, and I needed him to put some money back in the account so I could pay off some loans. He went to the outfit he was working for and drew ahead on his wages and paid back what he'd spent. I owed Zuck and Zule a note in Kansas City which I paid off with the money. We eventually lost twenty-five hundred dollars on our steers, but that was the way it went.

I stayed in New Mexico awhile longer until I noticed people were dying. Everywhere. They just died in bunches. I think they called it Spanish flu then. Later they likened it to the swine flu. A ditcher worked overtime in Taos burying people, and they had bodies stacked and waiting. Anyhow, they passed the emergency Volstead Act and the Army arrived in Taos with a truckload of whiskey for people to doctor with. I grabbed me a bottle or two. It worked fine for the living. Then I caught a train to Las Vegas, New Mexico, and connected on to Alpine where my younger brother Knox picked me up and took me out to the squat to get my jitney. I'd bought this little old secondhand, runabout jitney with carbide lights, crank, and running board for thirty-five dollars, and had driven it out to the squat and parked it. I run the jitney over to Pecos and left it at the rail station. I was afraid to take it to the Panhandle because it was so old and wore out. Then I caught the train to Sweetwater and made connections to Tulia the night before I was to report to the Army. I spent the night of November tenth at the Tulia Hotel. The next morning I went over to the draft board. They looked at me and asked if I could walk and breathe proper and I told them yes. They said there would be a man on the two p.m. train to induct me into the Army.

I sat down and talked with a few other cowboys they was drafting until around eleven when a telegram came saying draftees were no longer being accepted. The war had ended. They told us we could go—just take a train and pull out if we wanted.

I didn't go out to the homestead near Tulia because my sister Tola's husband, Roy Ross, had died that night with the flu. The next day, Mrs. Ross, two of their girls, and another boy died. Just like that. Within twenty-four hours. They took them out and buried them the same day.

I saw the druggist there in Silverton that afternoon, too, and even talked with him. The next day he was dead. I told Tola I was leaving and got on the train and made it as far as Sweetwater before I started getting sick. And scared. I got off at Pecos and picked up the jitney and started towards the shack. There was a little old four-inch snow on the ground, and I come to this arroyo that was hell to cross even when it was dry. I run into it and couldn't get the jitney out. I could tell I was getting weak, and it was about five miles from there to the Jeff Ranch headquarters, so I started walking.

When I got to the ranch, Mrs. McCutcheon was there. I said, "Mrs. McCutcheon, would you drive me back to the arroyo? I had to leave my jitney there."

Mrs. McCutcheon looked at me and says, "You're not going anywhere. You're as sick as you can be right now, and you just go in there and pull your clothes off and get in that bed and cover up real good and I'll bring you some medicine." In a minute she come in there with a big glass of hot whiskey and herbs and lemon and honey and something else. It was strong. I drank it and just passed out until noon the next day.

Frank Heulster and I went back and pulled the jitney out of the arroyo and I went on up to the shack. But Mrs. McCutcheon sent word I was to come back down there to the ranch right then. She said I could run up and see how everything was from time to time, but if I didn't come back down, she'd send somebody after me. I was still too weak to ride or walk or argue, so I went back down and she gave me another one of those drinks and the flu went away. I guess her hot whiskey sweated it out of me. As it turned out, I'd somehow missed the swine flu and World War I. I never realized how lucky I was until long years later and I got to reading about them both. The flu killed a lot of people. The McKenzie boy was young and strong and had a ranch up there by Fort Stockton. He'd gone up to New Mexico for something and was on the same train with me coming back. He got sick at Fort Sumner and passed out by the time they got to El Paso. His wife had him took off the train in El Paso, but he turned blue and died right there. She shipped him back to Stockton to be buried. That flu killed people so fast they didn't know what hit 'em.

★   ★   ★

**From an interview with
Bob Reid (1885-1976), older
brother of Wade and Roy Reid**

When the flu hit New Mexico I was camped with a government trapper named Max in the mountains north of Santa Fe. I guess being up there saved me. Silvertip grizzlies were killing our cattle and we were trapping them. A drought had hit and our grass had played out. Our steers were losing weight so we leased the Santa Fe Railroad's Rancho de Taos and moved them to the mountains.

The Santa Fe's ranch took in about a hundred-thousand acres in the Put Mountains southeast of Taos, which didn't have more than eighteen or so white people in it at the time. They were mostly artists who came there to paint the canyons and mountains on the Santa Fe's land. The railroad only used the land to cut cross-tie timbers, so they leased grazing rights to ranchers for fifteen hundred a year. Railroad crews cut trees during the winter, hauled them to the Rio Grande in wagons, and floated them down river to Albuquerque where they were cut. Sometimes the crews found a mountain stream big enough to carry logs to the river, and they'd work their way up both sides, clearing as they went.

Those mountains were some of the best range in the Southwest. Rich bunch-grass grew on top, sometimes as thick as wheat fields, and there were clear streams everywhere. During the Spring and summer a beautiful columbine and wild rose covered a lot of the mountains. The roses never got over ankle high and were the most fragrant flower I've ever smelled. Sometimes you could smell a small bunch a hundred yards before you got to them. I haven't smelled anything comparable in my seventy years since.

We packed our supplies up a ten-mile trail that topped out near our campsite which consisted of bedrolls and two tents—one for the trapper and me and one for his Airedales. We cooked in Dutch ovens over an open fire and killed meat for the dogs. There was plenty of wood and game, and we were near an ice-cold mountain stream that we bathed in and drank from. Those early mountain mornings were so clear it hurt your lungs to breathe, and I sometimes thought about never coming down from up there.

The grizzlies seldom ate the cattle they killed unless they just happened to be hungry. They killed the cattle to keep them out of their territories, which each silvertip had. If a steer or anything came into his territory, the silvertip just killed it or, if it was faster than he was, he run it off. They weighed up to a thousand pounds and there wasn't an animal in them mountains—wolf, cougar, lynx, bobcat, anything—that could challenge those grizzlies. We baited our traps with either apples or burro meat, which we bought from the Indians. The first thing we did though was sew some big thick logs together with rawhide to make a heavy three-cornered chute. The logs had to be big because those old bears would come in from the rear and flip them aside *like matches to get at the bait. Lord, they were strong. It was an all-day job just building a trap site. We used a big five-foot trap with springs that had to be clamp set. Each trap had a heavy five-foot chain with a big ring on the end of it. We always cut a tree about the size of a fence post and drove it through the ring. You couldn't anchor a silvertip to a tree because he'd pull his leg off in a minute to get away. Then we'd put our bait up in the corner and bury the trap, ring and all, in front of it. The idea was to force the bear to come around and walk up to the bait inside the log chute.*

When the grizzly stepped into the trap, he always tore up the pen we'd built, no matter what size the logs. The tree through the ring slowed the bear enough for Max's five Airedales to pick up his trail and catch him. Those Airedales were as fine a bear dog as I've ever seen. They'd nip the bear's rear, which he hated, and force him to turn and fight. When he turned at bay, they'd hold him until we caught up and shot him in the neck—about the only place you could shoot a grizzly with a 30-30. A bullet anywhere else in a silvertip was useless; wouldn't even faze him, and you didn't get caught around a wounded grizzly and live to tell about it. They were tough and mean and after we knocked a bear down, we always shot him a couple more times in the head to make sure he was dead. The fur on those old bears' humps was bluish and about three inches long. It glistened in the sun when you stroked it and gave off a silver appearance. That's where those old bears got their name. We killed twelve during a twenty-four-month-period and didn't have any more problem with them after that.

6

Now you always run the risk of getting hurt whenever you was working. We generally just laid up until we got well and didn't think much about it. We didn't go to no hospital because we didn't have any. First time I ever met old Sid Sibley his horse had fell with him and hurt his back and he couldn't use his legs. He was crawling around the bunkhouse on his hands and couldn't walk or stand up. He finally got to where he could walk. During the Fifties, Doc Sam Dunn, a family friend and doctor from Lubbock, was giving Wade a physical. The X rays showed Wade's neck had been broken, so he asked him what had happened. Wade told him about catching his neck on the telegraph wire. Doc asked, "Did it hurt?" Wade says, "It was sore for awhile, but I got over it."

I broke my hip one fall. Craziest thing. I was riding along out there bringing a bunch of bulls to the house so we could ship them. The old boy we'd sold them to had come for them that afternoon, and I'd ridden down to the little trap there below the house to gather them.

I was on the hill just east of the house when it happened. My horse was slinging his head, fighting flies. He slung his head around and when he did, my rein somehow hooked my spur and jerked my foot up side of his head. That boogered the old horse and he made a jump and went to bucking. I couldn't get my foot back in the stirrup and he dumped me off. I hit right flat of my back on one of them old rocks about the size of a grapefruit. Broke my hip in two.

The old pony stopped bucking after he dumped me and just stood there with the reins on the ground. I saw I couldn't get up so I rolled over and crawled towards him until I felt like I was going to pass out. I'd rest a minute and crawl some more. Just about the time I'd get to where I could reach out for those reins, that old horse would back up three or four steps. Lord, that made me mad. Anyhow, I finally went to cussing and throwing rocks at him trying to make him go to the house. I knew if he showed up there empty they'd come looking for me.

Finally the old horse turned and started the damn bulls toward the house. Hell, any other time he'd a lit out straight. But no, he took them bulls on to the house. When he got there, Wade knew something had happened so he got in the truck and come down there and found me and took me back to the house. They set me in the backseat of our old car while they loaded the bulls. Well, I couldn't lay down and I couldn't sit up and I was sure enough hurting. When they finished loading out those bulls, Wade took me over to old Doc Wright in Alpine. He takes a look at my hip and says, "You broke it." I told him I knew that. And he said, "Well, gonna have to put you in a cast." Called it a plaster of Paris cast. Damn thing musta weighed three hundred pounds.

★   ★   ★

From an interview with
Mrs. Lou Reid, Alpine, Texas,
sister-in-law of Wade Reid (1888-1974)

Roy's horse came back to the house without him one afternoon in the Fall of '36. When Wade saw him, he knew something was wrong. So he got into the pickup and drove around to the pasture where Roy had been and found him down there on the ground crawling toward the house. Wade lifted him into the front seat of the pickup and asked him if he was hurting real bad. He said no, he didn't reckon he was, and for them to go on and load the bunch of bulls headed for El Paso. So they put Roy in the car while they loaded the bulls. It was nighttime and the autumn air was chilly by the time they finished. When the cattle trucks were loaded, Wade drove Roy to Alpine and came by to get Knox to help him. I guess it was about two a.m., and Roy was cold and shivering. Knox took a blanket with him and draped it around Roy's shoulders, then they went down and woke Doc Wright up. He told them to carry Roy on into his office at the Holland Hotel and he would work on him. Doc Wright slid a big can between two tables, sat Roy's rear on the can, then made him put his shoulders on one table and feet on the other. Roy was so stiff from sitting upright so long in the cold, Doc Wright almost had to break his hip again to get him laid out flat. When they finally got him straightened out, they removed his chaps and boots and cut off his Levis.

Doc Wright set his hip right there without an X ray, then set about wrapping the lower portion of Roy's body. Doc had asthma, and every few minutes he'd give out and have to stop and wheeze. When he finally got Roy wrapped, he took a big washtub, mixed up his plaster of Paris and started building Roy a stomach-high cast. It took him the better part of an hour, wheezing and all. Ever once in awhile Roy would wince, but Doc never did give him a shot or anything while he was fixing that hip. When Doc finished, they brought Roy and a hospital bed over to the house, and we put them both in the west end of our living room.

The next day we hired an Army nurse who lived two blocks from us to bathe and dress Roy every morning. I tried to find things to help Roy pass the time. He tried reading Gone With the Wind *lying on his back, but the book was too heavy to hold up over his head for long periods. He couldn't bend except from the diaphragm up. He just hated having that cast over his middle and having to lay flat. One day I gathered up all my kitchen knives and a whetstone, spread a cup towel over Roy and the bed, and set him to sharpening knives while I went back to the kitchen. After awhile I was struck by the silence. When I went to see if Roy had fallen asleep, I found he'd whittled out the front of that cast so he could bend up at the waist. There was plaster of Paris all over the bed and floor.*

After Roy had been with us about eleven weeks, Doc

Wright come out and cut the cast off, and Roy had to learn to walk all over again with crutches. His legs were weak and he tired easily, and there was no way he could go home because he would never have been able to make it up those steps in front of their house on crutches. He stayed with us a couple more weeks struggling to walk again and did. Doc Wright finally told him to go home. Wade came into town and picked him up.

The year I came back from New Mexico Wade was already working part time at the Jeff Ranch and looking after our cattle when he could. Soon as I got there he went full time with the Jeff, and I rode our country, taking care of our stock. I slept outside our shack on the ground.

Then Wade's right arm got to hurting him again. Arthritis and rheumatism was withering it away, and it was getting so he couldn't use it. The pain had even gone down into his legs. So he decided to go to Hot Wells and start taking hot baths again. The second morning he was there Joe Kingston's wife's father, who was a doctor, saw Wade climb out of the bath to dry off. Old Doc Olive looked at his back and said, "I'm gonna tell you something. You needn't take another hot bath of any kind because it won't do any good." He said, "Your back is out of place. You're gonna have to go to a chiropractor and get it put back right."

Now different things had happened to Wade. He'd had his neck hurt and had horses fall with him a time or two, but the worst thing happened to him was at Hovey one morning, right when his rheumatism was hurting him so bad. He kept trying to work and had gone out that morning to gather a few horses we had at Jim McElroy's. We were gonna take some cows and calves back to a trap.

Anyhow, he must have been making a run when his horse stepped in a hole and rolled over him. Whatever happened didn't knock him completely out. Just stunned him. His neck and upper back was hurt bad, though. Somehow Wade got ahold of his horse and got back in the saddle. The horse followed the others to camp, but Wade didn't remember the ride in. We started the cattle on back toward the ranch, and he come riding alongside me and says, "Where we at?" I says, "What's the matter with you, Wade?" He says, "I don't know. I just don't know anything." He says, "Have we left the corrals yet?" I says, "Yes." He said, "Well, I guess I'm just beginnin' to come to. My horse fell with me. Last thing I remember."

Soon after he talked to the Doc at Hot Wells, he tried a chiropractor. The chiropractor worked on him two months, and do you know after about ten treatments, his right arm and hand commenced getting better and he could work them? He took sixty treatments and got to where he could use his right arm and hand as good as his left. The soreness disappeared from his leg and it got to where he could use it too, but his back was still kinda weak. It stayed that way the rest of his life. He says the chiropractor saved him from being a cripple. I just don't know, but Wade was better. Finally he come back out to the ranch and went to work for Mrs. McCutcheon again. I was still tending our cattle in the mountains and living at the squat. Bob, you know, ran the U-Ranch for awhile.

★   ★   ★

From an interview with
Bob Reid (1885-1976)

I was in Amarillo visiting with a few of the riders who'd worked for me on the Frying Pan. They told me Al Popham, who owned the U-Ranch in Pecos County near Balmorhea, had died. His health started failing him about 1917 and he'd gotten progressively worse. He lived in Amarillo, but his wife lived in Kansas City. They weren't divorced, however. He'd gone to Kansas City to settle up with her and had paid her for her share of the ranch. Before he could get the papers drawn up, he died. That left the ranch belonging to her and his nephew, Francis Popham, a bookkeeper who'd married Judge Wallace's daughter at Tascosa. Like Al, Francis lived in Amarillo. There were about five other Popham girls living there around Amarillo, but they'd all married local boys, none of whom knew anything about running a Davis Mountain ranch, which was a lot different from a Panhandle ranch.

An old cowman was running the U at the time, but he was getting on in years. Milt Cunningham, one of the men I rode with on the Frying Pan, told me Francis Popham was looking for someone to replace the old man. I looked Francis up, and he asked me if I would be interested in running it. I'd run the Word Ranch and the Sly Livestock Company in New Mexico and had the experience. I decided I'd take the job providing he let me run it and didn't interfere. I wasn't about to be told how to run a ranch. I said, "Francis, I'll go down there and run the U for you for a year. If I don't suit you at the end of a year, you let me know and I'll move on. I'll take care of the ranch, the roundup, and the crew. You take care of the selling and the books." He offered me a hundred dollars a month. I told him I'd take it and he hired me on the spot. I loaded up my gear, headed for the Davis Mountains, and stayed on at the U-Ranch the next six and a half years.

When I got there, it had about a hundred twenty-five thousand acres, a good remuda, and about thirty-five hundred cows. That Spring had been a good one and everything was fat. I personally counted all the cows and learned the waterings as soon as I could. Didn't take me long to find out those old cows knew what to do with themselves better than anyone. I'd work them and their calves in the Spring, and we'd gather and wean and ship their calves in the Fall. Francis took care of the selling and bookwork and I took care of the cattle. We never failed to show a good profit every year.

The U was, in my opinion, one of the best cow-calf operations in the Davis Mountains. The calves started about the first of March and by May, when we started branding, they'd all be on the ground. Nature took care of them. Each winter the old bulls congregated in groups of five or six all over the ranch and the cows moved off by themselves. We had about a hundred ten head of good saddle horses and when we finished the roundup each Spring, we'd take their shoes off and turn them back to pasture. The country had good springs everywhere then, and we just let the horses have the run of the range and drift with the grass. In the Fall we'd gather and shoe them, make our roundup, then turn them loose again to winter with the cows. I never kept bad horses because they hurt good hands. And good hands didn't really like to fool with bad horses while they were working.

The U had good springs everywhere then, including the big Palomas Spring and the big spring near Dick Riggs' old headquarters. Running water was all over that ranch when I got there, but as soon as they got to drilling those irrigation wells down there on the flats north of the Barrilla Mountains, the springs dried up. A geologist told me the springs from Phantom Lake to the Escondidas on the Pecos were up against a fault, and that it was part of the same waters they had in Carlsbad Caverns. He said the water had come in there millions of years ago, and when you took it out, it was gone.

Whenever I started the U roundup, I always had plenty of good help on hand. I think the reason was I always had a good cook, good food, and fresh beef. Them was the main things with a good cow outfit. Work and horses never worried good cowhands. Good fresh beef was probably the most important item to a wagon crew. We'd kill one about every three or four days. I'd pick out a big fat spotted heifer calf—never a steer—and we'd kill it, skin it, and dress it out near the wagon. Manuel, our regular wagon cook, would sit this spit next to the campfire and put the ribs on to broil about mid-afternoon. They had to be cooked first because they spoiled first. By evening the ribs would be done, and when the riders came in, they'd tear off those ribs and chew on 'em like a bunch of hungry wolves. The next thing Manuel did was cut up the calf's liver and heart and sweetbread and marigut and put them in a big pot to make his son-of-a-gun stew. He never would tell us what all went in it—tomatoes, peppers, corn, other vegetables—but it was always good and the riders usually finished off a pot the next meal. Then he would start into the steaks and roasts—which he either fried or broiled. Our meals usually consisted of meat, red beans, stew, sourdough biscuits, and fruit. The fruit was either dried apples or apricots, boiled. We preferred apricots because they kept better and kept the riders loosened up.

Coffee was another mainstay around the chuck wagon. One roundup Manuel was sick and we had to start without him. I'd hired an old man who was crippled—horse fell on him or something—but nevertheless who was a good cook. The second morning out we were camped on the Sandia down near the old Saragosa store. Now the first thing the men did when they rolled out each morning was to go take a leak in the brush. Then they'd head for the chuck wagon and a big five-gallon pot sitting on the coals. When the boys got up and headed for the coffee that second morning, the old cook stopped them. He said they drank up all his coffee the day before and, by God, they wasn't going to drink it up again. I was out aways from the wagon slipping on my boots and heard the ruckus going on around the campfire. I got dressed and eased over to the fire and asked the cook what was the problem. He told me they was drinking up all his coffee. Roy was squatting out there away from the fire with his cup. He always was kinda shylike, except when he was mad.

I knew right off I'd have to remedy that situation because them boys wouldn't stand for no coffee in the mornings. So I turned to Charlie Oates, a cowboy there, and asked him to ride down to the Saragosa store, buy some extra coffee and the biggest coffeepot they had, and charge it all to the U-Ranch. He did and I never heard another grumble that whole roundup. You could work good hands fourteen, eighteen hours a day and never get a grumble out of them cowboys. But a little thing like not enough coffee in the morning or a bad cook could make your whole crew mad, and next time you went to roundup you might have trouble hiring good hands.

Al Kountz, the Heulst boys, and Joe Hayter, one of the strongest little fellers you ever saw from down on the east side of the U-Ranch, always come and worked the round-up each year with me. Joe flanked calves because he was strong and Kountz, a big older feller, always brought two or three good gentle horses with him to help hold the herd. I'd also hire seven or eight young fellers and a Mexican boy or two for the roundup.

We made one roundup a day at each U watering. I knew about how many cows there ought to be from the swing. We'd throw them together at the spring, and I'd make a quick tally while the crew started to work. I'd have three men holding the roundup, two helpers dragging the calves, and two or three two-man crews stretching the calves. The mother cow usually followed her calf to the branding fire. When we finished working the calf, it always hopped up and went right back with her and they'd both go back to the herd. I always done the castrating and dehorning and vaccinating myself, and never lost a calf to blackleg the whole time I was there, thanks to the Franklin vaccine.

We'd get through a gather about midafternoon, eat dinner, move camp to the next watering, then lay around the wagon and repair equipment or shoe horses if any of them had lost one. The boys generally played a small ante game of poker if they didn't have any repairs. We used a good span (two) of mules to pull our wagon. A lot of big Panhandle outfits like the XIT or JA generally used four horses because they had so much stuff on their wagons. We camped at the waterings where we were going to make a roundup.

It took us about ten days to two weeks to brand everything. I always told the riders to cut back the baby calves that couldn't walk, the bulls, and the dry cows because they disturbed the roundup. I also scattered the riders myself each morning because I knew them old cows would be headed in towards water, and I could send the riders out beyond and just ease everything on in. When the

61

roundup was over, I'd keep one man and we'd ride our waterings. When we found a calf we missed, we'd rope it. I carried my vaccine and branding iron on my saddle, and we'd brand and work the calf on the spot. The rest of the time we spent taking care of the windmills and the waterings. We also rode and repaired the fences, and we always made sure our fences and gates was in order. I generally took care of everything myself. I'd watch the waterings pretty regular during calving season. Every once in awhile an old cow would lose her calf and come to water with a big bag. It happened a lot on the Word Ranch in the Panhandle, but the U cattle never did have that problem. That's why it was so unusual to see one. Truth was, you just didn't bother those old U cows.

Up in the Panhandle a lot of ranchers gathered up their bulls so they could sort of control when their calves arrived. The U-Ranch never had that problem either. Nature took care of everything there, and we seldom had winter calves. If we had one, we'd just cut him and keep him over until next Spring when we shipped. Then we rounded up each Fall, worked any late calves, separated the yearlings and shippers and trailed them to either Hovey, Saragosa, or Balmorhea, depending on where we could get a doodlebug in with the cattle cars.

The two roundups, fence and windmill repairs, the extra rider and my salary, and the ranch supplies was all the expenses the U had. It come to about seven thousand a year and worked like that for over six years. Then one Fall Francis drove out to the ranch and announced he'd decided to cut the U up into four pastures. I knew right off that idea had come from some of those Panhandle shoe clerks.

I asked, "Why?" He says, "Well, you can handle the cattle so much better." I said, "Damnit, you can't handle 'em any better than they're handling themselves right now. We've made money every year—drought and all—and we've never lost a cow or calf to blackleg." I told him if he would take the money he was going to spend on fences and buy out

*the Short place—a little five-section pasture that joined his
Eclipse pasture—it would give him all the grass and water
he'd ever need. "No," he said, "you can handle 'em so much
better with the fences." I said, "Well, you don't need to handle 'em. I never penned a cow or calf in my life on this ranch
'cause there isn't any need for it." So I told him again his
fencing idea wasn't no good and tried again to explain why.
All those old cows, you see, were born and raised on that
ranch. They knew where to water, how to follow the high
grass when it got dry, and how to winter and still drop a
healthy calf each Spring. Nature took care of their cycles,
and they took care of themselves. I told him if he started
chopping that ranch up, it wouldn't be no time until he'd
have those old cows walking the fences and parts of his
ranch grazed down to a nub. He said, "Well, my mind's made
up." I said, "So's mine 'cause I don't want my name associ-
ated with these fences. If I stay, someone might think I had
something to do with it. Make me out a check."*

*I dropped back by the ranch a year or so later and there
were fifteen or so Holstein cows clustered around the house
and barn. I asked the fella they'd left in charge, "What are
you running here, a dairy?" He said, "Oh, them's for
dogies." I just shook my head and went on.*

8

Wade and I shipped cattle from Hovey and Balmorhea and Alpine at first. We didn't have any trucks then, and we trailed most of them to the railhead at Hovey which was on the rail line about eighteen miles northeast of Alpine. When we shipped from Alpine, we'd take a couple days going so as not to draw down the cattle. People then didn't mind you crossing their land long as you didn't bother their cattle. We also shipped one bunch from Balmorhea to the plains in 1916. We'd bought them from old man Ikey south of Marfa, watered them near Alpine, trailed them to Balmorhea, and had to ship them to the Panhandle somehow. L. W. Addison had a little railroad company with a spur to Balmorhea where everyone from the north side of the mountains shipped from. L. W. said he couldn't get no stockcars, that all he had was boxcars. I said, "What's wrong with shipping them in those boxcars?" He said, "I'll give you two boxcars for each stockcar you'd normally get." We agreed, put sand in the boxcar floors, three two-by-sixes across each door, and loaded our cattle. I boarded the train with them and headed for Tulia where we'd leased nine sections near Kress. We got as far as Sweetwater and the Santa Fe Railroad said they wouldn't take those steers any farther unless we released them for all liability. I climbed down out of one of the cars and walked the length of the train checking the steers out. Hell, they was laying in there on that sand and was ten times better off than if they'd been regular cattle cars. I walked back and told the Santa Fe man if I shipped any more cattle to the Panhandle, I'd prefer to ship them like this. He said, "No more, 'cause someone has to clean them boxcars out." Anyhow, I released them, he was satisfied, and we headed for Tulia. We got up to Kress, unloaded them, and trailed them to pasture. Before we left, I knocked the two-by-sixes off the doors and sold them to a farmer for about what I give for them. Like I said, we didn't have no trucks then. Only horses and railroad.

We always worked hard during those early days, but every once in awhile we'd have a little fun, too. One of the things we enjoyed was the prizefights in the loft of Walter Graef's barn in Alpine.

Billy Crews (or Cruise, Cruiz; spelling unknown) was our champ. He was a sergeant in the cavalry at Balmorhea and was a boxer—I mean a good boxer. First time I ever saw Billy was outside a saloon there around Balmorhea. He had four or five people stretched out on the ground, and quick as someone stepped in front of him, why he'd knock 'em out.

Well, a bunch from over there at Saragosa had this big old boy who weighed about a hundred-ninety that they thought could whip Billy. Billy only weighed about one-seventy, but he was short and solid and all muscle.

The match was made and we crawled up in Graef's barn one night and this bunch from Saragosa got to betting heavy on their man. Billy strung him along—they fought bare-knuckled stripped to the waist—until all the bets was down and then knocked him out cleaner 'n a whistle in the fourth round. Wasn't nothing that bunch from Saragosa could do about it except pay off. We took their money and they went home. There was another big, tall, lanky kid with long arms from Fort Stockton who fought Billy once, but he wasn't no match at all and Billy knocked him out the first round. Billy never was beat as long as I saw him fight.

We always pulled the ladder up after everyone got into the loft for one of them matches. That way the peace officers couldn't sneak up there and arrest everybody while the fight was in progress or stop the fight. Everyone always paid off, too. If you didn't,they politely dropped you outa that barn head first.

Another thing we enjoyed doing was getting together and roping on a Sunday or July the Fourth. I always went to roping contests when I had a little time, which wasn't often. We'd get together and some old boy would furnish the steers

65

and we'd hold what they called breakaway ropings. Me and old Charlie Norton won second once in Alpine. Didn't have an arena or anything like that. We'd just get out there in the open and the people would form on each side of a flat space and we'd throw up a temporary corral for the steers. There wasn't no so-called professionals then. Just cowboys getting together. It was a break from hard work. George Jones, one of the better ropers in this area, had some fine roping horses.

Anyhow, we'd just turn a steer loose and let him run. The cowboy had to catch and rope the steer either by the head or horns, flip his rope around the opposite side of the steer, lay him down by himself, get off, and tie forefoot and hind foot while the steer was on its side. I've done it a lot like that. One man. And if you crippled a steer in the process, you were disqualified. Automatically. The way we laid a steer down by ourselves took skill. Whole purpose of it, of course, was that a man could doctor or handle one out by himself while he was riding and working. Very, very seldom would we even break a horn or injure an animal. Just wasn't done.

We got together a little goat roping contest at Toyahvale one Sunday. There was myself, Jim Cooksey, Pab Cooksey, Bob Reid, an old boy from down on the Pecos named Aubrey, and a fella named Carruthers who was always beating us. We finally figured a way to beat Carruthers. We gave him an old billy to rope that was fast and smart. Carruthers chased him about seventy-five yards and threw his loop. The goat saw it coming out of the corner of his eye, stopped, took a couple of steps back, and the loop just hit the ground in front of him. We musta laughed about that for fifteen minutes. Later we gave him a regular goat. I drew a little old yearling kid that could run like a rabbit. Damned if I didn't catch him first throw and win first money that day.

Our riding events consisted of outlaw horses people brought in. I've pulled many old horse's head down and held him until the rider got his saddle on and said he was ready.

People always brought their toughest broncs to see if anybody could ride them. We'd see who could ride these broncs and who couldn't. Whoever made the best ride got twenty-five dollars. Most of the cowboys couldn't stay with them old outlaw horses. We did some bulldogging, but I never could see the point of it. I agreed with what Asa Jones said about 'dogging—man who went in for that had to be a man who wore a number six hat.

Those ropings and get-togethers were always a lot of fun and entertaining for the men who were working. They were a chance, really, for us to match skills we was using everyday. That was the real origin of rodeos. Rodeos today are all professional, and there's not much to it when all an old boy does is travel from town to town and crawl over a chute. When we started we didn't have no arenas or nothing. We just went out and found us a good wide open space that didn't have no holes where our horses could fall and went to roping. Everybody had a good time and we enjoyed it.

Sometimes we'd go to Saturday night or July Fourth dances at Fort Davis or Balmorhea or Pecos. An old boy come down from Chicago—his dad had moved him and his wife down there for some reason—and built himself a three-story house on the Cayonosa towards Pecos. They had this big house that just sat there on the flats with a few acres around it. The top floor was a ballroom and from time to time he'd have a dance. It wasn't too far across there horseback from the ranch, and I made several dances at his place. Later we'd drive over in those little old jitneys. People from Pecos and Fort Stockton came too. The house stood there for many years, even after they left, then burnt down.

Wade met his first wife, Happy McAfee, when he was in the Panhandle. She took a liking to him right off. She'd gone to college at West Texas State in Canyon and had come to Alpine to teach home economics at the high school in 1924 and 1925. Then she'd gone back to college in Illinois. Wade caught the train up there and married her. They went to

Detroit on their honeymoon, bought themselves a little Chevy coupe, and drove it back to the ranch. It didn't last long in the rocks, and we traded for another Model-A Ford. Paid three hundred and eighty dollars for it.

About the only girl I ever called on was the Word girl. They told me the Mayfield girl liked me, but I didn't get to see her again after I came to this country. Dave Mayfield had about three sections that neighbored our homestead in the Panhandle. There were four girls in his family.

★　　　★　　　★

From an interview with
Myrtle Beights McAfee (1892-1984),
sister-in-law of Wade Reid's
first wife, Florence "Happy" McAfee

I guess the first time I ever met Florence—"Happy" as they all called her—was about 1918, a year before I married her brother. I was visiting a friend on a neighboring farm north of Loraine one Sunday and we went to church. That's where I met my husband, Russell. It was summertime, and he was working on a farm for extra money, even though he taught school at County Line. The next year he taught at Champion, then at Valley View. Florence was staying at Carr at the time, and we would sometimes see one another when we were all together. Florence and Russell's father had moved from Alabama and bought a farm outside Winnsboro, Texas, around 1880. His first wife died after he arrived. A few months later he married a Miss L. C. Redding. There were four children by this second marriage, the last two being Russell and Florence, the baby. Then Mrs. Redding just dropped dead on the floor one afternoon. They think it was a heart attack. Russell was two at the time, and Florence was three months. When the other kids came home from school, Russell was holding her head in his lap saying, "Mama's asleep. She won't wake up and the baby's crying."Russell's older half sister, Maggie, from his father's first marriage, took Florence to raise. Another half-sister from the first marriage, Agness Pearl, took Russell and the other two children.

When Florence and Russell's father died in 1909, one of the family members heard that Russell wanted to go to college, and offered to buy his part of his father's farm. Russell accepted and used his money to enroll in college at West Texas State in Canyon. Now everyone said Florence was smart and had always wanted to go to college, too. So Maggie helped get Florence enrolled in West Texas State using money she made from seamstress work. Later, Florence taught at Carr and Alpine. She also attended college in East Texas for awhile, then moved to Bloomington, Illinois, where she got her degree. Now when Florence was in school in Canyon, she became engaged to a young man named Harry Word.

The Words were wealthy people and their family owned a big ranch. The Word boy gave Florence a three-carat diamond for an engagement ring. Before they could get married, though, a horse threw the Word boy, paralyzing him from the neck down. Florence wrote to him and went to see him, but each time she could tell he was failing and his mind was going. Finally he died. She gave his mother back the ring. Afterward, Florence met Ted Reid in Canyon who introduced her to his brother, Wade. Well, Happy just fell in love with Wade the first time she ever saw him.

When Happy went to Illinois, Wade took the train up to be with her. They were married there in Bloomington. When she graduated, they came back to Texas to Wade and Roy's ranch. Since there wasn't a house on the ranch then, they lived in a tent for awhile. Roy was with them. They all pitched in and got the house built shortly afterward, though.

When Wade and Happy got back, we built our adobe house near the Miller Spring. It was 1927. First house we'd ever had. In between we'd managed to put together about a hundred-fifty head of good cows and we were shipping calves each Fall. Wade was still working at the Jeff when he left to go get Happy, and I was taking care of our place and our cattle. When he got back, we switched. He and Happy moved into the house and I went to work at the Jeff. That was how we made it — doing all the work ourselves while one of us worked for the McCutcheons.

Eventually, Jim and Beau McCutcheon divided the Jeff Ranch and the 7-Ranch. Beau wound up with over a hundred sections. I think Jim had about eighty sections. Willis and Bennett McCutcheon had about seventy sections each and were sandwiched in between Jim and the Jeff Ranch on the east side and Beau and the 7-Ranch on the west side. Mr. Beau's brand was 7L. Jim McCutcheon's brand was 7K, which became the Jeff Ranch's brand. Willis had the 7-Springs Ranch.

After Jim McCutcheon's first wife died, he eventually married Mrs. Lee Killough — everyone called her Mrs. Lee — a sister of John Killough in La Grange. R. C. Williams was a nephew of Mrs. Lee, and she raised him there at the Jeff Ranch. His mother had died when he was born and his father left shortly afterward, so Mrs. Lee took him to raise. Mrs. Lee left a third of the Jeff Ranch to R. C. Jim and his first wife had had one child — Marie — so when he and Mrs. Lee married, they already had two children to raise. She and Jim never had any children of their own. When Mrs. Lee died, she made her brother, John Killough, executor of the Jeff Ranch. John Killough was a successful businessman in La Grange. He and his wife and two daughters lived in that big house on those two blocks there near downtown La Grange, across the street from the Methodist Church. Pat

Mulloy married one of Mr. John's two daughters, Nellie Lee, and Mr. John asked Pat to come run the Jeff Ranch for him when Nellie Lee's health began to go bad on her at La Grange. He did and did a good job. Pat, you know, was always a good businessman and served on the board at the Fort Davis Bank for years.

Anyhow, Pat ran the Jeff for at least twenty-five years or so, then found a good family—the McKnights from over near Odessa—who wanted to buy the Jeff and had the money to do it. In order to sell it, Pat had to get the signatures of all the Jeff heirs—Mrs. Lee had named a bunch of them in her will—and it took him a year or so to get the job done. Eventually, though, he got it sold right to the McKnights in 1964.

★   ★   ★

From an Interview with
Beau McCutcheon, Jr. (1904-1980)

My mama died in 1912. I was eight and Papa felt like I was too young to go to school, so he kept me with him at the ranch. I made my first roundup that year. We covered a lot of territory then because the McCutcheons owned and leased so much land. Papa started gathering yearlings the first of September, and I didn't get back to Fort Davis until December. I slept in a camp bed on the ground and my hair got shoulder length.

The McCutcheons started their gather on the west side of Star Mountain. We'd round up four or five hundred cattle a day and cut out the steer yearlings plus any two or three year olds we wanted to ship. Then we'd turn the rest of the cattle loose and either push those yearlings east, holding them at night, or drop them in a holding pasture to pick up later. The McCutcheons did this day in and day out, working their way east until they'd gathered several thousand head,

71

then they'd trail them on over to a rail line near where Hovey would later be. Joe and Mackie Mitchell usually took delivery of the cattle at Hovey and helped with the receiving before shipping them on to California or up north. We had men out working year round. It was a real luxury for them to get to come into the bunkhouse and take a bath. We'd work all day or until we got through. Papa would say, "Today we'll work Horsethief Canyon country," which had a nice big spring and watering hole in the rocks there. There was a crew of eighteen that went with the McCutcheon wagon—the cook and his helper (the horse wrangler), and fifteen or sixteen cowboys.

Frank Millan was Papa's cook. He was a German who'd been raised in Mexico. He had to leave during a revolution. When the Germans headed back to Mexico after the revolution, Frank decided to stay and work as a chuck wagon cook year round for Papa. He did that until he died. He had a boy who spoke Spanish well. I taught the boy how to speak English and he taught me how to speak Spanish. Eventually he learned how to read and write English, too. We also had a Negro couple—Agnes and Lee Huff—who went to work for us there at the headquarters the day after they got married. The man worked for Papa all his life, too, until he died. He was as fine a bronc rider and cowboy as there was in that country. He never bossed anyone, even though Papa let him run the crew there at the ranch. Lee always suggested things while we worked, and whites and Mexicans alike worked with him because they all respected him as a cowboy. His wife stayed on and worked until she died. She raised all us kids, really. They were like part of the family.

The McCutcheons' remuda had at least a hundred fifty head of good horses in it that were quiet and easy to handle and worth their weight in gold. They'd all been moved and pastured together so long that they naturally stayed together at night. A good horse wrangler could take care of them by himself.

Every cowboy who worked for the McCutcheons was given a thirty-six foot rope if he didn't have one. Funny thing was, about the only way you could get in trouble working for the McCutcheons was roping something you wasn't supposed to. In the mornings after we finished breakfast, the cowboys walked out away from the wagon, pitched one end of their rope to another cowboy who stretched it until they formed a big circle with the ropes held about waist high. The wrangler would bring those horses into the rope corral, and the last two men in the circle would walk together to shut the "gate" and those horses would stand inside that rope corral perfectly still. Papa and one other man would shake out their ropes and the cowboy nearest them would call out the name of the horse he was going to ride that day. Papa or the other man would rope the horse from outside the circle and lead him to the cowboy. The cowboy would drop his rope, the horse would step over it, and the roper would hand the horse to the cowboy and hold the cowboy's corral ropes for him while the cowboy slipped his bridle on the horse. When he finished, the cowboy slipped the rope off the horse's neck, took hold of his corral rope again and waited until every cowboy had his horse. Then everyone made up their ropes, saddled, and started the day's work.

Papa also had two great big old sorrel horses to pull his buckboard, either of which could have pulled it by themselves. We'd started to Balmorhea one morning when I was about seven or eight. I was sitting up there beside Papa and he spied this group of men over in a little arroyo loading up their wagons with wood. Papa whirled the two sorrels around and whipped out across there and slid that buckboard to a stop in front of those men and gave them the awfulest cussing you ever heard. I was only a kid then, you understand, but I've never heard anyone give a man a cussing like that one since. He made them unload ever stick of wood and hitch up their teams and get off his land right then. There wasn't any argument, and there wasn't going to be any argument. All the men had axes, and I kept waiting for one of them to throw one at him. But they didn't. It was a good thing because he always carried a .32 pistol tucked inside his shirt where he could get at it. They always sewed a shirt button on the outside of his shirt so it looked like it was buttoned all the way down, but it wasn't. When it was all over, we rode on down to Balmorhea and bumped into those old boys. Papa told them if they'd come and asked him for the wood, he'd have given them all they could carry, but the thought of them coming onto his land and taking it without asking didn't sit too kindly with him.

There was bear and panther all over the Davis Mountains then, too. Every Fall, Joe Espy, a rancher and president of the Fort Davis Bank all his life, would invite these El Paso bankers and some area ranchers out to hunt bear and deer on the Powell Ranch near Star Mountain. He usually hired Mack Sproul and his dogs to run bear for the hunt, but one year Mack was working and couldn't come so he told most everyone to bring what dogs they had. Clay Espy and Frank Jones had a couple, I remember, and there were a couple others with some hounds. Papa was going and asked me if I wanted to go along on the hunt. I told him yes. I figured Mac would be there with his dogs, so I left my pack of redbone hounds in the pens and asked everyone around the house not to let them out while I was gone. Two of them got away anyway and started trailing me. They were both good dogs and knew I was going somewhere to hunt when they saw me saddle up with my gun scabbard on. They'd been whining and pushing at their gates when I left. Well, I was almost to the Powell Ranch when I looked back and saw one old dog trotting along behind me about fifty yards and the other one about fifty yards behind him. I stopped and whistled them on up and told them, "As long as you're here, you might as well hunt." When we got to the Powell Ranch, I could see it didn't set too well with Mr. Joe that those dogs were there, and he says, "Them dogs any good?" I says, "They'll catch

*any bear you got in this country if that's what you mean."
He says, "Well, get some chains on them so's they won't run
tonight, and we'll try them out in the morning."*

*We left the ranch house early the next morning. Clay
Espy was riding beside me, and those two old dogs of mine
were trotting along behind us. The whole party hadn't gone
two miles before we hit a ruckus of white tail deer and every
dog in that bunch except mine took off after the deer. Clay
says, "Well, we might as well turn around and go back,
hadn't we?" I says, "Naw, let's ease on around here, and
we'll jump us a bear in a minute." He says, "Your dogs run a
bear?" I says, "Sure they'll run a bear." So we rode on along
another hundred yards or so, and I whistled and my older
dog trotted right out in front of Clay and started working.
The other dog just stayed behind like he was supposed to
and let the lead dog work on out ahead of us. Directly the
lead dog barked once and my other dog joined him so fast it
made you blink. They laid into the track with Clay and me
right behind them. Wasn't a minute until we looked out
ahead and saw the bear, and the race was on.*

*The bear turned up a big rock slide towards the top of Star
Mountain with these two dogs nipping at him every step of
the way. When they put him out on top, Papa was sitting up
there on his horse and killed the bear as he came toward him.
The dogs and some of the other men on top came over to look
at the bear. My dogs kept barking and growling and worrying the bear a minute. Directly the dogs stopped and sat
right down and rested. Couldn't have been two minutes
more until they both got up and started back down that
rockslide toward Clay and me. I says, "Looka yonder, there
comes the dogs. Let's wait on them. They'll be here in a
minute, and we'll follow them on around here and jump us
another one." We were working the bluffs there under Star
Mountain. Clay says, "Ah, you don't mean that?" Well sir,
by four o'clock that afternoon we'd killed five bear on top of
Star and around the bluffs. Mr. Espy shot the last one*

himself. The dogs had this big old boar bear cornered. There was a helluva fight going on, and this bear had hooked one of my dogs and had him down trying to bite through his head. He was about to kill him when Mr. Espy got there. He rode right into the middle of that fight and put his rifle to that bear's head and killed him.

I rode up and started doctoring the one dog. The other one was laying over ther panting. I looked at Mr. Joe out of the corner of my eye and says, "You reckon these dogs'll run a bear, Mr. Joe?" He just laughed and said, "Hell, if I'd known how good they were, I'd have told these other fellers to leave theirs at home." I says, "I left three in the pens at home that were better than these." He just laughed again.

Another time Charlie Oates and I ran a black bear down into a rockslide there alongside Star Mountain. I asked Charlie if he'd ever shot a bear, and he said no. So I gave him my rifle and said, "Now I'm going to drop some rocks down in here on this old bear, and you shoot him when he comes out by you." Well, sir, that old bear came woofing out by Charlie and he levered every shell in the gun out and never fired a shot.

Those old hounds of mine mostly trained themselves. They were natural hunters like that. We'd saddle up to go to work of a morning, and I'd turn them out and let them come with us if they wanted. They'd go along and jump a fox or coon or bobcat and kill it, then move on and hunt some more. You couldn't get them to run a deer or rabbit or trash like that. They were all pure redbone hounds except old Rowdy. Rowdy was an English bloodhound. He was also the meanest son of a gun you ever laid eyes on. He'd let me turn him loose in the mornings, but he by God wouldn't let me chain or pen him in the evenings. Only person who could do that was my wife. She could step outside and holler, "Come here, Rowdy," and he'd come no matter where or what he was doing. Made me so darn mad. Rowdy kept killing my chickens, though. One day after he'd killed another bunch I went in and got my saddle gun and come out there and had that old dog in my sights. I was going to kill him when my wife steps outside and asks me not to shoot him. She says, "If he kills any more chickens, you can get rid of him, but don't kill him. I don't think he'll kill any more chickens." I says, "Hell he won't. Dog kills one chicken he'll kill a hundred. I'm going have to shoot him." She says, "Give him another chance." I lowers the hammer on my rifle and says, "All right, but if he kills one more chicken on this ranch, he's a dead dog." You know that old dog never killed another chicken? He was standing there listening to our conversation, and it was like he understood.

Papa divided up the ranch in 1926. He made a purchase agreement with each of us so we wouldn't have to have a lawyer. Papa wanted it that way. He sold each of us our sections for one dollar and other considerations. We had a hundred twenty horses at the time. We corraled them and drew straws to see who roped first. I got second rope. My brother roped a pretty horse that was no-account. I roped a big old brown horse with a blaze face that was mean and tough and that you had to tie down to shoe. After we'd separated the rest of the horses, I tied that horse down, started cutting the witches' knots out of his mane and tail, and shoed him.

The next day we were going to start the roundup and separate the cattle. I caught the big brown and finally got my bridle on him. He started backing away when I approached him with a saddle, but eventually he stopped and I got my blanket and saddle on. Everyone was watching me when I stepped aboard because they knew damn well I was going to get thrown and maybe stomped. That was a mean horse.

Well sir, I stepped aboard that old horse and nothing happened. So we went on, worked all that morning, and come to the house at noon for fresh horses. Everyone's mount was lathered and give out except mine. I noticed this old brown horse wasn't the least bit tired, so I just kept him and rode him that afternoon, too. And he still acted fresh that after-noon and never pitched with me once. It was like there was something about me this old horse didn't mind.

Then one day I came riding up to the Jeff Ranch. There was a fellow there breaking horses and he sees this big old blaze-faced brown of mine and says, "That's a mighty stout looking horse you got there." I stepped off and says, "Sure is, you want to try him?" He nods and steps aboard that old horse, and they hadn't gone ten feet when that brown horse broke in two. I've never seen a horse pitch like that since. He threw that fellow and took in after him and put him under a fence. Hell, it was like he went crazy or something. That guy gets up and says, "Mr., I don't know how you ride that son of a bitch." I says, "Hell, I don't understand it. He's never pitched with me like that. I just don't understand it." That old boy just laughed. I knew he didn't believe me. Come to find out, I was the only person around that old horse would let ride him. A few years later the Depression hit and things got bad. I had to sell the ranch and that old horse with it. Don't know whatever become of him.

10

Right before the Depression hit, Bob and Charlie Oates went in together on a bathhouse in the McCamey oil fields. They had stalls in it and would charge roughnecks a dollar for a bath, which was five gallons of water. They shipped their water from Alpine to McCamey by rail by the carload. It was a paying proposition. Bob came out to the ranch and wanted me to go down there and help them run it. I said no, but I'd come down on Friday and look the thing over. They was wanting to sell it, and I told them I wanted to look the thing over first. They figured I'd buy into it. I got down there on Friday night, and the next morning they turned the thing over to me while he and Charlie went off to a poker game. I stayed there taking in the money from them old boys bathing, and collected seventy-five dollars. Bob and Charlie come in that evening and says, "How'd you come out?" I told them, and they said, "Let's have the money." I divided it up. Gave each one of them half and kept a little for me. They disappeared and come back the next morning broke. They'd lost every cent in the poker game that ran twenty-four hours there around McCamey. I got in my jitney and come on back to the ranch. Bob wound up with a bunch of good oil leases over there, but the Depression hit before he could sell them.

The Depression drove cattle prices down almost over-night. During the Fall of 1930 an old boy from El Paso come down to the ranch to look over our calves. We had about seventy-five head of five-hundred-pound steers. He bought forty head at ten cents a pound. We got that bunch out and had about thirty left that we were going to have to sell on the open market. We loaded them out for El Paso about the same time the stock market broke. Luckily we sold them for six cents a pound.

By January, 1931, you couldn't sell a cow. John Killough, who was overseeing the Jeff Ranch then, and Bill Addison who ranched east of us, decided they'd ship some cattle to Fort Worth to see if they could get something out of them. What they got was a bill for the freight.

Then the government went in with their buy-out program that paid ranchers twelve dollars a head for cows. We sold them our old cows, moved them down to the Jeff Ranch with a bunch that John Killough had sold, shot four or five for meat, and took the others to Hovey where we shipped them. The Jeff Ranch then went to trying to sell calves, but there wasn't no market for them. So we tried to sell them at any price just to get rid of them, but couldn't.

I guess the drought during the Depression was one of the worst we ever had, especially in '33 and '34. It was so awful dry and we had no money and no feed because there just wasn't any to be had. We got through it by feeding our cattle sotol and prickly pear. Terrell Smith, Wade, and Bennett McCutcheon was on a committee trying to figure out what could be done to help matters. There was nothing for our cattle to eat, and it had been twelve months since it rained enough to settle the dust. About all the cattle had left to live on was prickly pear or sotol. Since we had quite a bit of sotol in our part of the mountains, we went to work cutting and trimming the briars and blades off—back to the heart of the plant so the cattle could eat it. The sotol had quite a bit of fiber and sugar and protein in its heart, and the cattle liked it. You had to cut the blades and briars off, though, or an old cow would eat them trying to get at the heart. When they did, they couldn't digest the sotol blades, and they'd swell up and die. We lost six or seven this way, but the rest survived. That's what we got by on. We also knocked or burned the thorns off prickly pear.

The government finally stepped in and started buying cattle—either killing them or selling them to anyone with a little money just to try to get some money circulating. We bought a bunch of little old scrawny calves from the government at four dollars a head—it was the last money we had—and threw them up on that mesa there back of the house. We had a lot of sotol up there we could cut and feed them—which we did—right on through until it rained the next winter and grass and things come back out. We just left those calves up there and let them grow. We sold them for thirty-five dollars a head.

We always lived on borrowed money most of our years until we got the ranch paid off. Once or twice during the Depression we had as many as three different loans with banks and people. We hung on and somehow made our payments, but that was about all we made. The key to our survival, I guess, was we didn't need—or want—anything other than what we had to have. Truth is, we couldn't afford anything else, but we had ourselves, our horses, our saddles and gear, our cattle, and something to eat. We did all our own work, too. A lot of ranchers who were leveraged went broke during that Depression. One month Wade wrote a check for a dollar fifty and almost overdrew our account, but we were better off than a lot of people. Another time our expenses at the ranch for a year was four hundred dollars. People didn't really know what we lived on. We'd gather our cattle with the Jeff roundup before we had any corrals. We finally built us some corrals there at the mouth of Lockhausen and Fonville Canyons.

It was the income from our horses that helped pull us through the Depression, though. The family had twelve Chickasay Bob mares up there on the Panhandle farm that they wanted to get rid of, so I bought them, loaded them into a boxcar at Tulia, and brought them to the ranch. About the same time Wade found out the Jeff Ranch had a hundred twenty-five head of mares they wanted to sell for fifteen hundred dollars, so we bought the mares and put them in the east pasture. Wade got sick again with his rheumatism shortly after that, and I went to selling them mares off wherever I could find buyers. I shipped one carload to

Schulenburg; another to Fort Worth. We kept about sixty of the best brood mares, though.

Wade finally got better and come back out to the ranch. I was working at the Jeff Ranch when word came the cavalry was buying horses in our part of the country. What they'd decided to do after World War I was to build a cavalry that could travel seventy-five miles one day and return the next. The cavalry's procurement officers found out the Southwestern horse had the stamina, but lacked the size they wanted. So they began buying good thoroughbred studhorses from Kentucky, Tennessee, and thereabouts, and crossed them with the Southwestern mares to get the kind of horse they wanted.

The cavalry was paying top dollar for good horses, so Wade and I got them to furnish us remount studs for our broodmares. The first one they sent was a big thoroughbred horse. He run out down there in the pasture and an old mare kicked him on the hind leg and broke it. We got hold of the Army rep who came out, shot him, and brought us another stud. We kept each stud three years. At the end of three years the Army rep came out, picked him up, and gave you a new one.

Over the years, the cavalry furnished us seven of their thoroughbred studs. The last one we had was old Copy Cat. He was an exceptionally good horse. We bought him after the cavalry discontinued the remount service, kept a couple dozen of our best mares for him, and sold the rest for a hundred dollars each. I think those were as fine a horses as you could find for working the Davis Mountains. When we finally sold the ranch, we were still riding descendants of the Army's remount studs and the horses we'd brought from the Panhandle.

One thing about studhorses is they seldom mix their harems or let a mare leave. They seldom let a new mare in either. I first saw this with those mustangs there in the Panhandle and later when we were raising horses. We kept about sixty mares with three government studs in the mesa pasture behind the house. Those studs separated the mares into three groups, and those three groups never mixed or mingled as long as we had them. The only watering we had in that pasture at the time was the big tub at the edge of our house corrals. I used to sit up there on the porch of an evening and watch each one of those old studs bring their mares in for water. It sure was a pretty sight. They did it one group at a time, and they never got in each other's way.

The Army rep always came to the ranch to inspect and buy our best horse colts. They paid whatever the market was at the time. Sometimes it might be two hundred dollars a horse, other times fifty or seventy-five dollars. This pretty much guaranteed the cavalry pick of the crop wherever they had their studs. It was a good business for us, especially when times was hard. The agreement was you had to break those horses to saddle yourself, or the Army wouldn't take them. We raised and broke a great number of those horses over the years. We knew how to break them, and it never took us long to get a bunch of young horses ready to go when the buyer came. The trick was to work with them from yearlings right on up.

The Army always picked up their horse colts when they were about three years old. Generally they brought their own rider, but then they might ask you to step up on the horse, too. I had one old horse that I'd held back one year because he was bad to pitch. The Army man asked me why I hadn't offered him, and I told him the old horse would pitch. The Army man says, "You go ahead and get on him. I don't mind if this one pitches. You get on him and ride him up this way." So I saddled the old horse up and he swelled up and I could tell he was gonna sure enough pitch. I stepped on the old horse and he bawls and pitches awhile around the corrals until I finally jerked him up. The old boy walked over to me and the horse and looks him over and tests his breath and all that kind of stuff—looking in his mouth and all—and says,

"I'll take him. Get down." Well, sir, I was surprised because this Army rep seldom took a pitching horse like that, and I was glad to get rid of him at the price. The old boy turns to me and says, "We got a bunch of men over there in the stockade in Oklahoma just waiting for a horse like this to ride."

Another time I was down at the corrals afoot helping load an old mean horse we'd sold to a rodeo producer. He balked just as we drug him up to the back of the truck. I didn't have a stick or anything to whack him with. About that time he went crazy and pitched back out by me. When he did, he reached out and kicked me right square in the chest. Knocked me out cleaner 'n a whistle. I come to up on our porch finally and got to where I could get around in a day or so, but it was about three years before I got back to normal and the swelling went out of my chest where that horse kicked me.

★   ★   ★

**From an interview with
Russell McAfee, Jr. (1920-1979),
nephew of Florence "Happy" Reid**

Every July Fourth they'd have a roping in Balmorhea. When they did, they'd build a temporary set of pens to hold the stock in. Wade went over to Balmorhea one year before the roping to make an offer for the lumber in those corrals because we needed it to build a set of mountain pens. The man who owned the lumber said he'd trade Wade the lumber for a good bucking horse. He was sort of a rodeo producer and traded in rodeo stock. Wade said he had just the horse.

Now the horse Wade had in mind was Chevy. Wade said he finally just had to quit riding old Chevy because he was the type that would buck up to the edge of a bluff with you and, instead of stopping, buck you and him both right on over the edge. Or he'd buck through a barbed wire fence, the side of a barn, an arroyo, anything. Wade said it didn't mat-

ter, and said he was the type of horse that would kill you and him both. A rider either had to quit Chevy or go with him whenever he bucked into something. Anyhow, old Chevy got so boogery and bad and crazy that they just quit riding him altogether. He was a big old stout horse that loved to pitch, even after a hard day's ride, and Wade figured he would make a good trade for the lumber.

So, this man come out—name was Lee—and wanted to make sure old Chevy would buck. Wade saddled him in a little corral by the saddle room, stepped on him, turned him around a couple times, then told me to go open the gate to a forty-foot alley that ran into the big corral, and to open the gate to the big corral at the other end. When Wade started down that alley, old Chevy exploded. Well, I'm ambling down this alley to open the other gate when I hear this full-grown bronc bawl behind me, and I look over my shoulder to see this crazy thing pitching toward me full speed, knowing full well he'll run over me, the fence, the barn and whatever else was in his way. I want you to know I hit the gate at the other end of the alley and start fumbling with the nail and piece of rusted chain holding it shut. Finally I shake it loose, throw it open, and roll out of the way just as Wade and Chevy come pitching by. Roy starts hollering at me, "Shut the gate, shut the gate!" I get up and shut the gate while old Chevy pitches out into the main corral with Wade aboard.

That was another ride Wade made I'll always remember. That horse was pitching so hard Wade's nose was bleeding, and Wade sat right there and rode him down until old Chevy was just too tired to pitch anymore. By this time Wade was so mad at Chevy he took his rope, stepped off, and give him the damnedest whipping you ever saw because Wade, you know, just didn't put up with any foolishness from a horse. He was strictly business. Anyhow, old Lee was sitting over there, and when the dust settled, he said, "I believe I could have done that a sittin' on 'em." Course that didn't help Wade's temper any.

The Cattlemen

Well sir, Lee agreed to take the horse, so he backed his pickup into the corral to load old Chevy, but Chevy had sullied up and was mad. Anyhow, Roy got a rope on old Chevy—Roy, you know, never believed a horse would ever hurt him—and we ran the rope down one side and out the front of the pickup's sideboards and got old Chevy's front end up in the back of the truck, but Chevy wouldn't budge. So we finally decided to put a rope around his rear end, run it out the sides of the pickup, and drag him up and in. We got the rope through both sides and started pulling on the slack, but Chevy got to fighting and bucking and squalling, and the rope slipped off and flopped on the ground alongside him. Roy walked back and reached over to pick up the rope, and when he did, Chevy kicked him hard right in the chest, right over the heart, with a hind foot. I guess if Roy had been a half inch closer, that damned horse would have caved his entire chest in. Anyhow, Roy dropped like he'd been pole-axed. I remember his face had turned gray. I thought, "My God, old Chevy's killed Roy."

Everyone run over and grabbed Roy and carried him up there on the front porch to his bed—that's where he slept—and stretched him out. We just left Chevy hanging out of the pickup. It seemed like ten minutes before Roy ever began to breathe again, and when he did, Wade reached over and opened his shirt. There was a perfect imprint—red and blue—of Chevy's hoof directly over his heart. The blow had knocked him cold, and to this day I don't know how it kept from killing him. He laid there awhile and finally said, "Well, I think I'm okay." Roy, you know, always thought of himself as indestructible.

We left him lying there and went back down and started loading old Chevy again. It took us the better part of an hour. Just as we fought him bawling into the bed, old Roy come walking back into the corral. He still looked white and weak. Lee took old Chevy, and we never heard from him again. I guess he used him in rodeos.

Wade and Roy Reid stretch and doctor a cow with screwworms. Circa 1920's.

11

Another morning during the Depression—I believe it was 1930—I was sleeping on the porch of our house when my bed slid left, then right, and started swaying. It was about five a.m. Wade and Happy was coming in on the road there on the hill in the horse trap when the ground went to shaking and their car went to wobbling and they said they didn't know what was happening. It only lasted about thirty seconds. My bed made a couple shifts across that porch, and I knew it was an earthquake. I made a grab for my boots, but they went the other way, so I come off that bed and stepped out on the porch there above the garage. Pablo Rodriguez was sleeping down there in front of the garage and he was standing up looking around, too. He said his cot had went to jumping up and down, and he'd got out of it. He said, "You guess it's over?" I said I guessed it was. About that time the coyotes started howling down east of the house and some more opened up below the house and three old polecats come around the little hill in front of the house with tails straight, going somewhere. There was no dust, and the damnedest calm you ever saw fell over that country. Wasn't any cracks in the earth I could see, but it had torn up the house pretty bad. There was a bowl sitting on a cloth in the middle of the table. The cloth had wrapped itself around the bowl.

Our house had some damages, so we got an old boy out there to start repairing it and saw he didn't know what he was doing, so we sent him off and got us one that did. He poured us a good foundation for the rock and helped us build a good solid house. We hauled rock off the mountain in back of the house and used it to finish the outside.

Happy died in 1932. Her and Jimmie Tom was sitting in the bedroom sewing and she stood up and told Jimmie Tom, "You know, I don't know when I've ever felt so bad." And she just fell over on the bed. Jimmie Tom run out there and called Wade. Doc Wright come out, and we made her a bed and loaded her in the back of his car and he took her to Alpine. He had a little old house he called a hospital there with a couple of beds in it. They took her in there and laid her on one of them beds. She was there about thirty days, then died.

An old boy also come through the country buying horses for the British Army during the Depression, too. He stopped down there at the Jeff Ranch and asked if they had any spirited horses for sale. They said they certainly did. What they had was a bunch of wild horses penned at the barns that nobody would buy or ride because they'd eaten locoweed. So this representative asks if someone would mount these horses so he could observe their movements.

Well, Bobby Rawls was the Jeff rider at that time, so everyone went down to the barn and the corrals to watch him. He'd catch these old horses and saddle them in the shade of the barn, mount, and ride them toward the sunlight. Now when these old horses hit that sunlight, they would jump right straight up and kick sideways. Bobby would ride them on around the barn, unsaddle and get another. The buyer would observe the horse jumping or pitching and say, "Yes, that animal has lots of spirit. I'll take him." I bet he bought every locoed horse in the country and shipped them over to England.

After Roosevelt took office in '33 there was a moratorium on the banks to not release loans on anything. Our livestock loans had been out of Fort Worth at ten percent, but they were cut. Wade and I needed expense money to keep the ranch going, so we went to San Angelo and saw the Rural Agriculture Credit Corporation (RACC) man. We told him we needed four thousand dollars to keep going. He okayed it on the spot. The RACC had Roosevelt's backing, you know. Anyhow, the old RACC at San Angelo loaned fourteen million dollars to ranchers and farmers. All but thirty dollars was paid back. Old boy that lost the thirty dollars tried to raise a bunch of onions. Everyone else paid off. Shortly afterward, Roosevelt got his people to form the Production Credit Association. The PCA offered low interest operating loans to all its members. That's why so many ranchers joined. At the time, the PCA interest rate was about three percent. We started with a Class B loan, then went to a Class A.

Water became even more important during the Thirties' drought. We brought John Cox with his drilling machine out to the Miller Spring after it started drying up. He dug us a seven-hundred-foot well, but the water always came up black. You could pump it into a tub, let it settle a couple minutes, and it would be crystal clear. Not a thing on the side of the tub. Still, it was black. We went ahead and used the well for several years until it got to going down and wearing the leathers out on the windmill every month, which meant pulling six-hundred-forty foot of pipe. That got old in a hurry, especially trying to keep up with the worms.

After the Fifties' drought, we got George and Diamond McSpadden out to drill us a good well on the east side below the house. They hit thirty-five gallons a minute at five-hundred-forty feet, then went down until they hit hard rock at six hundred. It was all the water we needed and to this day, it's a good well.

Now we'd laid the headwater pipe in Lockhausen in 1927. A wetback crew dug our pipe ditch by hand. Couldn't dig it no other way. Most of the ditch was about three feet deep. We laid about eight miles of pipe in all. Later years we extended it on around to the Old Lake above the Fonville. When the spring got weak during the Fifties' drought, we dug a well at Headwater and hit water at sixty feet. We tried to tie it into the waterline near the well and force it back up the line through a check valve to our storage tank. The gravity was too great and we wound up having to run a small string of pipe about half mile back up the canyon and into the tank at the headwater. It watered all our mountain pastures.

At first, we cooked on a wood stove and used two fireplaces to keep the house warm in winter. We burned mesquite wood and mesquite roots because there was plenty of them. We'd pull those old roots out of the ground, shake them off, let them dry a little and burn them. They burned a good, hot fire, just like coal. That's why that little hill out there in front of the house was so barren. We cleaned all the mesquite off it. Had an old boy out there working for us one day who said it was the damnedest country he ever saw—man had to dig for wood and climb up canyons for water.

The best thing that ever happened to the cow business, though, was the Franklin blackleg vaccine. That company did more for the cattle business than anyone has ever done before or since. Without it, you couldn't go from now until weaning time and frost without riding up on a pile of calves dead from blackleg. And the thing was, you might have looked at those same calves the day before and there wouldn't have been one of them looked sick. That blackleg would hit the calves sometime during the night, and they'd all die. Some wouldn't live three hours, others would make it a couple of days. I don't ever recall seeing an animal get over blackleg. I come down Barrilla Canyon one evening in the Fall—the Jeff Ranch was getting ready to deliver their calves in November—and rode up on a pile of dead blackleg calves in that Barrilla pasture where they was holding them for shipment. They'd died during the night or late the day before. I rode on down to the Jeff Ranch and told Mrs. McCutcheon what I saw at the watering. Now Beau McCutcheon was in charge of both the Jeff and the 7-Ranch at the time. Mrs. Lee McCutcheon, Jim's widow, lived at the Jeff and Beau lived at the 7-Ranch headquarters, which was several miles away. The Jeff had one of those old crank phones in the house, though, and Mrs. McCutcheon says, "Let me call Brother Beau and you tell him what you just told me." She got Beau on the line and I told him how I'd read about a blackleg vaccine they'd come out with, and that I'd ordered enough doses out of Amarillo—at fifty cents a dose—to vaccinate all my calves. I told him for the first time since I could remember, I hadn't lost a calf. I think I got some of the first batches of vaccine right after they started producing it.

Beau says, "Will you get in touch with that outfit and order me enough doses for our roundup? Find out if they got it and how soon they can get it to me down here." Beau had seen blackleg wipe out calf crops before.

So I called the Franklin people and told them Beau Mc-Cutcheon needed three thousand doses of the vaccine at Fort Davis soon as possible. They said they would load it and ship it out that night. I called Mr. Beau back and told him what they'd said. He said, "We'll start the roundup wagon tomorrow morning. You go ahead and get that vaccine there to the Jeff headquarters and start gathering and working those Jeff calves. I'll have the 7-Ranch calves ready as soon as you finish." While fifty cents a dose may seem high back then, it was nothing compared to losing twenty or thirty percent of your calf crop. There's one other thing I always praised the Franklin people for doing and that was as soon as they found out the serum worked, they went to work reducing the price of it. I think you can buy it for about eight cents a dose today. They also kept the serum in the family and didn't let it out or sell it to a big chemical company that would have held us up with the price and patent. They done all the cattlemen a big favor. Soon as most of these modern companies find out there's no competition for a product like blackleg serum, they drive the price right on up out of sight. The Franklin Company didn't do that.

Worms was another big headache for the early cattleman. We used just about everything for worm medicine until Koral come along. It killed worms outright and kept them off an animal for about seven days. I tried it out before we started using it. We had a cow die up there on the

Lockhausen Flats. So I mixed up a Koral solution and went up there and covered that old cow with a dip and dampened the ground around her for a couple of feet. We come back about three days later and I knew the stuff would work when we saw her. I bet there was a million dead flies on her and not a worm in sight. Worms were always a problem. You had to ride and watch and doctor your cattle ever day, ever week, or the worms would kill them.

Nowadays some of the ranches are reporting four and five cases again. That sterilization program they had going was working fine until they moved most of the experienced people out of it. When they come up shorthanded, it began showing up as screwworm cases on the ranches. When that screwworm program started, we all donated to it based on the number of cattle we had and helped establish the sterilization station there in Mission. Cattlemen out here raised over a million dollars to help get it started. They put a good man in charge who really knew what he was doing, and we didn't have a screwworm problem anymore after them flies were killed out. After an administration change or two, they lost the good people running the program, and the first thing they did was scatter a bunch of flies that wasn't sterile. Next thing we knew those flies had worked their way out to West Texas and we began finding worms again.

Most everyone rode those Miles City saddles during the early days. I finally traded mine and forty dollars to the saddlemaker in Marfa who made me a good one. I rode that saddle forty-seven years. It had a double rawhide cover. Horse could fall back on it and it wouldn't hurt it.

Kurt Lange in Alpine made our boots for forty or fifty years. He made you boots that lasted, too. Wouldn't put one out his door that didn't and he wouldn't make a pair of boots out of kangaroo or ostrich or fishskin or the like. He said it wouldn't last. He always bought his tanned hides from Germany. It was good, soft, tough leather that wouldn't bend out of shape and was easy to wear. It fit your foot good, too.

He charged us about fifteen dollars during the Twenties for a pair of his handmade boots. He was the only person who could make boots that would fit Wade's feet, and that Wade could get his feet into.

Man come by here the other day and said he was writing a book and could he talk to me and ask me a few questions. I let him in and turned up my hearing aid and we talked a few minutes about a little history. Directly he pulled out this contract and said, "Now if you'll sign this, it will guarantee you a copy of this book for a hundred twenty-eight dollars."

Well, I didn't sign nothing. I got caught in a similar deal about fifty years ago when I signed something I shouldn't have and forgot to keep a copy. An old boy brought this so-called book contract by, supposedly about what it was like being a cowboy, and a bunch of us signed it one Sunday at a roping. What it turned out to be was a note. I told them I'd be damned if I'd pay the damn thing. There were four or five others there at Marfa that got caught in the same jam, so we all went together and hired us a lawyer. It cost us ten dollars apiece to beat this guy and prove he was a crook, but we did it.

Anyhow, the fellow that came through here the other day got a hold of Pat Mulloy, and old Pat made him give him a copy of what he wanted signed. Pat's a good businessman, you know, and he kept this copy and gave it to his lawyer. We plan to check it when he brings the so-called book by. But then, he ain't gonna bring no book by. He'll just come by wanting the money saying he needs it to finish the book. World's full of crooks like that. Can't turn around without running into one of them. They've always been around, though.

One of the things I am proud of is the way the sale of the ranch went. We had several offers, but when four oilmen called, I asked Bob McKnight what he thought. Bob, you know, bought the Jeff Ranch. He said any one of them could buy the ranch by themselves. Once I knew these fellas could afford the place, we got down to some serious talking. One thing Dot and I didn't want to do was sell it to one of these fly-by-night fellers that had to borrow the money for that place hoping to make a quick sale for profit. Likely as not, we'd a wound up with the ranch in receivership and nothing to live on. When you're in your eighties, you can't afford that.

Bob called last night and said all those little springs and creeks were running clear water right on out onto the flats. Last time it done that was when we first came to the Davis Mountains, near as I can remember. Bob said the rains sure have helped that old ranch. Started falling about the middle of June and just kept right on coming. They stopped last Thursday, but then they started Friday and it's rained everyday since. None of them very heavy. Just little old showers. I guess the biggest was about eight-tenths of an inch. But they add up, and I'll bet we've had fifteen or twenty inches of rain down there on our old place and all across the old Jeff Ranch. Bob told me that Carrizo Creek was overflowing and about half of the old tabosa flat below the house had come up stirrup high in sidegoats grama. Man, he said you never saw such grass. And that old mountain country of ours, he said, is knee high and headed out in that old black grama. He says it's pretty. I'd like to see it like that again. Course, the men who bought it ain't got nothing on it right now. Man said he bought a little bunch of cows and calves here the other day. Paid two hundred fifty dollars a pair for them. Said the calves was pretty good size so that means he got them cows for about a hundred twenty-five. Damn cow market has gone to pot again. Know a kid that operates a cattle truck, and he can barely afford to run it. He's an independent. I don't see why somebody don't come up with an alternative fuel of some kind. Hell, when we started out they had the White Steamer and the Stanley. They run just as good as the gasoline car. But the oil companies bought up the patents. For a long time afterwards they made those steam cars in Mexico, then you never saw them no more. A couple of the ranchers had them in the Panhandle. They sure was smooth riding cars.

One of the early Cole cars manufactured by an independent parked in front of a Fort Davis home. The car probably belonged to a ranching family. These early vehicles could be used only for road travel and did not replace the horse (as many eastern experts predicted) in the Davis Mountains. The country was simply too rough, and rocks would shake these early cars apart. Cole went out of business during the Depression. Circa 1920's.

The most popular cars among the early Davis Mountain ranchers were Ford's Model C, Model K, Model T, and Model A series. Later, Chevrolet also became popular. The cars held up well on the rough, rocky Davis Mountain ranch roads and were reasonably priced and relatively easy to repair. The car, once introduced in the Davis Mountains, was a novelty to many of the early cowboys. Circa 1920's.

Above: The first structure (a wood shack) built by Wade and Roy Reid on their ranch. Circa 1915-1917. Perishables like food and feed, along with a cook stove, were kept in the shack. Wade and Roy slept in their bedrolls on the ground outside the shack for more than a decade.

Below: Their first house—an adobe—built shortly after Wade Reid married in 1927. The house was severly damaged in the 1930 earthquake. Note pre-earthquake crack down the left side of the house. Ground beneath their ranch house shifted each year throughout the century.

Part II

As Others Remembered Them

12

From an interview with
Russell McAfee, Jr. (1920-1979)

The first trip I ever made to Wade and Roy's ranch was in 1928. That was the same year Maggie Jo and Jimmie Tom, Happy's nieces, spent their first summer there. I was eight. There wasn't a paved street in Pecos except the Bankhead Highway, which was Highway Eighty. It was one of the first, paved cross-country roads in the Southwest, and it was named after the senator who got the funds to have it built. They also had watering troughs with big catfish in them at every intersection on main street in Pecos. I remember looking in and wanting to catch one.

It was all dirt road to Balmorhea after you left Pecos, and dirt road from Balmorhea to Toyahvale, and up Limpia Canyon to the ranch turnoff. Truth is, there was no pavement in Jeff Davis County period, and the only pavement in Brewster County was from the county line into Alpine between Fort Davis and Alpine. Senator Berkley lived in Alpine then. He'd fathered the state cigarette tax in Texas and got that ten miles of blacktop built. Berkley could see people were hooked on ready-rolls and knew they would be a steady income for the state.

Wade and Roy had just built the ranch house that summer. Until then, they used a two-room wood shack that they cooked out of and kept their feed in. Before that they used a tent. They told me they just slept out on the ground unless it was raining. But when Wade married Aunt Happy, they built the ranch house.

There wasn't anything around the house in the way of fences then. Just the water trap fence east of the house and a little trap there west of the house where they kept a couple of milk cows. Pablo Rodriguez milked the cows, took care of the wood gathering, and helped Aunt Happy with the house chores. Old "Pab" they called him. He could cowboy when he had to.

We drove up to the ranch that first summer afternoon and found Happy and Wade sitting on the concrete porch railing out back by the kitchen. They were both mad at Roy. He'd gone to Toyahvale to pick up a Servel Electrolux icebox. It was the first one they'd ever owned, and they'd ordered it through the hardware there. It worked off kerosene with two burners under it like a coal oil stove that had to be filled and lit every night. There was a little door on one side down close to the floor that you opened and pulled the burners out to light. Then you shoved them back in and closed the door. The burners sat near a bottle and their heat activated gas in the bottle and some coils, which, in turn, cooled the icebox enough to last until morning. Like I said, they hadn't had an icebox until then. They just used a big urn filled with water to cool things like jars of milk. They hung a wet dish towel between the jars to keep them cool. Aunt Happy took this milk and churned butter each Friday, then sold it or traded it for groceries at Don Adams' store in Alpine if they got to go to town on Saturday. She had one of these hand churns and a set of wooden bowls to work and salt the butter in. When she finished, she wrapped it in wax paper and set it in the icebox to get it good and cool for the trip to town. I imagine the churn's still up under their old ranch house somewhere.

Anyhow, Roy was overdue, not just a little, but a day or two. He'd bumped into Bill Kingston there in Toyahvale. They'd got to drinking and visiting, and he'd just spent the night and then the next night, and he finally got in about dark the third night with the icebox still in the crate. Course it was too dark to unload it so they had to wait until the next day. Anyhow, that's the first time I ever saw Wade and Happy, sitting out back there on that flat concrete porch railing, thinking we was Roy.

Now their house was built on a slope beneath the bluff. The lower part of the house had a garage, a washroom, a storeroom, and a canning room. To get upstairs, you climbed a couple dozen concrete steps to the front porch. It was screened. Roy slept in a little bedroom off the west corner of the porch. Behind Roy's room was a guest bedroom, then a bathroom, and finally Wade and Happy's bedroom—all connected by a hall on the west side of the house. When you crossed the porch, there was a door to the living room beyond which was the dining room and finally the kitchen out back. The east and north side of the kitchen had screen doors that opened onto a concrete porch about six feet wide with a three-foot concrete wall. The slab on top of the wall was wide enough to sit on. You could climb a dozen concrete steps or so to this porch on the east side of their house and enter the kitchen through either screened door. The "junk room" was the dirt slope up under the back part of the house. Roy kept a big wooden box full of rawhide and leather to patch saddles and chaps with up under there. He made thongs and quirts, too. They stored all the meat they canned up under there alongside about twenty regular automobile batteries wired in sequence for house electricity, and a little old thirty-two-volt Delco gasoline generator that charged the batteries. One of your first chores when you came in of an evening was to crank up that one-lung motor so the batteries would stay charged while you had the lights on. Roy had wired Happy's old Maytag washer, vacuum cleaner, and house lights for low voltage. The generator ran as long as you kept the lights on.

Now you had to crank the generator to start it. After supper someone went up under the house, filled it with gas, and gave it a twist. And I want you to know, we spent many an evening up under that house cranking on that damned generator when it decided to quit. Sometimes, if it wouldn't start, we'd just go upstairs and light a kerosene lamp. Next evening after work and supper Roy would be back down there with his tools. He'd have the generator torn completely down trying to find out what was wrong. You could hear him cussing and muttering to himself, then he'd give it a turn or two and it would fire. Roy always was good at fixing motors, you know. He did all the mechanical repairs at the ranch.

Ever so often Roy would take the generator apart to grind the valves. He did this with a screwdriver, a little ratchet tool, and a brace thing he'd built to seat his valves in and grind them. What you did was put the screwdriver in the brace after you smeared the valves with this compound. They always had teeth across the top, you know. Then you crawled up on top, gripped the screwdriver, bore down, and pulled up with everything you had; running the valve back and forth until you'd smoothed out the edges. That was the way we ground our valves. We did it at night, by ourselves, time and again.

There was a wooden cookstove in the kitchen and two fireplaces for househeat. One fireplace was in the living room and the other was in the back bedroom where Wade and Happy slept. We either dug for mesquite roots to burn or took their old Ford jitney up Lockhausen Canyon. We'd gather up dead mountain oak, load it, bring it back, and pile it by the clothesline where we chopped what we needed for heat and cooking. It was good stovewood. They'd burned up most of the mesquite around the house by the time I started going to the ranch.

The country had big live oak groves then, and we watched for dead oak when we were riding and looking for worms. You didn't have the screwworm program then like you do now, and the ranchers either rode and doctored their cattle or went broke. We rode every day, all day. We'd find a cluster up on the side of a mountain somewhere. On Sunday, if we had time, we'd drive the jitney up as close as we could to the dead oak and get out and go to carrying wood. Roy said most of the live oak groves eventually died out after the farmers started heavy irrigation in the Balmorhea Valley.

They just didn't have many electrical appliances then because there wasn't any electricity in the Barrilla Mountains. Even when Wade married again in the Fall of '45, they had to buy an icebox that ran off butane. The icebox prompted them to buy a new butane-powered generator. They set it in a rock storehouse they'd built out back. Roy rewired their house for a hundred ten volts and put in an automatic trip switch on the generator that kicked in any time you flipped a light on in the house. When you cut off the last light, the motor shut off automatically. When anyone ironed or ran a vacuum, they left a light on so the motor wouldn't shut off every time you stopped using the appliance. These butane generators around ranch houses were mostly post war. Up until then, ranchers used the little one-lung generators and car batteries, if they used anything at all. A lot of ranchers, when they first got their butane generators, always left a yard or shed light on so the generator would keep running. Wade and Roy figured that was hard on the motor and a waste of electricity, so Roy put in their trip switch. It sometimes got worn out, and you'd have to go out back and push it manually. When you did, you watched for rattlesnakes. They liked to crawl at night when it was cool. Even when the switch worked, you could walk in the front door, flip on a light, and get halfway across the room before it kicked in and the lights came on. That always fascinated city visitors for some reason. Sometime during the late Fifties or early Sixties, the REA got around to running a line to the ranch, and they bought their first electric icebox.

Wade's and Roy's day back then always started with the same breakfast. You got coffee, a bowl of oats, one egg, two pieces of toast, one slice of bacon, and red beans if you wanted them. The first thing Wade did every morning before daylight was drop some wood in and fire up their old stove. While the stove was getting hot, he sliced everyone's bacon.

He bought it by the slab, and you got one slice. No more, no less. These were lean years and nothing was ever wasted. He used the bacon rind to flavor his red beans, which he kept in a gallon, half-lidded bucket. The bucket sat on the back of the stove, stayed full of beans, and was the only thing you could eat all you wanted each meal. I grew to love pinto beans. They often saved me from starvation. When they were gone, he'd make a fresh batch, and they'd last another three or four days. Each time he fired the stove the beans boiled, which kept them from spoiling.

Anyhow, we always ate before sunup. When we finished, Roy went down and cranked the Model A while I got my saddle and bridle and handful of cake from the barn. It was my job to catch old Big Boy in their horse trap east of the house. Big Boy was the only horse on that ranch you could walk up to. He was gentle and was the one horse they started all the kids on. After you learned to ride old Big Boy, and they decided you could take care of yourself horseback, you graduated to other horses. By then you either had enough sense to make a hand horseback, or they quit you, which meant you stayed at the house and didn't ride with them anymore. Roy and I would drive down and hunt up the horses there along Carrizo Creek. Old Big Boy would start to the truck when he saw it. I'd slip his bridle on and let him eat his cake while I saddled him. Then I'd climb aboard, gather the horses, and head them toward the house corrals. Everyone would catch a mount, saddle up, and we'd start the day's work.

Now it took me about two years to catch on to the fact that they decided their day over breakfast. I never paid them no mind at first, but then I began to notice each morning they'd discuss the cows that ought to be close to calving and those due next month and so on. And it began to dawn on me that Wade and Roy knew every cow they owned, what she looked like, and how many calves she'd had. They could describe her to you and tell you where she ran in their mountains which, except for property lines, never had a fence in them. They knew because they rode everyday and saw all their cattle and waterings at least three times a week. That was the rule. The cattle had to have water to survive and baby calves had to be doctored because they only lived about three or four days if they got worms, which meant you kept right on riding and checking those two things if you wanted to stay in the cow business. Every calf and colt was important financially to that ranch. And if you were lucky enough to have a rainy year, then you could count on worms being twice as bad. We roped and doctored wormy cattle wherever we found them. Didn't matter if it was a big bull or cow or baby calf. You stretched it where you found it and doctored it right there. Sometimes it took one person to fight off one of those old wild cows while the other one doctored her calf.

Anyhow, we'd be saddled and away from the house before sunup so we could be where we wanted to by daylight. We always rode all of their mountains in a day. When you got in from those mountain pastures after dark, there was no doubt in your mind you'd put in a full day's work, too. We'd start through Bill Addison's country there east of the house, swing into their pasture by the Old Lake and split. Wade would ride the lake country there below the bluffs. Roy would turn up a deer trail and top out above the Old Lake. I went with Wade when I first started riding. I guess I was eight or nine. When I got a little older and Roy began to have a little confidence in me, I got to go with him. Wade usually circled the Old Lake and the country below the bluffs and swung up Fonville Canyon from the U-fence. Roy would ride the top of the bluffs and check Barrilla and Wood Canyon. They'd come together at the Fonville tub. Then they'd separate again, and Wade would swing up Fonville Canyon to the Jeff fence by the Camp Tub and over the ridge. Roy covered the Rincon country and topped out by what they called the Spanish Peaks. They never seemed to say anything about which way they would ride. They just did. Like I said, they'd been doing it so many years they didn't need to talk about it. They'd come together at the Tub-On-Top and discuss what cattle they'd seen—or hadn't. Then one would drop off into Lockhausen Canyon while the other rode the high country north of the canyon. They'd come together again at Headwater Springs where they had a fire pit and chuck box.

The little spring there watered all their mountain pastures by gravity. People who bought the ranch at the end were amazed at that. Wade had laid the pipeline out by himself. He couldn't afford a surveyor or engineer to help him, so he rode the pipeline route horseback, marking it so "wets" could hand dig the ditch. When they started laying pipe from the spring, Wade got himself a pressure gauge and used it to see if he had enough pressure to push the water over the next rise. If they did, they'd lay another mile and he'd check it again. That pressure gauge was the only thing he used. Every quarter mile or so he put air vents in the line. Wade would screw the gauge on top of one of those vents and read it. If there wasn't enough pressure, he'd ease the line around a mesa or ridge until he found enough pressure to get it over the rise. He strung all the mountain pipeline like that. Horseback. That's how they packed their pipe and equipment in, too. The only addition to that pipeline was fifty years later when Wade extended it from the Fonville around to the Old Lake below the bluffs. He didn't use the gauge then—even though he still had it—because he knew there was enough pressure for the water to get over the little mesa there east of the Fonville. And he knew the Old Lake was lower than the mesa.

Anyhow, when the line was finished, it left Headwater and ran east, filling two troughs in the floor of Lockhausen Canyon. One leg of the line T'd south from the canyon floor, topped Lockhausen ridge, filled a tub there, and dropped on south to another tub where they later put in a storage tank.

They called that the Yellow Tub because of the yellow-colored dirt in an arroyo there. The main line continued on down Lockhausen Canyon, filled a second trough at the mouth of the canyon, crawled straight up a quarter mile to the top of a mesa, filled that tub—called the Tub-On-Top—and ran east another mile or so and filled what they called the Camp Tub. The main line then ran from the Camp Tub across a corner of the Jeff Ranch's Barrilla pasture and on up to Wade and Roy's Barrilla storage tank.

The tank held about five thousand gallons and was a later addition. They had to put it in because Barrilla was the highest point on the line. If a float or pipe broke anywhere else on the line, the water couldn't make it to Barrilla. During droughts, the spring would get weak. Cattle up line from Barrilla would keep the troughs drunk down and the line pressure so weak that Barrilla would dry up. So Wade put the storage tank up there to keep water in the trough when times got dry. They lugged the steel up there in pieces, built a cement and rock bottom, and bolted the thing together with wetback help. They only used wetbacks for jobs they couldn't physically handle themselves.

Another line T'd northeast off the Barrilla-Camp Tub line and ran up into what was called Wood Canyon. They had to hand carry everything up to that tub, too, because it was so steep and rough. It was located on the side of the canyon, but there was good grass there and cattle used it. The main line left Camp Tub and dropped down into the Fonville Canyon and filled the Fonville Tub there at the corrals.

Originally there were at least five springs around the Lockhausen Headwater, and the canyon ran cool, clear water year round when Wade and Roy first bought it. Then it dropped down to just the main spring and one small seep spring. When I first saw it, I couldn't figure out how it watered their whole ranch. It was just a small stream that came out of the side of the canyon there, over a rock strata, I guess. They had a one-inch pipe with a fine screen over the end cemented into a small, hand-dug catch basin. The pipe ran from the spring into the storage tank. Whenever they stopped for lunch, they cleaned the screen and checked the spring's strength. It never ran over a few gallons an hour, but it was steady and dependable and kept them in business in the mountains for over fifty years. If the canyon flash flooded, the first thing we did was pick-and-crowbar our way back up to the Headwater spring to get it cleaned out and running.

The seep spring came out of the rocks above Headwater. They'd buried a number three washtub there to catch it. The washtub always stood full of springwater and tadpoles. A small, barbed wire fence kept the cattle out of both springs. They also kept a chuck box at Headwater stocked with condiments, some cooking and eating utensils, and a big, blue coffeepot.

Anyhow you wound up at Headwater about noon when you rode the mountains. And the first thing you did when you got there was gather up some firewood to boil coffee water. Roy always made the coffee, even at the house. Sometimes Wade would make his biscuits at noon. When he did, it was a real treat. Especially if there was a little syrup in the chuck box, which was about as fancy as they ever got sweetwise. I think Wade made better biscuits than any person I know—woman or man. At least I never ate any better. And maybe it was because I was young, but that springwater coffee always tasted better than any I've had before or since.

Every few weeks they'd restock their chuck box when they came to the canyon to put out salt. After we unloaded the headwater supplies, we always gathered up a load of wood for the house stove. Canned corn, like the breakfast menu, was the one item that never seemed to vary at the Headwater meal. The rest we carried in a morral on our saddles. It usually consisted of a can or two of meat, red beans in a lard can, and maybe a potato or two. They usually hung the morral on my saddle when I was with them so they wouldn't lose it chasing a wormy cow or calf.

Once the fire was going at Headwater, Roy would fill the coffeepot with springwater, and Wade would start frying the steak and potatoes while the coffee boiled. When the coffee water was boiling good, Roy would dump the grounds in, let it make a minute or two, then lift the pot off the fire, sprinkle it with springwater to settle the grounds, and pour everyone a cup. When Wade finished cooking, he would fill the Dutch oven with springwater and a little soap and let it boil while we ate. After we ate, everyone dropped their plate in the hot water and washed it with a bar of Lux soap and one of two old rags that hung inside the chuck box. The other rag was for drying. I don't know why, but the Lux soap never came off the plates, and the next time you stopped to eat, you had to take your plate and cup down and wash it off in the springwater. Otherwise, you ate potatoes, cream corn, meat, and Lux. If the women were riding with you—and usually they were—everyone rested a few minutes after lunch. The chuck box was built right on the side of the mountain beneath those old oak trees, and the ground was steep and rocky. You never could find a comfortable place to stretch out and rest. What you usually did was tie your horse, pull your saddle off, spread the blanket out to dry while you ate, then stretched out on the blanket and tried to rest a few minutes.

13

After you rested, you saddled up and rode the rest of the mountains. Roy always topped out on the Southside bluff. I would ride the ridge separating the Southside from Lockhausen. Anything wormy I couldn't handle, like a cow or bull, I pushed off the ridge towards the Southside watering where we roped and doctored it.

Wade would swing beneath the rockslide and work the canyons and twin peaks while Roy was coming off the top and I was working the ridge. Now that ridge between the Yellow Tub and Lockhausen was my first responsibility with them. When I'd meet Wade at the Southside Tub, he'd want to know how many cows and calves I'd seen, what they looked like, and how close they were to calving. I learned what cattle stayed along that ridge, and I learned to describe what I'd seen to Wade. You'd have a droop-horned cow with a red spot around her eye or yellow cow or a lug-horned cow or a wide-horned cow or high-horned cow. They knew them all and where they'd be and if you missed one and no one else had seen her, you went back and found her if she was getting close to calving. Roy could make a baby calf sound and usually force an old cow to go check on it. You stayed until you found the calf if it wasn't with the cow. Especially if it was a new calf, which you caught and doped, worms or no. Because if he didn't have worms when you found him, he would have in a day or two.

We killed worms with chloroform back then. Each of us carried a big wad of cotton and a bottle of chloroform in old boot tops tied on our saddle skirts. When Wade and Roy wore out a pair of boots, Roy cut the tops off, sewed one bottom with rawhide and mounted them on their saddles.

When you found a baby calf with worms in its navel, you worked a wad of cotton down into the wormhole, soaked up the blood, took the cotton out, poured the hole full of chloroform, reinserted the cotton, and waited a few minutes for the worms to die. If you had an old cow trying to hook you while you worked on her calf, you learned how to keep the cotton in and the calf between you and her. Long as you kept the calf between you, she wouldn't hook you.

After a few minutes you removed the cotton and either scraped the dead worms out with the cotton or picked them out with a little stick. Then you refilled the hole with chloroform, smeared the navel good, inserted some clean cotton in the hole, mounted, and pulled out for the next one. You knew you'd be back in a couple days to check the calf, so you remembered what the cow and calf looked like. Where the trouble started was when those old mountain cows left their baby calves lying up on a ridge somewhere while they made a pasiado for water. When you found a fresh cow at a watering, you just had to wait her out and let her lead you back to that calf. Sometimes it took a couple hours and the patience of Job to find one, but you had to do it or lose the calf.

When worms really got bad, only one of them went to town on Saturday—usually Wade with Happy—and the rest of us just kept riding and hunting worms. Once in a great while we'd have a wet year and an old cow could just lick herself and there'd be an old green blowfly laying eggs on her. They didn't have to scratch themselves or draw blood or anything during wet years. They just got worms. Period. Especially in their rear ends where it was tough to doctor them. You'd stretch an old cow out and those worms might have a pocket the size of a coffee cup eaten out four or five inches up inside her, and you'd have to go up in there and doctor her. Usually she'd crap on your arm at least once. Worms was why ranchers did all of their branding and dehorning in the early Spring or late Fall when the blowflies weren't so bad. You just couldn't do it after worm season started.

Sometimes we'd find old cows having trouble calving, and we'd hook a rope onto a baby calf's front legs and back him out of a cow with a horse, which usually meant ripping the uterus of the cow out. Or sometimes an old cow would just prolapse and slip her uterus trying to calve a breech calf. Whenever this happened, we pushed the uterus back inside the cow, placed a half-pint whiskey bottle inside it to keep it shaped, and sewed her shut with a rawhide string and a sacking needle.

After they'd sewn an old cow up, they keep her in the nearest corrals with water. They'd feed and doctor and check on her and her calf every other day until the stitches rotted out or the womb healed. When they felt it was time to take the whiskey bottle out, they'd turn her back to pasture. Almost all of those old cows recovered.

They tried to weed out their wild cattle over the years. They had cows that would run off and hide from a gather or drive, which meant you just had to outsmart those old cows to look at them or check their calves. One of them watered at the mouth of Lockhausen Canyon. She seemed to have a case of screwworms every time you found her. When we'd come off the ridge there by the Tub-On-Top and start down the trail into Lockhausen Canyon, we'd unlimber our ropes and try to locate her in the canyon brush.

By the time we got to the bottom of the hill, we'd have her spotted. Now she'd already learned what we meant and by the time we hit the canyon floor, she'd be going away at a dead run. And I want you to know she could run. You can't believe the chases we had up and down that canyon. She'd hit that catclaw brush high as your head on a horse, and knew every trail through it. You were definitely at a disadvantage when the race started.

But once you started after her, you stayed with it until you caught her. That was another one of their rules—whatever you started, you finished. Didn't make any difference if it took a half day. Most of their horses had learned, too, that the quicker they caught whatever it was they were chasing, the quicker they didn't have to run and jump those big rocks and catclaw bushes. So they'd just build to her. And you'd better have a deep seat when they started because it didn't make any difference if it was a hackberry tree or catclaw bush or white brush, they were going through it to that heifer. Roy usually swung up the side of the canyon to try and get ahead of her while Wade and I fell in behind her along the bottom. When we caught up with her, we stretched her out and doctored her.

Now I thought those canyon runs were fun the first time or two. I'd come in real proud of the fact the catclaw had tore my shirt off and my arms was all scratched up. But about the third time on, I want you to know I dreaded coming off that hill into Lockhausen because I knew what was about to take place, knew we were going to have to catch that damn heifer, and knew we still had a hard ride to make to finish the day. I got to where I hated riding the rest of the day with my shirt tore off.

After we rode the Yellow Tub country, we'd meet and come down the road to the mouth of Lockhausen, cut by the Jeff's square trough, and head for the house across the flats. We always passed the Jeff's Barrilla tank in the flats below Barrilla Spring. It was probably the only dirt tank in that country that never dried up, and even had a few fish in it.

The Jeff had run a pipe from Barrilla Spring down to the tank to keep it full. An old stage station had been at the spring. There were three graves there, too. I understand an early stage stop keeper, his wife, and his little girl were buried there after Apaches killed them. Wade and Roy's country started right above the spring.

When we only had time for a half-day swing in the mountains, we started out up Barrilla Canyon. Roy would take the right-hand trail back up into the rough country behind the house. Wade and I would go left, split, and work Barrilla and Wood Canyon. We'd meet Roy on top of the northern bluffs, drop down to the Fonville Tub, and ride out the Camp Tub, the Tub-On-Top, Rincon, and the Spanish Peaks. Then we'd start back toward the house and ride the Old Lake country and the breaks beneath the northern bluffs, and come in through Bill Addison's and the horse trap east of the house. Soon as you got in you ate and did whatever it was that kept you from riding the rest of the mountains—like changing windmill leathers or fixing water gaps. You were usually horseback twelve to fourteen hours a day, though, and you still had to feed your horses, cook supper, and start the generator when you got in.

The next day we'd saddle up and ride the flats on the east side of the ranch below the mountains. Every other day we rode one side of the ranch and then the other. Had to or the worms would put you out of business. We used our ropes a lot. Truth is, you really didn't have time to pen everything. There was a corral at the English well in the flats, a corral at the Fonville Canyon, and a corral at the mouth of Lockhausen, but we seldom used them. If they found three or four wormies at Barrilla, they might pen them together at the Fonville rather than scatter them. Later they added corrals at Barrilla.

Now everything at that ranch was always done a certain way. There was no deviation except in emergencies, and how they did it was arrived at through trial and error years before you got there, meaning there was a reason they did things the way the did. Before he married, Wade cooked, cleaned, and looked after the yard. Roy milked, fed the house stock, and took care of the machinery. The coons, coyotes, and hawks made short work of their first attempt at a few chickens they bought for yard eggs. We tried to varmint-proof a chicken pen by dropping chicken wire in the middle of cement to keep coyotes from digging under it. We'd planned to cover it with the wire to keep the hawks and coons from coming in over the top, but the varmints cleaned out the hens before we finished the project, so we shut it down. The empty chicken pen sat out back for years.

116

One evening we were sitting on the front porch after supper. Roy had gone down to milk. Now the milk pen was partially obscured from the porch, so the first thing we heard was Roy cussing. Then we got a glimpse of Roy and the milk cow circling the pen, him limping and whining and whopping at her butt with a two-by-four every time they came around. Roy finally limped up to the house with about two inches of milk in his bucket. The cow normally gave a couple gallons. He slammed the bucket down on the kitchen cabinet, and someone asked him, "What happened to the milk?" Roy said, "That sonofabitchin' cow dried up." Wade started chuckling and said, "If I had someone chasin' me around a pen with a stick, I'd dry up too."

Roy had squatted down beside the cow and started milking. She swished her tail and knocked his hat off. He whomped her in the flank with his fist—as he was prone to do to things when he got mad—and she promptly stepped on his foot and broke it. He jumped up to push her off his foot and she kicked the milk bucket over.

Now Roy's mad, so he grabbed a two-by-four off the ground to whack her, and she takes off around the pen, Roy hobbling behind on his broken foot, cussing. When he finally got calmed down and got the cow settled, she only had a couple inches of milk to give. The only reason Roy and Wade had a milk cow was they both liked fresh cream on their oats at breakfast. Finally the cow got old so they sold her. Truth is, they both hated to milk. Roy never did go to a doctor for his foot.

Wade and Roy canned all their beef then too. They'd use two, sometimes three beeves a year. After Alpine got its locker plant and they got their butane icebox to keep meat frozen, they just hauled their beef to town, had it killed and dressed, and put in their locker box. When they went to town, they'd fill a cooler chest with frozen beef, bring it back to the ranch, and put it in the icebox freezer for a week or two.

Before iceboxes though, they'd kill a beef late some evening, bleed and clean it, then hoist and tie it to a barn rafter with fence stretchers to cool. After supper, Roy returned to skin the carcass with his pocketknife, split the beef exactly in half with a wood saw, and cut off some T-bones for breakfast. Later years I went to school at A&M and the professor who taught the meats course there offered an A to anyone who could take a meat saw and split a carcass in half—down the backbone, one end to the other—without leaving bone. It was a standing offer, and he didn't award any while I was there. Yet time and again I saw Roy take a common wood saw and split a carcass right down the vertebrae without ever leaving bone. I never could do it.

The first thing Wade did on canning day was put on a pot of son-of-a-gun stew composed of heart, liver, sweetbreads, and I don't know what else he'd saved from the beef. Then he'd cook the T-bones for breakfast. It was the only time breakfast ever varied, and you needed the extra meat to get you through the day because canning was a hard, hot job.

After they finished breakfast, they stoked the stove, backed their old jitney out from beneath the front porch, set up some long tables in the shade there, and brought the beef up from the barn a half at a time. Bill and Maude Addison, their neighbors and good friends to the east, always came over and helped.

The steaks and roasts were chunked first—about three fourths of an inch thick, twelve to fourteen chunks per number three can, or enough to feed about six people. Unseasoned. You did that when you ate it. A few roasts they rolled and canned whole, but most everything was chunked. Anything left over—shoulder, shank muscle, anything —was ground for chili. My job was to seal cans and grind chili.

You sat the can on a stand and placed a lid on top that hung over the rim. Then you slid a handle up that clamped the can while you cranked and rolled the lid halfway round.

Then you stopped, shifted the clamp and handle, and finished the job. Soon as you had a half dozen or so cans you took them upstairs to Mrs. Addison who ran two pressure cookers sitting on a full-stoked wood stove in a kitchen that always felt like it was a hundred-thirty degrees, and probably was. Sometimes it became unbearably hot as the day wore on and the sun rose, and she would have to sit outside on the concrete slab in the shade of a tree between pressurings.

The meat had to be cooked close to an hour, the stove kept red-hot and the pots clamped tight to keep the pressure. Finally Mrs. Addison would lift a cooker off, set it on the drainboard, bleed off some of the pressure, and fish the cans out with wood tongs, immersing each in a dishpan full of water. Air bubbles marked the leakers, which had to be reopened, resealed, and repressured. This went on all day until we worked down to gristle and muscle. Then it was chili grinding time, and I can't think of a job on that ranch I hated any worse than grinding a dishpan full of shoulder and shank gristle with dull blades. They never sharpened those damn grinder blades the whole time I was at that ranch, and my arms would ache sometimes until I thought they would come off. But they'd just keep piling the meat up for me to grind, never throwing away anything.

After we finished, we labeled everything. And this was the beef we ate along with our red beans and biscuits and corn. The steak, when you opened it, never did really taste like steak, but it was tender and you could cut it with a fork and it wasn't bad with a little salt and pepper. Mainly, it was nourishing.

They used their Model-T truck to put out salt around their waterings. Roy finally sold it in '47, I think, for fifty dollars. That and horseback was the only way you could get salt to those waterings on top of ridges or along canyonsides. They didn't have their mountain road cut through the Jeff Ranch then. To get to the mountains they had to go east across the flats from their shack, cut back under the bluffs through the

Addison Ranch, circle north through the U-pasture and come south up Fonville Canyon on an old dirt road. The U-Ranch at that time belonged to a man named Francis Popham. When old man Popham died, he left it to his granddaughter who sold it. It passed through two or three hands until the King Ranch bought it. There was a rough road up Fonville Canyon, but there wasn't anything to Barrilla.

To get there they just followed the pipe line. The same was true for the Tub-On-Top. We'd crawl along that pipeline in their old truck with a load of salt. My job was to ride in back. There was an art to keeping yourself and the salt from bouncing out. There wasn't any sideboards. I'd stand, hanging onto the cab. It was easy to grip because it had no top, and I'd brace the salt blocks with my feet to keep them from sliding off. When we got to a tub, we dropped a block off and pushed the float down to check the air bubbles. They could tell from the size and amount of the bubbles if there was trouble in the line. Wade could also tell if the pipeline had water in it by checking the pressure at the tub halfway up Lockhausen Canyon. He also checked it below the Tub-On-Top because if the water was out, it would pull back down the hill and give the appearance of pressure in the canyon. He knew, too, exactly which air vents in the line were valid tests and which ones weren't. There'd be times when we'd ride by three air vents then Wade would stop and say, "Let's check this one." Some I did understand. Air rises in the pipe, for example, so you checked the springside vent just below a rise because that's where the air would be.

We moved John Fonville's old windmill from Fonville Canyon around to the Miller Spring at the house one summer. We just pulled the windmill over and loaded it onto the old Model-A. We made about five miles an hour. Took us all day.

The Miller Spring came right out of the bottom of that bluff, just above and west of Wade and Roy's house. It watered the house, the house corrals, plus all of the east side.

In fact, there wasn't a well anywhere on their east side except for the old English windmill, but it didn't run enough to fill anything but the English trough. That left their north and south sections, the horse trap, the house trap, the house barns and pens, and the house itself all depending on the Miller Spring for water.

Wade and Roy had caulked the spring up and made a small watering for stock there around the house, but they didn't have enough slope or enough pressure to get water to the east side. That's why we moved the Fonville windmill to the spring. Before they put the windmill on it, Roy hand-pumped water every night into the tin storage tank at the house so they would have water. Ever notice how they hated to waste water? Anyhow, Roy finally got tired of the hand pump after several years, and we spent a day moving Fonville's old windmill over to the house. Wade and Roy said the spring never failed until farmers started heavy irrigation north of the Barrillas.

Truth is I hated having to clean springs on that ranch when I was young. They'd find those little old seep springs around and dig down to the outcrop, trying to get a better flow so they could water a cow or two more somewhere. They had one coming out of an old white clay bank with a hole about six-foot deep down to it. When the hole filled up with mud, we'd have to clean it out. Roy would pull off his boots and roll up his pants and get down in there and muck around with a five gallon bucket. He'd scoop it full and hand it up to me. I'd be standing on the edge. My job was to reach down and get a grip on the bucket handle, come up outa there with it, then walk away from the hole and dump it. You talk about backbreaking work for a youngster. I didn't have my strength at the time. I'd be wobbling and Roy would be ducking the mud I was sloshing. Finally I'd get it dumped. This went on for an hour or so until we had the spring cleaned out and running again. I'd be half wore out time we finished. Usually we'd go on and make a day's ride.

14

Cavalry horses were a major source of income for Wade and Roy during the Depression. Wade told me their mares kept them in business when the cattle market disappeared, and that the income from their cavalry horses was how they made their land payments. They kept their saddle horses in the middle trap east of the house and their mares with the cavalry's remount stallions on top of the mesa in back of the house.

When you used a cavalry stallion, the remount service had first pick of the colts when they were old enough to sell. A Major Vorhees put out the studs and did all the buying for the cavalry. At the time, Fort Reno, Oklahoma, was head-quarters for the remount service.

Now a cavalry horse had to meet certain qualifications. First, they had to be physically sound and without defect. He also had to be at least fifteen hands and a solid dark color. The government kept a half-breed studbook to register their horses each year. Wade and Roy named all their colts and described them so the government could have a record from each breeder.

One of the early studhorses Wade and Roy got from the government was called Repine. 'Pine we called him for short. He was a big, black thoroughbred horse. One of my first jobs at that ranch was to feed old Pine when he came to water at the house with his mares. It meant walking about fifty yards from the barn up to an old two-by-foured, tin-lined feed trough that sat on the ground off up the side of the mountain there behind the barn. Anyhow, Pine was always the first one in to eat, and I want you to know I was as afraid of that studhorse as I was a mountain lion. He'd see me start to the feed trough with that bucket, and here he'd come, wringing his neck and snorting and pawing at rocks. Hell, I was only ten and had no way of knowing he was just hungry. When I dumped that feed, I checked it to him and never looked back. Course, Pine just downed his head and went after that feed and forgot about me.

When we rode the mountain pasture where Pine kept his mares, we had to get off and gather up a hatful of rocks—big rocks—to throw at him. Whoever opened the gate into his pasture provided everyone else with an armload of rocks big enough to chunk and hurt him with. Because if that studhorse saw you come into his mountain pasture, he was going to try to run you out. And when he did, a handful of pebbles was the last thing you wanted.

Wade was usually out front. He'd meet him and bounce a rock or two off his head, then Roy would hit him and holler at him. I'd bring up the drag. All of us would be throwing rocks with our horses jumping and fighting their heads. It was pretty exciting times, especially if you've seen one of those old studs bite or kick something. Their jaws look like a lion's mouth when they're open.

Copy Cat was the last government stud they had. He was a big bay horse with a black mane and tail and was powerfully built. Wade's bay—Highball—and Roy's horse—Bobby Socks—and Prissie and Mac and some of the others—all of the last horses they rode—all come out of old Copy Cat. That's why all of them were such tall horses. They stood a little over sixteen hands you know.

Wade wrote the Army each fall and let them know about how many horses he thought he had that would meet their color and physical standards. Then they'd make a date and come to the ranch. You had to show the horses under saddle. That was another requirement. The horse had to be pretty well gentled or broke, though the Army didn't *really* care. It was just a regulation. The buyers for the Army were old-time cavalry men, and you couldn't hoodwink them. They'd come out and look over the horses, cull the blemished and bog spavins and off-colored, ask to see the rest under saddle, and conclude the sale. Sometimes they'd brand them right on the spot—a U.S. on the left shoulder. From that moment on, they belonged to the Army.

Except for the government remount service, the horse business wasn't all that good though. Occasionally eastern polo players or endurance riders would make a swing through the country looking for the type of horse Wade and Roy bred. Whenever they bought one from Wade and Roy, they always did good because the horse would have the heart and stamina and speed they needed.

Now raising horses wasn't easy in those rocks. When you finally got one up to a yearling, you really felt like you had something. Navel illness was a problem in their colts. It was an infection they didn't know how to treat very well back then, and they'd lose a bunch of colts from time to time. Then, knee and ankle joints would just swell up and run and get worms. Or colts jumping and playing in those rocks would scratch an ankle and get worms and die. Hell, when one of those horses made it to a yearling, just having survived a year on that mountain there back of the house gave a colt a certain quality.

Usually when they were yearlings, Roy would rope them out the first time and fool with them a little bit. Then he'd turn them back to the mountain and bring them in when they were past two and begin breaking them.

Anyhow, Wade and Roy always got top dollar for their horses from the government because they had such a fine bunch of mares, and the cavalry was after as near perfect horses as it could get. That's why the government always went first class with their remount studs. It sure was a pretty sight to see that bunch of old mares come into the water there at the house. All of them with little colts running and jumping, playing and raring over one another. Wade and Roy always checked them like hawks whenever they'd come in, seeing if any of the colts or mares had worms.

From what people told me, Wade and Roy always had good mares around even before they started doing business with the cavalry. They had several Steel Dust mares they'd bought in the Panhandle. They'd bred them to a ranger's stallion up in that part of the country. They said this stud was a big, solid dun horse. Back then, you know, the entire country was horseback, and you didn't get off your horse except to relieve yourself. The first thing you did each morning was saddle up and you stayed on until you got done with whatever it was you were doing. All of the early cattle work was done horseback.

Anyhow, it was no job at all for this old ranger to get up and cover sixty or seventy miles in a day on this horse. This was the type of studhorse they used on those Steel Dust mares, and they said they got some fine horses out of that combination.

Then, when paints became popular in the early Twenties, they used a paint mare called Maxine. She was a strong breeder, whatever else she was, and always dropped a paint colt. Wade would keep one or two of the better paints at the ranch to work, then sell the rest. The last paint at the ranch still had Maxine's markings, and it had been almost fifty years since Maxine was on the place. Mary Lou was one of Maxine's colts, and all of her colts always dropped paint colts; even when they were bred to solid-colored studs. Mary Lou was mostly thoroughbred herself.

Wade and Roy would bring their young horses in as soon as their seeds dropped—usually as yearlings and always in the winter to avoid worms—for Roy to castrate. Roy always did the cutting, and never lost a horse that I know of. Castrating a horse isn't like cutting a calf, and you can kill one quick if you don't know what you're doing. Then they'd turn them back to pasture, and the horses would be maybe two-and-a-half or three years before anyone fooled with them again. They just grew and got big and stout.

Now working with these broncs was something you did after you were caught up with your worms. On days when we rode the east side, which only took us until noon, we'd come in, eat, pen the broncs, and spend the afternoon riding them.

Of the two, Wade was by far the better rider, going away. And when Wade got on a horse, he was there. I don't recall him ever getting thrown while we worked young broncs. He was strictly business on a horse; up there to get a job done. And he expected his horses to help him do that job. If the horse didn't or couldn't, he got rid of him and broke him another one that would. He just didn't have time to waste on a bad horse.

Roy, on the other hand, liked to fool with horses and seemed to have a natural touch with them; wasn't the least bit afraid of a horse. Any horse. He just believed a horse wouldn't treat a man mean, and he always rode one of those early roping-type saddles with no seat or swells to speak of, and he'd baby those horses and talk to them all the time like they was spoiled children or something. When he got where he thought one was pretty gentle, why he'd just step up on him. I don't know how he kept from getting killed, but I don't ever recall Roy being thrown either. He had a way with horses and always made a pet out of every horse he kept for himself at the ranch.

When it came time to start gentling the broncs, we'd pen them and cut one off into the forty foot alley in front of the barn. The alley was about ten or twelve feet wide. Roy would try to get a loop on the colt without having to rope him; but if he couldn't, he'd rope him, take a couple turns on a post, and hand the rope to me. My job was to hold the rope and give him slack. Roy would start down the rope towards this two-and-a-half- or three-year-old bronc, talking to him as he went. Usually the bronc would choke himself down. When they did, Roy would holler at me to give him some slack. He'd walk up there and loosen the rope around the colt's neck. When the bronc got back on his feet, Roy would be standing there, rubbing him on the nose, talking to him. Sometimes they'd paw at his head and knock his hat off or rip his shirt, but it never worried old Roy none. Like I said, Roy never saw a horse he was afraid of. He just didn't believe they'd hurt him.

We'd work with one twenty or thirty minutes, then we'd go get another one until we'd worked our way through the entire bunch. You kept this up until they knew what a rope was, and you could work your way down a rope to them without getting run over or pawed. Then you'd begin to catch them in the big pen and lead them. Finally, you'd step up on one. We all rode them. I was the only one that ever got throwed. That always tickled Wade and Roy, and they'd laugh and chuckle about it the rest of the afternoon. Eventually I got to where I could stay aboard a few and made them a pretty fair hand. Anyhow, this was their gentling process, and it went on whenever we could find a spare minute.

I guess the last time I saw Wade ride a hard-pitching horse was right after World War II started. Everyone had gone off to fight, and there wasn't anyone left to help around the ranches, so we'd all ridden down to the Jeff Ranch to help them gather their cattle.

We started out early that morning to gather what they called the Rooney Pasture. Everyone was loping along to warm up. We all rode up and over this big, long, dirt dam the Jeff used to turn water out of an arroyo. Wade was riding a horse called Strawberry. Now Strawberry was stringhalted and he had a habit of jerking one hind leg up while you rode him. Anyhow, when old Strawberry come down the other side of that dump, he just bogged his head and turned it on. Talk about pitching. I want you to know, he and Wade put on a show out across those flats for about sixty yards. Wade just sat up there and rode that horse as fine and easy as you'd ever hope to see. He never touched a piece of saddle leather with his other hand, and when he finally pulled him up after a minute or two, old Strawberry was out of breath and had had all he wanted. We all just went on about our business and gathered the pastures. Wade, I guess, was in his mid-fifties then.

Wade told me when he was a boy they didn't pamper horses. He said they'd bring four- and five-year-old horses in right off the range. They'd rope and stake them overnight on an anchored halter rope to get their necks and heads good and sore. Then they'd put them in a pen, ear them down, put a saddle on them and step aboard.

If you could stay on one in the corral, they'd open the gate. Since it might be thirty miles to the nearest fence—if there was one—you either rode him when you went out that gate or walked in. He said they did this three or four times with a horse, then stuck him in their remudas. That's what a man drew when he rode out and went to work on a ranch. That's the way they broke their horses then. They were called green broke horses. Wade said you either rode them or walked. And if you couldn't ride them, they found someone who could.

Now Wade and Roy had certain horses they'd give you each summer when you come down, and you could measure how good a hand you were making by the kind of horses they were giving you. The year they gave me old Jigs, I knew they'd accepted me.

Old Jigs lost his mother in the mountain pasture one year, so Wade and Roy raised him on a bottle at the house. He was just as gentle as he could be when he was a dogie, but then he got mean. I didn't know until later that Wade had rode Jigs all winter the summer before I got there. I guess he was afraid Jigs might hurt me. I wasn't too old then. Like I said, though, Wade didn't brook foolishness from any of his horses, and when Jigs got lazy and mean, Wade went to riding him hard. He'd stopped Jigs from pitching and boogering, and the only thing he hadn't cured old Jigs of that winter was kicking your foot out of the stirrup whenever you went to get on or off him. And he whammed it, I mean. Would break a leg or ankle like a pretzel if he got in a good lick.

That was the summer I learned to step on a horse from

the front. Fast. Wade showed me how. Once. That's all they ever showed you anything. You grabbed a tight rein and a handful of mane with your left hand, pulled the stirrup up under old Jigs' neck with your right hand, stuck your left toe in it, and swung from right there up into the saddle. And if you were the least bit slow, Jigs would kick your leg out of the stirrup so fast it'd make your eyes blink. When you got off, you swung off under his neck, too. Otherwise, you paid the consequences. I learned to get on and off in a hurry that year.

Anyhow, we'd come in one day after a long, hot afternoon ride—hunting wormy calves—and we were sapped. I mean, it was one of these days when everyone was just tired and hot and hungry and half mad by the time we unsaddled.

I rode in under the barn, swung off, pulled my saddle off old Jigs and carried it in and plopped it on the saw horses. When I went back to slide my bridle off Jigs, he'd run off in a corner of the corral and there he stood, his rear end to me. Well, there wasn't no way you could get to old Jigs' head without passing his hind feet. And if there was one horse you didn't walk behind on that ranch it was Jigs. Because he'd as soon kick your brains out as your foot. I guess he just liked to kick. I flicked him with a little rock or two, but he just humped and sullied and stood there waiting for someone to try to get to his bridle so he could kick them.

Finally everyone had their horses loose but me, and Wade happened to walk around the corner of the barn with his bridle in his hand. He saw Jigs standing there with his head in the corner, knew what he was up to and, I guess, it hit him wrong. I imagine Jigs had whammed him a time or two during the winter. Anyhow, Wade walked up behind old Jigs and lashed him across his ass end with his reins. I mean, you could've heard it pop clear up at the house. Jigs spun around and Wade had ahold of them reins faster than you could blink.

Without saying a word, he led Jigs down to the big corral,

tied him with his head against a fence post, backed off about ten feet and started gathering up an armload of fist-sized rocks. Then he started chunking them at Jigs' rear end. Hard. I mean hard.

Well, that just beat all. I hadn't ever seen Wade act like that before. Not that I wasn't enjoying seeing Jigs get his, you understand, because he'd dumped me off and kicked my stirrup out from under me no less than a dozen times already that summer. But it looked to me like Wade was going to stand right there and rock that horse to death. He stood there gathering and chunking rocks at Jigs' ass, whopping him; the rocks just bouncing off Jigs' rear end. Directly he stopped. I guess he'd got his frustration worked out, and when he started towards Jigs to untie him, Jigs did his damnedest to put his ass end against that fence and turn his head toward Wade. He wanted to see where the next rock was coming from. Wade untied him, led him back to the barn, slipped the bridle off, and I never had a bit of trouble with Jigs sticking his head in a corral corner after that.

The thing about old Jigs was that he wasn't partial. I mean, he'd kick or throw anyone he could, given the chance. He was a pretty decent cow horse, though, and I think that's why Wade kept him.

That mesa there above the mouth of Lockhausen Canyon was where Jigs got Wade after he roped the bull. The bull had worms, and Wade and Roy were going to stretch him out and doctor him. Roy missed his first loop and pulled away to remake. Wade fell in behind the bull and caught him first throw, just as the bull headed off the mesa and down the trail into Lockhausen Canyon. When the bull hit the end of the rope, old Jigs decided it was time to pitch. Now Wade's cinch had worked loose, and when Jigs went to pitching and the bull hit the end of that rope, Wade and the saddle skinned right out over Jigs' head. Roy said they just sailed out of sight—in the air—over the edge of the mesa. The bull never broke stride, and Wade never left that saddle until

130

he had to. Old Jigs pitched on down the trail, stopped, and surveyed his handiwork.

Wade managed to get loose from the saddle without getting hurt and had to watch the bull head down into Lockhausen Canyon with his saddle bouncing along behind. The bull got about halfway down the trail before the rope and saddle hung up between two big rocks. Roy was sitting back up there on the mesa rim laughing so hard he couldn't talk. Finally he managed to ask Wade if he was hurt. Wade told him no. So Roy caught old Jigs and handed him to Wade, then went on down the hill and roped the bull. Wade come hobbling down the trail afoot and helped Roy doctor the bull, then saddled old Jigs and stepped aboard. He must have slapped old Jigs five or six times between the ears with his rope. He was hoping he would try his hand at pitching again. If he had, Wade would have worn him out and rode him hard the rest of the day for good measure. But old Jigs was too smart for that. He knew he'd caused a mess and wasn't about to compound things.

★   ★   ★

**From an interview with the late
Dorothy Reid, (1904-1990),
wife of Wade Reid (1888-1974)**

One year some people from back East—Connecticut, Vermont, somewhere—came to the Davis Mountains looking for horses that could win some type of endurance or marathon race. The race was held each year back East. They needed horses that could hold up over great distances. Not race horses, understand, but horses with stamina that could cover a lot of country. I remember the men came to the ranch in January because it was a very cold day. I had some tea ready, thinking they might be from England, but it turned out they were from the U.S. and they all drank coffee. They bought two of Wade's and Roy's horses. I think one was named Angel and the other was named Dark Age. They were both beautiful horses. Tall and big-boned. They took them back East, and I believe won their race with one of those horses.

When Wade and Roy finally sold all of the mares, they sat up there on the porch and watched the trucks leave with them. I think that's the saddest I ever saw them both at one time. Wade kept four or five good broodmares back.

Johnny Fitzgerald came by and asked if he could try to get another colt out of one of our mares before they got too old, and Wade and Roy said okay. Johnny always liked those horses, you know. One of the mares they kept was a paint called Maxine. She had two colts, Roy and Dorealles. Wade rode Dorealles and Roy rode the other one. Maxine's last paint colt was Prissy. She became one of the gentlest and smoothest riding mares on the ranch. They always kept one paint mare with their stock. Wade kept a big bay horse called Highball and trained him to cover country in a running walk. Lord, you could ride that horse all day and not get tired. Roy kept a big black horse with whitefeet he called Bobby Socks. When Bobby Socks died, I thought we were going to have to bury Roy with him. Wade kept the broodmares on the mesa in back of the house. Prissy finally had a little paint colt called Candy. Wade's other mares threw one more colt. Roy worked with them around the barn. By this time I'd quit riding. After Bobby Socks died, Roy rode Gato, one of our last saddle horses.

The one horse I do remember on that ranch was old Jigs. Everyone hated Jigs. You could ride Jigs all day long without a thing happening. Then late in the morning when you were least expecting it, which is very unusual with horses, he would just drop his head and start pitching. I mean hard. That's how he threw me. We were starting home through the English; and Wade said, "Let's swing back down this draw. I want to check a gate." When we turned,

Jiggs dropped his head and caught me completely off guard. Off I came onto some rocks. I got up and Wade said, "You hurt?" I said, "I don't think so." He said, "We'll trade horses and saddles," and I said, "No, I'll ride this same horse." By the time I got back on Jigs, I'd just lost my sense of direction, everything. I would start to say something, but the wrong words would come out. Roy was gone at the time, so when we got back to the house, Wade says, "Now you lay down, honey. I'll fix lunch. You'll be all right in a little while." I never hurt so bad in all my life. My neck and legs ached where I'd landed on the rocks.

15

Interview with
Russell McAfee, Jr. (1920-1979), continued

Wade and Happy never went to a dance that I know of. I guess because of Wade's feet. But they did everything else together it seemed, riding included. Me and Jimmie Tom was there the day Aunt Happy passed out. It was in 1932. She'd miscarried that Spring and had been kind of under the weather ever since. Jimmie Tom was madly in love with some old boy in high school and had written him a letter to come see her. Trouble was, she hadn't told anybody this old boy was coming until he walked around the point of the hill west of the house one day, wore out. He'd walked all the way to the ranch from the highway.

Jimmie Tom saw him and run out the front door, hollering, "Oh, it's him. It's him!" 'Course Aunt Happy didn't know who he was, so she run out there on the front porch and hollered at Jimmie Tom to get right back up there. The old boy stayed around the ranch house for a day or two. Soon as Wade and Roy put him to work, he pulled out for Wichita Falls.

Anyhow, it was about three or four days after that when Aunt Happy got sick. Roy had gone to town earlier, and I was down at the barn working one afternoon when Wade stepped out on the front porch and hollered at me, "Aunt Happy's real sick. Go down there and catch old Spot and ride down to the Jeff Ranch and call the doctor. Try to hurry."

I had old Spot saddled and was going out the gate when he hollered, "No. Don't ride old Spot. Go get old Big Boy and ride him." I don't know what made him change his mind, except maybe I was still pretty young and old Spot had a bad habit of stampeding with anyone who couldn't pull him up. I guess Wade didn't want him running through a fence with me.

He said, "Leave the gates open and ride hard. Happy's real bad, and she needs a doctor." I guess that was the wildest ride I ever made. Old Big Boy was fast and tall and had legs like rock. I got it all out of him that afternoon. It was about two or three miles down to the Jeff headquarters as the crow flies, and we covered it fast and hard.

When I got there, I put my horse in the corral and run up to the house. Mr. and Mrs. Killough was there, and Roy had just come in from town and was visiting with them. I told them about Happy. They called the doctor, and Mr. and Mrs. Killough jumped in their car and drove up to Wade and Roy's. Doc Wright finally got there from Alpine. He took one look at Happy, then asked us to help him load her in the back of his car. They took her to town. She never did come back home. She was there about six weeks, I guess, then she died. Wade just moved to town and lived in the hospital with her.

That was the summer I spent by myself with Roy. I was just a growing kid, and I never come as close to starving to death in all my life. I also found out that summer that if there was one thing Roy loved, it was ice cream. I think it was because he never had none as a kid. Anyhow, soon as Roy took over the cooking chores in Wade's absence, all the cream from their old cow went for ice cream. Now the old Servel only got things semihard in its freezer. It also had one deep ice tray that Roy promptly laid claim to for his ice cream. He would skim the cream off the milk jars, fill the tray, dump in a tablespoon of vanilla and three heaping tablespoons of sugar. He stirred this a couple of times and sat it in the freezer. The sugar never dissolved, and you could see streaks of vanilla up and down the tray, but that, by-God, was his ice cream. He'd stick it in early each morning; and when we hit the kitchen twelve to fourteen hours later, that was the first thing we'd eat. Roy would get us a couple of tablespoons, draw a line halfway down the tray, and we'd sit down and start in on it—him eating from his end and me from mine. You don't have any idea how good it tasted, gritty sugar and all. I'm convinced the few extra calories we got out of that tray kept me alive that summer. I always suspicioned Roy snuck a little extra ice cream for himself when he split it, but then my stomach was usually in control of my mind by then and it didn't matter. After we ate that tray of ice cream, we ate dinner. It never impeded out appetites at all. Roy could make good biscuits, too, but he never touched nothing in that kitchen except the coffee and oats when Wade was there.

Mrs. Killough invited us to eat supper with them at the Jeff Ranch about twice a week that summer. We'd go down to wait for Wade's call to see how Happy was doing. You talk about a treat, her suppers were it, and I really stoked up. Wade and Roy had run the Jeff Ranch for both Mrs. Lee McCutcheon and for John Killough off and on. Wade was there for several years until he married, then Roy took over for several years.

Nellie Lee and her sister, Annette, John Killough's daughters, usually came to the Jeff during the summers and spent a lot of time there. They had a cousin named Myrtle, a school teacher in Houston. She was Dave Killough's daughter, I think, and she stayed with them at the Jeff from time to time. Myrtle was a pretty woman and always liked Wade, or so they said. Mrs. McCutcheon and the Killoughs always thought the world of Wade and Roy.

The old stage stop had been at the Jeff Ranch, you know. When they first moved there, Mrs. Killough said Frank Heulster told her he saw one of the last Apaches in that country there at the Jeff's headquarters one morning. She said he told her he looked up and this Indian was standing there, looking at him. Then he said the Indian just disappeared into the brush. Afoot. It was sometime around the turn of the century. They said a few of those old bronco Apaches lived down in the mountains in Mexico after all the fighting was over, and ever once in awhile one would come back up into the Barrilla country. Mrs. Gregorea Bencomo, her husband, Alfonso, and their boys also worked at the Jeff then. Chone Bencomo, one of Alfonso's sons, was about my age. He later opened his own business in Fort Davis. It was Mrs. Bencomo who taught me to speak Spanish.

The Jeff Ranch used carbide lights then. They had this big metal tank buried between the garden and the house, and they'd dump carbide and water in it and close the lid. The carbide-generated gas ran up copper lines, I think, from the tank to the Jeff's house lights. They sat about shoulder high along the sides of the walls. They bought the carbide in five gallon cans. Welders, you know, used it for years to make acetylene. The carbide turned white after it ran its course, and they'd just keep adding to the tank until it was full of this thick white slush. When they couldn't add anymore, they bailed the residue out and whitewashed all the fences and barns around the Jeff headquarters. That was the best painted ranch and headquarters' corrals in the Barrilla Mountains.

Anyhow, we'd go down to the Jeff nearly every night while Aunt Happy was in the hospital. Since Wade and Roy didn't have a phone, Wade would ring the Jeff—a long-short-long—to let them know how she was doing. We'd get the report. After supper, Roy and Mr. John always went out on the porch, talking baseball or settling world affairs or politics, which wasn't any fun for a kid—I guess I was about thirteen—and I'd go down and visit the Bencomos. They always moved their chairs out back of their adobe after it got cool in the evenings. They only spoke to me in Spanish, too. I learned to communicate pretty quick. Chone and I would usually fall asleep in the grass. He and I both were old enough to ride and work everyday. Roy always came by and picked me up on the way back to the ranch.

Roy told me they always helped the Jeff gather and drive their cattle to Hovey each Fall. It meant a little extra money for them both, which they were always needing. He said they stopped shipping at Hovey long about '35. Later, when they knew they were going to make it, they still went down and helped the Jeff at roundup. Both of them always cared a great deal for Mrs. McCutcheon, and afterwards, the Killoughs and Mulloys. After Pat Mulloy took over as Jeff manager, he always sent his hands to help Wade and Roy work their cattle if they needed them.

Roy told me that during the Twenties and Thirties they'd get a large herd ready to ship and just trail them right on down through Indian Springs and load them out at Hovey for Kansas City. Then the Santa Fe started losing money on the spur, so they shut it down, even though they shipped cattle on a doodlebug line out of Alpine for years afterward. They just never used Hovey anymore. The Alpine depot was still in operation during the Thirties. Cattle then were selling for a penny a pound, if you could sell them. That was during the Depression, you know. Funny thing, they said as much as they hated to admit it, it was the War that saved what ranchers were left after the Depression, and the agricultural business in general for that matter.

Anyhow, I don't think I'll ever forget that summer with Roy. I remember he was breaking a black colt he called Nigger Baby. He was a big, black, good-natured horse and broke out just fine. Panthers killed him a couple years afterward, though, right there at the water trough east of the house. Caught him when he came in for water and ate a big part of him.

Roy and I were on the south side of the Fonville one morning and had come around making the swing. Roy was riding old Nigger Baby and I was riding old Big Boy and we'd found this old cow with a new calf. The calf had worms, so Roy says, "You know, I don't know whether to rope off this bronc or not. Why don't you step off, hold old Nigger Baby, and I'll get on old Big Boy and ease up there and catch that calf."

So I did. Roy eased up behind the calf until he was in range, then whipped a little old loop on him slick as you please.

Well, the calf went to jumping and bawling when he found out he was caught, running around the end of that rope—which looked to me like it was sixty foot—circling right towards me with its mama right behind. She was a big old wide-horned, wild-eyed cow looking for something to hook because she knew her calf was in trouble. And they both were coming right at me, standing in the middle of a mountain pasture holding a bronc I knew would throw me the minute I stepped on—if I could even get on in the middle of that ruckus—and a mad cow coming at me from the other direction. You talk about decisions. Every time that calf swung by, that old cow would hook at me. Roy, he's sitting out there watching all this, chuckling and hollering, "Catch the calf. Catch the calf." I said, "You get off and catch him yourself!" He finally steps off and says, "Now keep that old cow off me."

Well, you didn't fight one of them old cows afoot, much less holding a green bronc. It just wasn't done. They'll by-God run over you and hook you on the way down if they're mad or excited, which this old cow was. But you could keep her from running over you if you kept that calf between you and the cow. As long as she could smell the calf and know he was all right, you were okay behind the calf. We both got behind the calf—it was a tight fit—and finally got it doctored. I slipped the rope off, got back on old Big Boy and grabbed Nigger Baby's reins from Roy. That left Roy holding the calf down with both hands full of worm medicine and cotton, the old cow hooking at him, and him hollering and cussing at her. Roy finally let the calf go and got back on his horse.

Roy, you know, had this knack for talking to inanimate objects. It might be a hammer or a screwdriver or a car or a tire or whatever it was. People working around him for the first time sometimes thought he was crazy. They'd hear him off down there by the barn somewhere, talking to himself. But that was just Roy's way. If something didn't suit him, why Roy'd just give it a good cussing like he was talking to a person or something. Wade only cussed when he was real mad.

One afternoon Roy and I had gone to the Fonville in their old Model-A jitney. We'd found a float off that morning while we were riding. We'd tied it up, finished our ride, split our tray of ice cream, ate our can of corn and meat, got us some parts and tools, crawled in the jitney, and went back up there to fix the water trough.

After we started working on the float, a cloud come up. When the first big raindrops hit us in the back, Roy looked up and said, "You know, we might ought to park that jitney up on top of that ridge in case the road gets slick." You had to drop off a straight clay ridge to get to the trough we were working on. There was no way to get back up if it got slick, and we were a long way from the house.

Wasn't a minute later the bottom fell out of that old cloud, and we run for the truck and got it about half way up the bank before the wheels started spinning. Roy hollered, "Jump out and push! Jump out and push!"

It rained harder, and we weren't making any headway, so Roy pulls the gas lever all the way down on the Model-A, opens his door and steps out to help push. The jitney's wheels are really spinning now.

Well sir, about that time those wheels worked their way down to dry dirt and the jitney jumped out from under Roy and me and run on off up the hill, up and over a great big old rock and died.

Well, I never in my life. Roy runs up there, kicking that Model-A's tires, hitting it with his fist, cussing it, muttering, "You dirty so 'n so. You wouldn't go when I wanted you to." He just give a good human-type cussing.

By then we were both drenched and covered with mud. I started laughing and then he got to chuckling and finally we both just sat down there on the running board, laughing until we almost fell over, water pouring off our hats.

A Saturday trip to town, if you went at all, was something special. The first thing you did was stop at Bill Fryer's Drugstore, pick up a week's worth of San Angelo Standard Times and get a nickel fountain coke. Bill's drugstore then was in the old Limpia Hotel, and the doctor's office was out back. The coke was the highlight of the week if we were lucky enough to make it in because they didn't believe in those kinds of frills at the ranch.

After you got your Co-Cola, you drove over to the Fort Davis post office across from the courthouse and picked up a week or two's mail. But they never read it. They just sifted through it to see if there was anything they could take care of while they were in town. Once the sift was completed, they rolled all the mail inside the San Angelo papers, tied everything up with string, set it in their jitney, and continued on to Alpine. Usually they'd have lunch with Mama Reid. They had her a little place there with a well and all. They always checked in with their other kin after they saw their mama's windmill was in good shape. They also took care of any business they could for her. After lunch, they split up and made their rounds, visiting with other ranchers and people, Wade buying the groceries and ranch supplies. Roy usually slipped down to the American Legion Hall and had a beer or two. There was always several ranchers there, too, and they'd talk cattle. Roy was the only one of the two who ever took a drink. Once in awhile Roy would take the jitney into Fort Davis for a Saturday night dance at the courthouse.

Wade and Roy's ranch was my first introduction to politics, also. Just because they lived off out down there away from town didn't mean they didn't keep up with politics and things. Whoever went to town on Saturday brought the week's papers home. They stacked them by date and read every word in them right after breakfast on

Sunday morning if they weren't riding or fixing waterings. This was one way they kept themselves informed. They remembered and talked about everything they read, too. Newspapers, the radio, and other ranchers were their main sources of information. At Sunday breakfast they'd compare notes from the day before—who'd sold calves for what to whom and who'd gone broke. This was Depression time and a lot of ranchers just didn't make it. Mr. Bennett McCutcheon had to let his place go. His house sat under the big mesa on the left as you drove up Limpia Canyon, right before you got to Wild Rose Pass. It was a beautiful home back up under those big cottonwoods there along Limpia Creek.

Anyhow, elections then were always held in a tent on the flats across the blacktop from Bennett's house. It was on Willis' land there near the windmill and water trough, about a mile from the cutoff road to Wade's and Roy's. It seems to me like they only had thirty votes in a precinct that took in all of Star Mountain, Jim and Rena Duncan's country, and on around to the McElroy's.

At the time, I think Mr. and Mrs. Casey were still living and voted there. People told how Velna Casey kind of run their outfit. They said she rode broncs and worked just like a man; and if a man gave her a hard time, she'd just as soon whip him as a bronc.

During the Depression years, Wade and Roy made very little money and almost lost their ranch in the process. They borrowed money from three different sources when they were just getting started and had three different loans out when the Depression hit. The only clothes they bought one year during the Depression was a pair of Levis. When I asked why they didn't buy any more clothes than that, Wade said, "I didn't have any more money to buy clothes with." They also borrowed money from an executive—one of the Jeff Ranch heirs—whom they considered to be their friend. He was well-heeled and had offered to lend them money.

Now the man wasn't a rancher, and his Jeff inheritance had been passed down to him. In fact, he only came to the Jeff to shoot rabbits in the summer and a mule deer in the Fall. Wade and Roy always let him hunt on their ranch, too. The man offered to buy Wade and Roy's place, but they wouldn't sell. So he offered to lend them operating capital at low interest rates, which they needed, and they took him up on his offer. But as soon as the Depression got underway good and the cattle markets disappeared, he wrote them a letter telling them he had to have his money back. He really didn't need it, but he knew Wade and Roy didn't have any money. What he wanted was their ranch so he could hunt rabbits and deer and vacation whenever he wanted to.

Wade and Roy tried to borrow the money to pay him, but there just wasn't any to be had except from people like him. Anyhow, the man started foreclosure proceedings against them and would have gotten their ranch if Roosevelt hadn't established the RACC and the Production Credit Associations (PCAs) just in time. As soon as they opened, Wade and Roy joined, borrowed money, and paid the man off. That was one of the reasons Wade and Roy always voted democrat. Several other ranchers in similar situations lost their ranches before Roosevelt's programs were established.

The PCA was set up so you couldn't foreclose on a rancher's land, just on production of his land. That way, the rancher couldn't lose the basis of his income if he had a bad year. The security for a PCA loan was his production. In most cases the PCA couldn't even foreclose on a whole herd, just on the cash crop for the year. They left the rancher his breeding stock to start again. Wade and Roy borrowed from the PCA each year until they paid their ranch off. When they sold their stock at the end of the year, they had their check made out to them and the PCA. If it paid the note, fine. If it didn't, the PCA credited their account and carried it forward until they sold some more calves. And even though they paid their ranch off in 1955, Wade and Roy used the PCA up until the Seventies. Wade, you know, was the Marfa PCA's director for years. Wade was also president of the board for over a decade and was reelected every year automatically. No one thought of not reelecting him. He was honest and everyone trusted him. People like him and Worth Evans always served on the board.

Now you couldn't vote in a PCA meeting unless you owed the PCA money. Or, you had to be a borrower in order to be a voting member. You could own Class A stock in the PCA if you'd paid off your note, but it was non-voting stock. The loan was the key. After Wade paid the ranch off, he would go over and borrow two hundred dollars every year so he could stay on the board. When he retired from the board, he never borrowed another cent. Wade was president of the board when he and Roy had their pickup wreck. He had to stay in bed with a bruised kidney for awhile after he got out of the hospital, so the PCA board decided to meet bedside with Wade at the ranch. Wade sat on the edge of the bed, recommending and okaying loans for area ranchers. The board knew all the applicants—and their country—and could tell right off whether or not a man could handle what he was asking for. Before they split the Marfa and El Paso PCA's, the Marfa PCA was the largest in Texas. They carried all the farmers in the El Paso and Pecos valleys and all the cattlemen from the Pecos River west. And they made big loans. Funny thing, Wade told me their losses out of that Marfa office were less than one percent. That's because they knew every borrower and hand-checked each loan. See, when Roosevelt put the PCA in, he said, "The best people to know the credit standing of a man are his neighbors. If you're farming and your neighbor is farming, you'll see his fields and how he works them and you'll talk to him, day in and day out, and you'll know whether he's a man who will pay his debts. Or who will at least make a sincere effort to pay them. And if you're a rancher, you'll know how your neighbor handles his cattle and horses, and how he handles his business dealings." This was the whole point behind the PCA. It was neighbors who made the loan decisions. One year some of the Pecos Valley farmers came to the Marfa PCA wanting to borrow money for fertilizer tanks. They said this man, Billy Sol Estes, had a million dollars worth of collateral in fertilizer tanks. Wade turned them down flat. I asked Wade why. He said, "Nobody could make a million dollars in Pecos, Texas, with fertilizer tanks."

15

Just about all the members of the Highland Hereford Association were PCA members, too. The association was organized by the Mitchells and by Mr. Bill Jones during the Twenties when it was hard to find good markets for their cattle. A lot of cattle buyers wouldn't come out all the way to the Davis Mountains, so the ranchers said, "We've got to start boosting our own product and let the country know we've got top quality cattle for sale out here." That's when they organized the Highland Hereford Association. Their dues—based on the number of head each rancher had—was used to advertise and market their cattle across the country. They succeeded. Wade and Roy were members of the association for fifty years. They were also members of the Texas and Southwestern Cattle Raisers and the American Hereford Breeders Associations.

Now the government paid ranchers to kill their cattle during the Depression. Wade and Roy had seen it coming and had already cut back and didn't have to kill many. But the Jeff Ranch wound up having to kill about eighty-five or ninety head. I rode down to help the Jeff gather these cattle. They had maybe fifty or seventy-five head in the little Garden Trap by the house. Mr. Killough sat his .270 in his wagon, hitched up his team of mules and came out to the pasture with us. Wade rode with the government inspector, who started shooting the cattle with a .22 after we gathered them. Every once in a while he'd wound one of those old cows, and she'd hike her tail over her back and head for the brush. Mr. Killough, who was sitting up there in his buckboard, would throw up his .270 and let her down before she got too far away. Alphonso and Falis Dominguez tailed what dead cattle they could into a hand dug pit there. I don't remember how much the government paid for each dead animal. The buzzards had a feast.

On top of everything else, one of the worst droughts in

history hit right in the middle of the Depression. Wade and Roy spent weeks and weeks cutting sotol to feed their cattle during the winter of '33 and '34. It was the only thing left to eat in that country then, but it kept their cattle alive. They'd go over there into the Indian Springs country in their old Model-A early of a morning, spend all day cutting and trimming out a load of sotol hearts, then haul them back late that evening and feed their cattle. It was all they could afford, and they did it day in and day out to keep their cattle alive and their ranch going during the drought. I think it was times like these that made them never waste anything. They wouldn't even throw away a nail that I can remember. They'd save their coffee cans, fill them with used, rusty nails, then stick the cans away in the tool shed. When they got ready to build something, they went down there, got themselves a bucketful of used nails, a flat board or rock, straightened the nails out, and used them again.

Bill Addison was helping Wade and Roy build a set of corrals at the house one day and got so mad trying to straighten his can of rusty nails he took the whole bucket down below the corrals and threw them in the arroyo. Then he went to town and bought him a new supply of shiny nails and went to building corrals. Wasn't three days before he was out of new nails and was back down there in that arroyo hunting the old ones.

Bill and Maude, you know, were good friends with Wade and Roy. Bill was a great big Indian-looking fellow, dark complected, with a huge hooknose. He was about six foot-five and always wore the biggest Stetson you could buy. He'd come from around Snyder where his father lived. We used to eat lots of Sunday dinners with Maude and Bill. They lived in a rock house Bill built six miles east of Wade and Roy. He'd come out there, homesteaded four sections, and went to work for R.C. Williams there at Deepwell. He also leased four more sections that joined Wade and Roy's mountain pasture to the east. He had eight. Anyhow, he'd work for

R.C., then go up and work on his place when he could. He didn't have any natural water anywhere on his ranch, and he built the first dirt tank in that part of the country.

At the time, everyone who lived on the east end of Limpia Creek used the Addison's for a meeting place. Old Ben Williams had a little old place down there, and Clarence and Mildred Hord had the old Fulton place leased next to Deepwell. Mr. and Mrs. Joe Hayter ranched down there, too. Later on, people would meet at the Hovey schoolhouse on Saturday nights and play dominoes. Before that, they always got together at Bill's and Maude's.

Wade and Roy saved bailing wire off hay bales to wire gates and fix floats and things. Their boots was another example. Kurt Lange, the German bootmaker there in Alpine, made everyone's boots in that country. He'd repair Roy's boots until they simply couldn't be repaired anymore. Mentally, Kurt was cut from the same mold as Wade and Roy, and when he finally told one of them he had to have a new pair of boots he by-God meant it, and they always accepted his decision without question. But instead of throwing their old boots away, Roy cut the tops off, sewed the bottoms tight with rawhide and tied them on their saddles to carry worm medicine. And he saved the soles to improvise windmill leathers in emergencies. Nothing was wasted. I remember they took out an operating loan one year for eight hundred dollars. Out of this they purchased their feed, food, gas, cow salt, grease, clothing, windmill oil, and fence supplies. I sometimes think they could have existed on nothing if they had to.

Like I said, Adams, who owned the M-System in Alpine, used to buy all of Happy's butter. Wade always traded there, even after Mr. and Mrs. Adams sold out. The store finally closed. Don Adams' daddy had owned the livery stable in Alpine when it was still called Murpheysville. They grew up there. Wade and Roy bought all of their calf and blackleg serum as well as their worm medicine from Mrs. Gentry who ran the Alpine Drug Store.

The only time I ever saw those two men argue was one morning the year they'd decided to hold some calves over and feed them there at the house. They'd figured out a way to buy cheap hygear—bundled—in the field there around Mentone. They'd haul it to the ranch, then grind and sack it themselves and use it for feed. They'd bought an old used cattle truck somewhere that Roy had overhauled. He'd also bought a motor out of some wreck there at Fort Davis which he'd rebuilt and got running. You had to hand crank the motor to start it. He'd rigged it with a pulley wheel and six-inch wide belt to power an old hammer mill that ground their feed. I don't know where they got the mill. The motor was mounted up on cross ties with a gravity gas line running to it from an old gas tank. The whole thing looked shaky and was.

To operate the mill, you cranked the motor, slipped the belt on the hammer mill's pulley first, then onto the motor's pulley. It was a dangerous operation, but Roy had worked him out a system for slipping the belt on the motor's pulley without losing his hand. Once on, the belt flapped and wobbled—it was about twenty foot long and usually slipped off several times while you were grinding—but it would run the hammer mill while they ground their feed.

Well, they decided to drive over to Mentone and buy a load of hygear one morning. Roy had been working on the old truck near his tool shed and had it parked facing down the slope away from the house. He had the flatbed hooked up and the side boards off so we could load hygear easier. Now the gas tank for the ranch was fifteen or twenty yards back up the slope behind the truck near the old cottonwood. It sat up on one of those high steel frames. To fill anything you dropped the hose, stuck it in, and squeezed the handle.

Anyhow, Wade climbed in the cab—he always drove whenever they went anywhere like that—and decided he'd back that truck and flatbed up that rocky slope behind him and fill it up.

Well, there wasn't any way you could back that old heavy

flatbed up that slope on those loose rocks and gravel, especially with that little old engine the truck had in it. Plus, Wade had broke his neck earlier in life. A horse had thrown him or something and his neck just grew back stiff. He couldn't turn his head either way to look behind him. To see where he was going, he had to turn all the way around. So whenever he tried to back up in a vehicle, why it was a disaster. Whatever was behind him he either run over or scattered because he couldn't look back.

Anyway, Wade started trying to back that truck up that hill to the gas tank. The tires were spinning and throwing rocks, but that flatbed wouldn't budge. Wade was determined to make it go. Wasn't long before Roy's truck overheated and was boiling and steaming and we hadn't even left the house.

Roy was standing out there shaking his head and cussing and whining; watching Wade tear up his truck right before his eyes. He always shouted when he got mad. Wade, on the other hand, just gritted his teeth and got red in the face.

Finally Roy couldn't stand it anymore. He threw up his hands and shouted, "Hell, I might as well take my half of this sonofabitch and go somewheres by God where it won't be tore up all to hell." Wade, he's sitting there behind the wheel, says, "Well, hell, if that's the way you feel, just by God go ahead and pullout."

The old truck is steaming. I'm standing there watching all this—just a big old teenager—and I suggest to Wade why didn't he just pull forward and make a wide circle and just pull up alongside the gas tank and fill up? Well, he did and we finally got filled up and pulled out for Mentone which was about forty miles north of Pecos. Everyone was sullied up the first part of the trip. We rode along in silence. Finally the old truck cooled off and by the time we got to Mentone everyone else had too.

Wade pulled into the farmer's field, stopped, and crawled up on the flatbed. Roy and I started pitching hygear bundles up to him to stack. We'd load as many shocks as we could around the truck, then Wade would pull forward to another area and we'd repeat the process. I guess we had about two-thirds of a load.

Now Roy had eaten something the night before, or maybe that morning, that had given him the scours. He'd work about an hour, then have to go squat down behind a feed shock somewhere.

Well, we cleaned out the first field there at the farmer's place, and Wade crawled back in the cab of the old truck and started over an irrigation ditch culvert—it was just wide enough for the truck—to get to another part of the field. He had to cross the ditch and make a sharp right. Now Wade never made allowances for anything when he was driving. And he could have crossed that ditch and turned right in a pickup without any problem. But, when he crossed it and turned right with the flatbed, his back wheels just fell in the ditch. 'Course the load tilted. Roy's squatting out there behind a shock watching the load rock and he starts to cuss and shake his head. Wade, soon as he feels his back wheels drop off in the ditch, guns the old truck and rocks it a time or two trying to get out. About the second time he guns it, off comes the whole load of hygear. It all just fell off on the ground. Every last bundle.

Roy, he's over there squattin' with his britches down watching all this, just giving it to high heaven. He's saying, "Absolutely, absolutely that boy, that boy will absolutely never learn to drive. Anybody that doesn't have any more damn sense than that—I swear I knew I should have driven over that ditch. Now we got to load the whole sonofabitch again. The whole sonofabitch. I swear..."

Well, we spent most of the day on that first load, then come back and got three or four more that week and unloaded them by the hammer mill. After the last load, Roy cranked the motor and slipped the belt on the pulleys so we could start grinding; but for some reason the belt kept slipping off.

151

It would run a few minutes and then start flapping real loud and flop off on the ground. I'd crowbar the engine around some trying to get it aligned. Roy was cussing. Nothing seemed to work.

Anyhow, after about the fifth time the belt started flapping—you could always tell when it was about to come off by how loud it flapped—Roy walks up to the motor's pulley wheel and just draws back and kicks it. Somehow the belt caught his boot heel—it would have crushed his foot if it had gotten a better bite—and flipped him straight up. He landed flat on his back. I turned around so he couldn't see me laugh. Roy hated it if you laughed at him in those kind of situations.

Eventually we got all the feed ground and put up.

A few winters after Happy died I caught pneumonia real bad and couldn't make the Spring semester my first year in college. Roy had broke his hip late that Fall and had been laid up at Knox and Lou's in Alpine. Wade wrote me a letter and said if I wasn't going to register for school that January, to come on down to the ranch and help out while Roy mended. I think he was lonesome.

Anyway, that was the first winter I ever made at their ranch. Mostly we kept ice broke at the waterings and wood gathered and chopped for the house. Worms weren't a problem during the cold months. We rode once a week to see how the livestock was doing. It was a good time to learn the country and the ranch and to talk to Wade about things. I remember it snowed a lot that winter and we had a lot of mornings that were cold and foggy and misty. Ever once in awhile we'd pull a calf as Spring came along and cows started calving. Wade and Roy always had a ninety percent calf crop every year—or better. They just looked after—and took care of—all their livestock.

Those two men had grown up in a certain era. If they told you they'd meet you on top of some mountain somewhere at five o'clock one morning, why they'd be there. They just believed if you told someone you were going to do something you did it regardless of how it affected your own personal business. In fact, you could make book on what they told you. And act accordingly. If a man came along and offered them so much a pound for their calves—and they accepted—then that was it. No money needed to change hands. If the buyer wanted to put some money down, why that was up to him. They didn't really care whether he did or didn't because once he said he would buy their cattle at so much a pound, and they accepted, they considered the cattle sold for that price. And if the price of cattle went up a dollar a pound between then and when they actually delivered the calves, it didn't make any difference to them. They'd sold the calves for what they'd agreed to sell them for. On their word. And the same held true if the price of cattle went down. They expected the buyer to purchase their calves at the price he'd agree upon. I never saw a written contract for anything the whole time I was around them. Ever.

They also believed in live and let live. They didn't want anyone trying to tell them how to run their business and they weren't about to tell anyone how to run theirs. I never heard them say anything unkind about anyone other than a politician, and them only because they lied so much. They might not approve what someone did—sometimes you could sense this when they were talking—but they never come right out and said someone had done wrong. They'd just wonder out loud "why so'n so had done that?" In their own way they were true gentlemen, even though they lived way out there by themselves.

For a youngster growing up in my day and time, working for those two men was one of the highlights of my life.

★   ★   ★

From an interview with
Mrs. Dorothy Reid (1904-1990)

My first husband was killed on duty with the border

patrol about the time Wade lost his Happy. Miles and I had only been married three years at the time. Jack was not quite two when we lost his daddy. So when I first met Wade at Mama Reid's boardinghouse, I understood how he must have felt about losing Happy so soon after they'd built their house and all. He and Roy had moved Mama Reid to Alpine from the Panhandle, and had helped her open her boardinghouse. Anyhow, soon afterward, my sister, Beth, met and married one of Wade and Roy's younger brothers, Warner, and we would sometimes all wind up over at Mama Reid's when Wade and Roy came in from the ranch. Then Knox Reid, another younger brother, married my friend, Lou, who I taught school with. Since it was the middle of the Depression and no one had any money, Knox and Lou stayed at Mama Reid's. So I'd come over to Mama Reid's and we'd all just sit around and talk or get a bridge game started, and I began to see Wade. It was unusual, but all the Reid brothers were good bridge players. How they learned I'll never know, but everyone in that family played bridge regularly except for Bob Reid. Bob was the poker player. Sometimes, though, they'd rope Bob into playing bridge with them at the ranch or whenever they needed a fourth. He always added an element of excitement to the game. If everyone passed, he'd open with three no-trump. Religiously. Nobody would know how to respond, especially his partner. Used to gripe Wade and Roy to death when he did it, especially if he was their partner. He made it more times than he lost, though. Plus he had a good knowledge of cards. Anyhow, that's how I began to get to know Wade.

Sometimes Knox and Lou would make a Sunday trip to the ranch to play bridge if Wade and Roy weren't riding. I first went out with them during the Thirties. Jack was ten years old at the time. Wade and I knew each other and dated and played bridge together then for over nine years. As time went on, I came to like him more and more. He was so good with my son and other children, you know. I will always be grateful for that. He would let Jack and a friend go to the ranch and work a couple months each summer after they got out of school. It was good for them. He did that for all of the young people in the families, nieces and nephews included. I think it helped them all later on, just understanding what real ranch work and hard work in general was all about.

We were at camp meeting in August of 1945 when I told Wade I'd marry him. Camp meeting, you know, was always one of our favorite places. Wade and I always went each year until he died. We built our cabin there during the Fifties. Up until that time we stayed in a large tent during camp meeting week. We were married September 4, 1945. Since I'd been to the ranch and played so much bridge with them, they both accepted me into their routines. Up until then Wade had always taken care of the house and cooked. Roy took care of the mechanical things, animals, the barn, and the out-side of the house, except the yard. Lord, how he hated yard work. He would do anything to get out of it, and whenever one of the family teenagers spent the summer with us, that was the first job they got right off the bat. As time went on, we made a few changes with the house. I put up some new drapes and added a few things inside. Later, we carpeted the upper level and converted that garage and storage room downstairs into two rooms with a shower. The year Wade and I married was the same year they got butane at the ranch for the first time. Up until that time Wade cooked on a wood stove fired by mesquite. The only other appliance they had was an old Electrolux kerosene-operated refrigerator. But at least we had a little ice. We finally got butane, but we couldn't get a stove or refrigerator to go with it. The war was winding down, and you just couldn't buy appliances. We did get a hot-water heater, though. Talk about a luxury. I cooked on the wood stove and even though I'd used one as a kid, it took me awhile to learn how to keep the fire going all day so I wouldn't have to start over to fix lunch or supper. Still, I was very content and glad to have a home of my own. We found a

155

butane stove and refrigerator the following year.

The next two years at the ranch— '46 and '47—we had snow for three weeks in January. I remember we crawled up on that old barn of theirs and shoveled it off because the roof was leaking on the feed. That much snow was unusual for our part of the country. Wade and Roy had a crew burning prickly pear when the snow came. It had been a dry summer, and there wasn't much forage of any kind. The crew got snowed in. They were camped there in the horse trap right around the hill from the house. Roy got to worrying whether or not they had enough coffee and cigarettes and all, so he decided to walk around there and see. I went with him and walked behind in his tracks. I remember the snow was higher than my boots. We found they were nearly out of food, and so were we for that matter. But we shared what we had. I hadn't yet learned to buy staples three or four weeks ahead for the ranch when we went to town. I learned after that snow. We ran out of flour for bread, but someone told me not to worry, that when we ran out of coffee, Roy would get on a horse and go to town and get his coffee and our supplies. The snow melted before then, however. I always liked the winters best because the men were around the house more. We would go out together in the pickup and check water and break ice. Sometimes we'd get in a little visit with relatives during the Christmas season.

The first years I always rode with them. They didn't use outside help then or have a trailer to haul their horses in. The thing that always fascinated me was that Wade and Roy, without saying a word, would get to a certain place on the ranch, separate, and each would ride and look at the cattle pasturing in a particular part of the mountains. Wade would pull his horse up and point to a canyon and say, "Now Roy will show up over there in a minute." And sure enough, Roy would show up. They always rode the same area. Every time. Never changed. Sometimes I rode with Roy just so I could see the other part of the ranch. They could see cattle a long way off, too, and could usually tell if one of them had worms. I learned to eat breakfast out there pretty quick.

We left the house one morning intending to be back by noon. All I had to eat was a half grapefruit and a cup of coffee. The more we rode that day, the more wormy cattle we found. It was past six before we got back. I thought I would faint I was so hungry. I ate breakfast every time I rode after that. Usually they would stop for lunch at Headwater when they rode the mountains. They had an old chuck box set in the rocks there with a couple Dutch ovens inside. I still have them. Someone offered me fifty dollars for them. Wanted to use them as flowerpots out front of their house, but I turned them down. I won't have them ruined like that.

Anyhow, they kept those Dutch ovens and some coffee, sugar, flour, salt, and other staples in the chuck box to use when we stopped. We carried our meat and potatoes and can of corn on our saddles with us. Then we'd meet at Headwater, unsaddle, and fix something to eat and rest. The springwater always tasted sweet and cold. We used it to make coffee and wash dishes with, too. Roy always gathered up the firewood and got the fire going so he could make coffee. You know how he liked coffee. Those two pear trees—the big one and the little one—that grew there near the chuck box made the best canning pears. You had to get them as soon as they ripened or the coons would strip the tree. They seemed to enjoy those pears as much as we did. We finally put tin around the bottom of the big tree.

Wade Reid holding a nephew, 1942.

17

From an interview with
Jack Scannell, Midland, Texas

You always hoped if anything went wrong with your windmills it would happen in the winter so you'd have water in the summer. I want you to know it was a job pulling sucker rods and changing leathers, all the time wasting days you should have been looking for worms.

Sometimes the wind wouldn't blow during those hot, dry spells in the summer, and the water would get low at the house or east side, and we'd fire up the old Briggs and Stratton and connect the pump pulley. Way you did it was after the engine got started good, you slipped the pulley belt on and let it pump several hours until everything got full.

Those old Briggs and Strattons were heavy and you were always having to crowbar them around to make sure they were lined up with the well pump. They were as dependable an engine as they ever made, though. Whenever you finished pumping, you reconnected your windmill sucker rod and hoped you got enough wind to keep your troughs full.

During those years we'd be riding the flats and those old cows would come across there to water, and it seemed to me like they'd drink a hundred gallons. They'd get so full their stomachs would stick up higher than their backs, and all the time they were drinking, you'd be hoping that old engine was still pumping back up there at the house. Lord knows how those things run. Roy would rig it so it would operate on its own for awhile—say a half day—while you rode. They had a gas tank sitting on a stand made out of wood scraps with a leaky gas line running to the engine. It looked delicate, but it worked. Wade mashed the end of his fingers off there one afternoon. It was sometime during the summer of '49 when it happened. Dry. We were hoping it would rain. Wade had been working around the house and said he was going down to start the pump. Like I said, the motor wouldn't start while the pump pulley was attached, so you had to take the belt off to start the pump. After you got the motor really churning, you slipped the belt back on the pulley. I always thought it was dangerous myself. Wade and Roy never thought about it. Roy wasn't there that day, and for some reason Mother said, "I'll just go with you to get a breath of fresh air." So Wade pulled the belt off—it was tight—and started the motor and was just slipping the belt on the pulley when it caught his glove and jerked his two index fingers into the pulley and cut the ends of them off. One was still hanging by a piece of skin, but the other just stayed in the glove when he peeled it off. Wade found it about three weeks later when he went to put his gloves on to go back to work. Both his fingers were spouting blood when he jerked his glove off. Mother helped him back into the pickup and Wade took his shirt off and wrapped his hand. Mother drove to the house, changed to the car, filled up with gas, and headed for Doctor Eaton's office in Fort Davis. Doctor Eaton sewed one finger back on and said, "If you'd brought the other one, I could have sewed it on, too." He put a big heavy bandage on Wade's hand and Mother took him back to the ranch. That's when she found out Wade was ambidextrous. The next morning she asked him if she could help him wash or shave. He said no, and proceeded to shave with his left hand.

Right after World War II uranium was the big thing. This young fellow with a geology background came out to the ranch with the idea of becoming the newest uranium millionaire. He'd decided there was uranium in the Barrilla Mountains, which there might have been. Anyway, he was prowling around in one of those planes that supposedly tested for uranium from the air and had flown across Wade and Roy's ranch for two or three days before driving out. He walked up the front stairs, knocked on the front door and asked to see the owner. Wade went out to talk to him. The boy said, "I'd like to do some prospecting for uranium." Wade said, "Well, we could probably work something out. Assuming you find something, what kind of lease agreement would you be wanting to make?" The boy said, "I was thinking in terms of a sixteenth." Wade said, "No, I don't think that would do. Oil companies work on an eighth. If you're willing to pay for a lease if you find anything, plus a royalty of an eighth for production, I think we could probably work out an agreement." Then the young man said, "No, Mr. Reid, a sixteenth is all you'll get since all you control is the surface. I could come out and prospect the land without your permission, and I just dropped by out of courtesy." I saw the color change in Wade's face and he said, "First thing you'd better do is learn a few things about this country and the people who live here. You don't set a foot on my land without my permission. Not now or anytime. And if you think you have the right to come on this land when it's not given to you by the people who own it, you'd better go back and take a course in land law and courtesy. You can go to the courthouse and see who has title to this land. Then you can go and connive with whoever you want to as long as you want. But don't you ever let me see you on this ranch again." The young man turned around, got in his car, and drove off. We never saw him again.

Truth is, they both had tempers. Wade just kept his under control better. The maddest I ever saw Wade, though, was during the drought of '49. The well at the house, which watered the east flats, finally started drying up and sucking mud. It had to be cleaned. We were desperate for water. Wade and Roy talked about hauling water to keep their livestock alive each morning at breakfast.

The first people Wade tried to get were the McSpaddin Brothers in Marfa. They were good well men and had a solid reputation among the ranchers. But everybody was in the same boat as Wade, and they were booked up until August. It was June. Wade knew he couldn't wait that long, but he went ahead and asked them to come on out in August and help him drill a well on the east side in the flats.

The McSpaddins told Wade about an old boy they'd heard of over in Pecos, but they cautioned him they didn't know if he was reliable or not, just that he drilled and cleaned wells sometimes. So Wade went to Pecos and hunted the fellow up. The old boy said, "Yeah, I'll come clean your well out." Wade told him it was a six-hundred foot well and to be sure and bring the equipment he would need to work on it. Then he asked him when he could come. The old boy said he'd be there the following Monday. Wade told him everyone would stay at the house that day and give him a hand. Now this meant we lost a workday because we were riding every-day looking for worms and making sure the mountain troughs had water. Nonetheless, we all stayed home that day to wait for the old boy because it was important we get water back down to the east side.

He never came. Tuesday morning and Wade said we couldn't waste another day, so we saddled up and rode the mountains. Before we left, he told Mother to tell the man not to start to work until we got back to help him, and to pitch camp and wait.

We made a hard swing through the mountains that day and when we rounded the hill above the house that after-noon, we saw the old boy's pickup up by the well. We all rode on down to the barn and Wade handed me his horse to un-saddle, which was rare, and hobbled on off towards the well.

Roy and I turned the horses loose and walked to the house. Roy poured himself a cup of coffee and went out to his radio to see if he could pick up some news. That and baseball was all he ever listened to. I'd just walked into the kitchen when Wade came up the back porch, stepped into the kitchen, and went over and sat down in Roy's chair by the door. He was shaking all over. Mother said, "Wade, what's the matter?"

He just shook his head and gritted his teeth. Now Roy I'd

seen get mad like that, but this was the first time I'd ever seen Wade that mad. He just sat there and shook for about three minutes. Finally he asked Mother to pour him a cup of coffee. She poured it and asked him if there was anything she could do. He just sat there and shook his head, sipping his coffee. He finally managed, "That man has ruined my well."

The fellow hadn't waited for us. He took a look at the well and decided he could pull the casing and rods together. So he disconnected the casing, forgot to clamp it, tried to pull the rods and six-hundred feet of casing, twisted off, and dropped the whole thing back into the well. Rod. Pipe. Everything was jammed together down in the well.

The fellow comes to the back door and says he'll have to go to Monahans to get a grapple and two hundred feet of cable. He came back the following day with a six-inch grapple. The well had a four-inch casing. Wade's face got white again. Roy, who'd been standing back letting Wade handle the situation, finally said, "To hell with him." He stomped down to his old tool shed, found himself a piece of pipe, rigged a coupling on the end of it, and took his homemade grapple up to the well.

Roy told the man's helper to help him drop his grapple in on the cable. Somehow they managed to get a bite on the joints and winched them out of the hole enough to slap a clamp on. The rods had broke somewhere downhole and the couplings were uneven because they'd been jammed. Consequently we had to cut each rod.

Finally we got the rod past the break, cut the broken rod off, then pulled the rest of the pipe and rod like it should have been done in the first place. By the time the idiot got back with his cable, we had the pipe out. That's when he told us he'd have to leave again and take the six-inch grapple back because it was costing Wade and Roy four dollars for every hour it was out there. He'd had it almost two days. Roy said, "Like hell you will. You clean that damn well out like we asked you to, and I'll take the damned grapple back."

I rode with Roy to the supply house in Monahans where the grapple had been rented. Roy walked in, dropped it on the counter, and told the man, "We'll pay for it, but it didn't do us no good. We got a four-inch well." The man studied Roy a minute, then said, "I told that damn fool it wouldn't work on a water well." Roy said, "What do I owe you?" The man said, "Don't worry about it. I'll take it out of the bastard's hide next time I see him."

When we got back that evening late, Wade and the old boy were already bailing the well. After about twenty buckets of mud, it changed to a soft brown liquid. The old boy said, "Well, I believe it's clean." Wade said, "I do, too. Now you get packed up and be ready to pull out first thing in the morning."

The next morning the old boy knocked on the front door and presented Wade with a five-day bill for a job that shouldn't have taken more than a day. It was for more than a thousand dollars, including the cost of the two-hundred foot cable. Wade studied the bill a minute, then said, "That cable belongs to you." The man said, "No, that's your cable, Mr. Reid. I'll never have use for it so you might as well keep it 'cause you're gonna have to pay for it." Wade said, "Like hell I will." Then he proceeded to whittle the bill in half. When he finished telling the old boy what he would pay him, he turned, went into the house, wrote the old boy a check for five hundred dollars, handed it to him and said, "Now, I 'spect you best leave."

Wade, I don't think, ever learned to drive. Riding anywhere with either of them was an experience. Of the two, Roy was a better driver, but not by much. Wade's way out of trouble was to step on the gas. And when he stepped on the gas, he always stepped on the clutch and rode it — simultaneously. And the more he gassed it, the heavier he rode. Finally he'd have the motor roaring but wouldn't be going anywhere,

164

and we'd be sitting still somewhere, smelling the clutch burn. They never did understand why they couldn't keep a clutch in their truck. It got wild if you were in the mud and Wade was driving.

Roy tried to drive his car up Lockhausen Canyon one afternoon, which he wouldn't have normally done except the clutch was out on the pickup and they were checking the Lockhausen spring everyday to see if it was keeping up with the cattle. It was a dry summer and the spring was weak. They'd worked the road so he could make it, but a flash flood had wiped out a couple creek crossings. Anyhow, Roy knocked a hole in his oil pan and tried to plug it with a tube of liquid solder he had in his glove compartment. But the oil pan was hot and the solder wouldn't stick. He worked on it about three hours, then finally had to walk to the house. It was after dark when he got in. Lord, was he mad.

★   ★   ★

From an interview with
Mrs. Dorothy Reid (1904-1990)

Seems like they were always thinking of their cattle. Remember when they had that wreck on the way to the locker plant in Alpine? First thing they did when they got to the hospital was get me to call someone to go find the calf they'd lost when the trailer flipped over. They'd forgotten to put the gate across the middle of the trailer to keep the calf up front. When they started down that second hill coming from Fort Davis to Alpine, the calf wandered to the back of the trailer. Well, the trailer started swinging back and forth. By the time they got to the bottom of the hill they were whipping back and forth so fast the pickup, trailer, everything flipped completely over and back up on the wheels with both of them still sitting in the cab. Threw the calf out.

The only reason I wasn't with them that day was my sister, Margaret, wanted to come to the ranch, so I'd taken

*the car in to bring her out. We were going to take some cattle
to San Angelo and she wanted to go. Well, Roy's lip and head
were cut. Wade had a bruised kidney and didn't know it.
Anyhow, Wade got out—Roy couldn't open his door—and
the first car he flagged down was one of the nurses who
worked at the hospital. She loaded them both in her car and
brought them on to Alpine to the hospital then called me.*

*When I got there, they were both in the emergency room
lying on tables. Wade was white as a sheet and Roy, who had
blood all over him, was cussing, saying, "I bet I've told him
a million times not to weave with that trailer." He was just
having fits. Wade said, "Honey, I have a check in my pocket.
Get it out, then call Mac and tell him to go out and get the
calf and get someone to check on the pickup." Anyhow, they
finally got them into a room at the hospital and Roy says,
"Dot, I want a cigarette." I said, "Roy, where do you want
me to put it?" He had stitches all across his upper lip. I finally found a place for Roy to smoke his cigarette. Then they
noticed Wade could either stand or lay down okay, but he
couldn't sit because of the kidney. That was the year the
Marfa PCA Board met at the ranch because Wade couldn't
sit for anytime at all without being in great pain. I called the
truckers and postponed the shipping. Later, Wade said he
didn't remember me being there at the emergency room.*

18

Interview with Jack Scannell, continued

You could get hurt on that ranch if you weren't careful. I caught old Gato one morning before daylight and pulled out to gather the horses in the horse trap east of the house. I found them in the northeast corner. I tried to start them toward the house, but they turned south along the east fence at a dead run. When they finally ran up on the south fence, they cut back north towards the house. When Gato saw them cut north, he cut hard, too. That's when my cinch broke. It caught me by surprise and I hit the ground head first. All the horses, Gato included, headed for the house. Now I had on a big, old thigh-length, heavy jacket with a box of shells over my left hip in the pocket. Somehow I came down on the shells, and it felt like my hip was broke. I rolled over on my hands and knees and steadied myself a few minutes, then I saw something dripping on the rocks and saw blood all over my gloves. My head was cut. I got to my feet, thinking I'd just walk to the house, but I couldn't make more than a few steps at a time. When I thought I was going to pass out, I dropped back down on all fours.

Wade was in the barn feeding some calves when the horses poured into the corrals. He shut the gate, then saw Gato come over the hill trailing his bridle, no saddle. Wade caught the horse and told Mother to get the truck. She asked him what he thought. He said, "It's probably not serious." He told me later he was thinking Gato had drug the saddle off. And if he had, I was probably dead out there somewhere.

They took me into Ft. Davis and Dr. Eaton sewed me up. It was four months before I could get a haircut. I still had blood and scab on my head, and the barber had to wash my hair.

Another time we were trying to pen the English herd on the east flats and had gathered a mean old one-eyed cow—wild as a goat—along with the rest of the cattle. We were going to spray them as soon as we got them penned. But every time we approached the corrals with the herd, this old one-eyed cow would spot the fence wings out of the corner of her good eye, and bolt back through the herd, scattering cattle everywhere. We'd gather them again and start them toward the pens and the same thing would happen. Roy started cussing her the first time she did it. The third time it happened I heard Wade start in on her. When she tried it again, Roy left the herd, fell in behind, and circled the pens with her a couple times at a dead run, slapping her on the ass with his rope. About the third time around they yelled at me to head her into the corrals. I turned her at the gate and she went all the way to the backside pen in the corrals. It looked like she would bust through the fence. I vaulted off my horse, wired the gate shut behind her, then helped gather and pen the rest of the herd.

Truth is, they kept that old one-eyed cow because she always raised a good calf. The year after we penned her in the English she had another good calf. Now most cows brought their calves to water with them soon as they were old enough to walk, but not this old cow. She would keep her calf hid out for weeks. Which meant the worms would kill it if we didn't find it. We finally found him lying in a mesquite near the northeast corner of the English. He was so still you almost had to step on the little bugger to see him. He had worms from his belly down between his hind legs and up the middle of his back. His whole rear end was solid worms. He was so weak he couldn't walk. We knew we'd have to take him to the English corrals and keep him there if we had any hope of saving him.

Wade said, "Just try to walk him as far as he'll go. I'll ride back and get the pickup." The little calf didn't get fifty yards before he just laid down and quit. I got off, picked him up and carried him about three hundred yards across a rough arroyo where Wade could get to us with the pickup.

We took him to the English pens, doctored him solid with fly dope and shut the gate on him and his mother.

Since there was no water trough inside the English pens, we had to go down everyday to doctor the calf and let his mother out to water. When he got well enough to turn out, she took off and hid him again. Every time we rode down to check on him she seemed to get smarter and wilder. It got so if she saw a rider coming, she'd hide her calf, then put a mile or two between them. The only time you could surprise her was in the pickup because she hadn't learned the association yet. That's how we were able to drive up on them out in the flats one morning. We'd driven down to check the water, saw them, and noticed her calf had worms again. Wade said, "You get out on the running board, and I'll drive up right beside him and you grab him."

As soon as I stepped out on the running board, that old cow took off at a dead run across the flats with that calf right behind her. We went bouncing over mesquite clumps and rocks, and I was trying to hold on and watch the calf at the same time. We were gunning it the first hundred yards or so. I could smell the clutch. Dust was boiling around us, and I was leaning off the running board grappling for the little bastard. Finally I said to hell with it. I dove for his head and caught a hind leg. We both rolled over about three times with him on top. People just don't have those kind of experiences anymore.

Anyhow, we doctored him, then drove them both back to the house the next time we rode the flats. That's when Wade said good calf or no, he was shipping her that Fall. That little calf never did do well. Eventually his tail fell off where the worms had eaten through.

They were both in their seventies the last time I saw them rope a full-grown cow. I think it was the last time anyone saw them rope. They'd found a cow with worms in her udder and had taken her to the Barrilla pens. She was wild, and when we got her into the pen, she made two circles, hit the corral fence and went through it like matchsticks. They both swung aboard their horses and run her hard out there a hundred yards or so. Wade caught her horns, Roy picked up her heels and they stretched her out, doctored her, and rode on. We came back later that week and fixed the corrals.

Roy kept trying to rope when he was no longer physically able. He just wouldn't quit. When Wade got to where he knew he was too old to handle himself on a horse, he quit riding. The thing that finally forced Roy to quit was when he lost his eyesight to cataracts and couldn't see where he was anymore in the mountains. The last time they rode together I guess they were both almost eighty. No one knows what prompted them, but they saddled up and rode away from the house one morning, all the way around to the Old Lake, on around past the Fonville, up by the Camp Tub and the Tub-On-Top then off into Lockhausen Canyon. When Mother found out they'd left without the pickup and trailer, she hooked up and drove around and met them coming in. That was the last ride they ever made together in their mountains.

They bought their first horse trailer about 1955, I guess. The only reason they got it was to save their strength. The older they got, the more those long rides from the house sapped them. Up until then they rode everywhere they went on that ranch.

Roy was always forgetting he was seventy. He was riding old Lightning down east of the house one day. Wade had found a bull in the Northside with worms. We were pushing the calf and its mother toward the pens. I rode on ahead and opened the gate into the little trap next to the corrals, then went back down to help with the cow and calf. We got them inside the trap. I'd left the corral gate open so we could pen the cow and calf while Wade was bringing the bull in from the north side. I shut the wire gate, and Roy said to me, "Hell, I'll just go ahead and doctor this calf out here. You go open the gate for Wade." I was a little skeptical about that, but then you never argued with Roy; so I said, "All right." Meantime, Roy shakes out a loop. Wade's still coming in with the bull, about a hundred yards out. Roy makes his throw, and it's a beautiful loop and would have dropped on the calf except the old cow boogered and lunged between Roy and the calf. She ran right into the loop, panicked and headed for the gate. When she hit the end of the rope, it jerked her flat, jerked Lightning to his knees, and jerked the saddle, Roy, and everything right out over Lightning's head. Roy hit the ground in a cloud of dust, hard enough to have crippled an ordinary seventy year-old man. I was trying to keep from laughing. Roy, you know, was not sympathetic with people who laughed at him in situations like that.

He was sitting on the ground, spitting out dirt, cussing the calf, the cow, the horse, the saddle, the blanket, the rope, the pen, and everything in sight. Meanwhile, Wade, who'd left the bull when he saw Roy go up and over his horse's head, had ridden up to the fence and was sitting there watching Roy spit and cuss. Finally Wade said, "You hurt?" Roy muttered, "No, gawdamnit." Wade said, "Well, that was a damned fool stunt for an old man to pull." Then just turned around and rode off. They were like that. Roy got up. Lightning was already on his feet, following the old cow around. I went over, picked up his saddle and helped him pen the cow afoot. We doctored her calf and Wade's bull, got Roy put back together again, and headed back to the house.

The older they got the more Wade stuck close to Roy so he could be there to help him out of jams. He never told Roy that, but he did us. It was a good thing Roy wasn't able to pull his shenanigans up in the mountains, or he might have killed himself on those rocks. Like the day Roy was down on the east side chasing a calf with worms—trying to rope, as Wade said, instead of using the pen. Roy found this calf with worms, so he said he was "just gonna pitch his rope on the calf and doctor him." He was riding old Bobby Socks and the calf was faster than he thought, so he and Bobby Socks was building to him through the brush when this calf cuts around a small mesquite bush. It was just high enough you couldn't see what was on the other side.

Anyhow, this calf cuts around the bush at a dead run with Roy and Bobby Socks right behind, and Bobby Socks decides to jump the bush. But what neither of them saw was the seven-foot gully on the other side. Bobby tried to extend his jump, but the wash was about ten feet wide and all he could manage was his front feet on the other bank. The rest of him went in throwing Roy hard against the saddle horn and cracking some of his ribs. It's a wonder they didn't puncture a lung and kill him.

Truth is, people lost track of Roy's broken bones. Roy, I know, broke both feet at different times, or at least cracked them; and he'd broken both hips, his back, and his ribs. It was in 1966 or '67—August, I believe—when he broke five more ribs. Understand, he was in his seventies. Bill Cotter had come to the ranch in his pickup to get a load of firewood out of Lockhausen Canyon for his place in town. Joe, who'd taken Melly's place at the ranch, said he'd go with Bill who was almost eighty himself. Roy was sitting on the porch and said, "I believe I'll just go with you." He wanted to look at the canyon country, even though he could barely see. They went back up into Lockhausen, found an old dead tree the waters had washed into the canyon, stopped the pickup and Joe got out and started chopping wood. Bill and Joe almost had a full load when Roy, who couldn't see a damn thing, got out of the pickup, started to walk over toward the tree, and stepped on one of those rocks that looks solid but really isn't. It tilted and Roy twisted sideways and fell sideways atop a big rock.

When he got back to the house, everyone could tell he was in pain, but he wouldn't go to the doctor. So they gave him this big old bronze dinner bell to ring if he got to hurting during the night. He slept downstairs, and I slept in the other room. Along about three in the morning I heard the bell. I got up and went in and he said, "Help me up." He couldn't make it by himself. I helped him. You could tell he was in misery. I said, "Your ribs are broken." He said they were just bruised. Then he said, "Get me that big wide leather belt of mine." And I said, "What the hell you gonna use a leather belt for?" He said, "Get it and I'll show you." So I got it, and he had me strap it around him real tight and help him to the bathroom. I said, "Let me go get Wade. We gotta get you to a doctor." He said, "Hell no, I'm not going to no damned doctor." He seemed like he could breathe a little easier, but I could tell he was still hurting. The next morning I knew for sure. You know how Roy always got up before daylight? Well, it was past daylight when I woke up because I hadn't heard Roy stirring. I always woke up when he did, so I thought he must still be in bed. I went in there and he was asleep. Roy Reid, you know, never slept past daylight in his life. So I knew he'd been awake all night. I went on upstairs and Wade said, "Where's Roy?" I said, "He's asleep." Wade said, "At eight o'clock in the morning?" I said, "Yeah." He said, "You think he slept last night?" Then I told him about how I strapped the leather belt on him. Wade said, "If he was awake that late and still asleep this time of day, there's something wrong. He's going to the doctor. That's all there is to it."

Wade went downstairs and Roy was laying there awake by then, and Wade said, "You're going to the doctor." Roy says, "Ain't gonna do it." Wade said, "You are going to do it, even if we have to carry you out to the car 'cause I'm not gonna have you put up with this." With that we loaded him in the backseat of the car, propped him up with pillows, and took him in. He was in the hospital for two weeks or so. He wanted to leave that day, but Doc Hill told him, "You're gonna stay here 'til them ribs have a chance to set enough to where you can move around on your own." Doc Hill knew Roy. Wade had told Doctor Hill that Roy had to climb the stairs outside for meals and so forth. That's why Doctor Hill decided to keep him in the hospital until the ribs mended. He knew Roy wouldn't give them a chance. Roy hated every minute of it.

Then Roy broke his back when he was almost eighty. Wade had ordered a load of hay. They delivered and stacked it in the barn, but Roy decided he didn't like the way it was stacked. So he went down to the barn by himself, grabbed a couple hay hooks, and started restacking. Wade and Mother were in the pickup in the east side, checking the water and cattle. When they got back, they found Roy with a broken back. He'd fallen, it seems, just as Wade and Mother left the house. They'd asked him to go along with them to the east side, but Roy just grunted he didn't want to go, not telling them why; Wade never thinking an eighty year-old, half-blind man in his right mind would go into a barn and start restacking several tons of hay. As soon as they got in the pickup, he'd gone to the barn and started restacking that hay. And he'd decided to stack it clear to the rafters since he planned to put some more feed in the barn and needed the space. He said it wasn't too bad for the first two or three layers. He was up to four layers when his foot slipped down between a couple bales. He lost his balance, tried to catch a bale with a hay hook, missed, and fell off the stack backwards onto the cement floor. Right flat on his back. Nobody knows how he crawled to the house or got up the stairs, but he was there when Wade got back and found him, hurting. He didn't tell them what happened at first because he was always embarrassed when he got himself in a jam. He just said his back hurt. But when they saw he couldn't move much and how it was hurting him, they took him into town. The doctor looked at the X-ray and said he couldn't have got from the barn to the house with that kind of fracture. Wade told him he had. The doctor confined him flat on his back for about two and a half months. He recovered from that, too.

★   ★   ★
From an interview with
Mrs. Dorothy Reid (1904-1990)

The best Wade and Roy ever got for cattle while I was at the ranch was in January of 1974. We got seventy cents a pound for some of the calves that year. It doesn't sound like much, but it was much better than the seven cents a pound they got when they started out. And during the Depression they couldn't sell their calves at all.

Wade normally shipped in the Fall, but the last few years he waited until the end of January and shipped the calves to either San Angelo or El Paso. He seemed to make a little more money that way. Why, I'm not sure. They branded baby calves as they came. They'd catch their cattle around their mountain waterings, put them in the pen, and brand and work the calves. They did the whole ranch like this during the Spring. They also had a little portable chute they put in the back of the truck. They'd set it at the end of the chute gate in the corrals, run the calves through it, lay them over and work them. It worked out a lot easier for them and a lot easier for the cattle. You've got to remember, they were both almost eighty at the time. Thank God, they weren't fighting worms those last few years. We worked, branded, and marked the little calves as they came.

If we had to feed, it was usually between March and June, because that was always the driest part of the year. During the summer, we checked waterings, you know. In the Fall we'd usually get some rain and have good winter grass, so if it didn't get cold early, our cattle really put on the weight in the Fall. I sometimes think that's why Wade would wait until January to ship. When all the calves were on the ground, our work would taper off. Wade and I would sit down and work the books and get all the registration papers sent in for the cattle. Wade kept all the books, paid the bills, and ordered the feed. He and Roy would discuss about what their cattle should bring each year. Whoever started a deal with a buyer for the cattle first, concluded it. The other never butted in, even if the market fluctuated in between the time a price was agreed upon and the time the cattle were shipped. They never argued money. Ever. I don't know many brothers or sisters that could do that. I guess that was one reason they got along so well all those years. I don't think there's anyone else in their family or mine—and we both came from big families—that could have gotten along as well as those two brothers did.

Towards the end, we had to have some help at the ranch to take the hard work off Wade and Roy—like digging postholes in the mountains—but good help was hard to find. It really didn't cost that much to operate the ranch. One year during the Fifties drought we spent ten thousand on feed, and that was more than all of our other expenses combined. When we made out income tax that year, we didn't have any income. Lot of people couldn't handle that today. That drought was the only time we ever had to feed the mountain pasture. We always fed our registered cows in the flats during the hard years, though. When we did, we just scattered cake on the ground. And we kept salt out year 'round. We felt like our mountain pasture was some of the best cattle country in the Davis Mountains.

When Wade and Roy put together their ranch, Willis McCutcheon, Sr., owned two sections of land east of their place. The sections were cut off completely from the rest of Willis' land because their ranch and part of the Jeff sat in between. Willis was running some steers out there one year, and they ran out of water. Wade and Roy saw they'd run out of water and turned them into their pasture and took care of them. When they got caught up, Wade rode over and told Mr. McCutcheon. Willis said, "I believe I'll just move those cattle off there." Wade said, "If you do, we'd like to lease those two sections from you." Willis said, "Okay." They agreed on a price and shook hands. For forty years Wade and Roy leased those two sections on that handshake from Willis, Sr., then his son, Willis, Jr. There was never any contract, never any written agreement, never any earnest money, nothing. On New Year's Day we always drove over to Willis', handed him a check for the year, and had coffee. When Willis died, we went over that January and asked his widow, Mallie, what she wanted to do about the lease. She said, "Wade, you do exactly like you and Willis agreed." And when the descendants took over his ranch, no one ever came by and said anything about Willis' and Wade's agreement. Now when Willis didn't raise the lease after twenty years or so, Wade had gone over and said to Willis, "Willis, I think we ought to raise the lease. Things have gone up these days." So Willis said, "All right, Wade. What did you have in mind?" So Wade told him and both agreed it was a fair price, and Willis raised the lease to that amount and went on with never another word. That lease was still in effect when Roy and I sold the ranch.

I'm proud, too, that I was able to get them both off that ranch and travel some. At first, we mostly went to the Production Credit Association meetings. Wade worked with the Production Credit Association for thirty-three years and was president of the Marfa PCA for fifteen of those years. I knew I had a good chance of getting them off that ranch at least once a year to go to the PCA's annual convention in Texas. We all met so many good friends at these conventions, and we really enjoyed it. Some of the people we met would come by the ranch and see us. Finally I got Wade to take a vacation. It was his first. Up until then he just wouldn't leave that ranch except for the PCA convention. I don't think they would have ever left it if I hadn't made them. Once they went, though, they enjoyed themselves. Roy would go with us only if the city we were going to had a professional baseball team. You know how he loved baseball. He played a little baseball, I believe, somewhere around Clarendon. I think that's the only sport, besides roping, he had a chance to participate in. The rest of his life he worked. He stayed interested in baseball, even when he was almost blind and deaf. He would get his ear right up next to the radio and listen to the Astros' and Rangers' games coming out of Houston and Dallas. Roy and Wade both finished high school in Tulia, you know. They only had ten grades back then. They added a grade the year Wade finished, but he didn't go back. He and Roy already had themselves some horses and a few head of cattle, and they just went on and went to work. They helped a lot of other young people in the family go to college, though.

19

Interview with Jack Scannell, continued

Wade had the shingles real bad three years before he died. I don't think he ever really got over them. They also found out he was anemic in the Fifties. The doctors said he was born that way, but in the late 1800's, they didn't know too much about that sort of thing. I guess he just suffered with it all his life. I was going to Sul Ross the summer he got real sick with it. I guess I was eighteen or nineteen at the time. I kept noticing Wade just wasn't himself when we were riding. He was still working those long days. Wade always worked. But I kept noticing when I'd ride with him, he'd look like he was about ready to fall out of the saddle. I knew he was sick. I mentioned it to Mother and she made him go to Lubbock to see his friend, Doc Sam Dunn. Sam and his brother Nelson—they were both doctors—always came for the Fall hunt at the ranch. Sam gave him the first thorough physical he'd ever had and found out Wade had no acid in his stomach. His digestive system just never had worked right, and that's what made him anemic. Sam told Mother she would have to give him a shot everyday, and Mother said, "Sam, I can't give anybody a shot. I'm the poorest nurse in the world." Mother did learn to give shots though. Then Wade learned to give them to himself. When Wade began to build up his strength, he took shots every other day, then monthly. He also took two or three drops of acid in a glass of water before every meal for the rest of his life. Later they developed a pill for people like him. It's a wonder he lived as an infant. Wade's mother had told the family he was always sickly as a kid and that Roy always looked out for him. Wade just had a hell of a lot of things wrong with him, and I guess that's why he took better care of himself than Roy.

Wade froze his feet that winter in the Panhandle. Their pasture and water was frozen solid, he said, and he had to get off and walk through that snow and slush to break ice for their cattle. His boots and feet were soaked and frozen. That was how his rheumatism started, he said.

Then when he was in his eighties, his right hand doubled up bad with rheumatism again; he said it was totally useless. Anyhow, he'd already learned to shave left-handed, and do so many things left-handed, that he'd become ambidextrous over the years. Didn't seem like anything could get him down. For the better part of a century, nothing did. When he finally got better in his younger days, he gave all the credit to the chiropractor. He said the chiropractor saved his life. He'd gone to doctors hoping for some relief for his rheumatism, and they'd told him there wasn't anything could be done for him. Then he tried the chiropractor and the man helped him. He was always a staunch believer in them from then on. He said when he got his call from the draft board during World War I, he reported on crutches because his feet were so bad at the time. They took one look at him and said, "My God, man, go home. We can't use you."

I think Wade's death caught Roy by surprise, but he took it pretty good considering how long they'd been together. I don't think he expected Wade to die when he did. None of us did. He knew Wade was in the hospital and sick. Wade had the flu, but then he'd had trouble like that all his life—got a cold every winter it seemed—so Roy stayed out at the ranch.

Mother called to tell me in March of 1974 that Wade had gone into the hospital. I was going to go see him that weekend, but she called back a day later and said, "Wade wants you to come now." That's when I got scared because Wade just never asked anybody to come help him, even in his worst moments. I knew if he was asking for somebody, he was afraid he was going to die. She said, "Wade wants you to come. He has something he wants you to do." I said, "All right. I can come tonight."

When I got there Mother said, "Wade's been asking for

you all day long. I told him you'd be here soon as you could." She said, "Something's really worrying him, and he thinks you're the only one that can take care of it." Know what was worrying him? A gasoline bill. Wade and this supplier in Balmorhea had been discussing the ranch's gasoline bill for several months. Wade felt he'd paid it, and the man said he hadn't. That's what was worrying him. He wanted me to go over and get it straightened out right away. He said, "If I owe it, I want you to pay it." Then he said, "I want you to get a statement drawn up tonight giving you authority to write checks on the account. I just never got around to doing it so you could." I said, "All right, I will." So I typed one out that night and took it up to the hospital the next morning and he signed it.

Then I went by the ranch and picked up the bill. Roy was there, and he asked me how Wade was. I told him Wade looked awfully weak and thin, but that he'd been in the hospital about ten days, so naturally he wouldn't look his best. I went on over then to Balmorhea and settled up with the man, got back to Alpine that afternoon, and went by the hospital. I told Wade, "I took care of the whole thing. The bill's paid in full. There's no more problem." He thanked me. I really think he'd been keeping himself alive until that issue was settled. He started choking while we were there that night. We called the nurse. They got him an oxygen mask, and he seemed to be breathing easier, but I think his lungs were filled with fluid then. We left for supper, then went by Mother's sister's for the night. The phone rang while we were there. It was the hospital. They said, "Mr. Reid has taken a turn for the worse." I really think he was dead when they called.

20

Roy broke his hip again the summer after Wade died. There was a little step just inside that basement room where he lived. Roy had gone down to his room, and Mother was upstairs on the phone. It wasn't quite suppertime and just a little before sundown. But the rooms downstairs always got dark first because the sun would drop behind the hills there west of the house. Well, his room was already dark, and Roy's eyesight was almost gone. He stepped in and reached to turn on the light.

When he did, his foot slipped off the step, and he fell hard on the floor, breaking his hip. He never really recovered from that one. Actually the hip recovered beautifully, considering, but with him still weak from his broken back and the other hip having been broken forty years earlier and him pushing ninety and almost blind and all, it was asking a lot of his old body. He was only in the hospital about six weeks, though. He should have been there twice as long, but he wouldn't stay. He had to lay flat on his back from that broken hip since they'd had to operate and put a new ball-and-socket in. The break was a pretty good one.

When they let him sit up in a wheelchair, Mother told them to give Roy a single room. She said she would pay the difference. They had him in a single room and everything was fine until the hospital administrator decided to close down the wing he was in and move everyone into another part of the hospital to save money.

They put a young fellow in the new room with Roy. About twenty I guess. Said he'd just gone to work for the Southern Pacific and was repairing a line outside of Alpine when he fell and cracked his back. He was laying there in the hospital bed on a steel plate, couldn't turn over, couldn't move at all with Roy in the room with him. Mother had been in Midland for a couple of days and had just got back and dropped by Knox's and Lou's before going on out to the hospital to see how Roy was doing. The phone rang while she was there. It was Roy, who by this time was in a wheelchair. He was calling from the pay phone in the lobby of the hospital. No one knows where he got the money because Mother had his billfold and change for him. They didn't like you to leave money in the hospital. Roy had gotten a couple of dimes and talked someone into dialing Knox's and Lou's number. Lou answered and Roy said to Lou, "I want you to come pack my stuff. I'm getting out of here." And Lou said, "Now, Roy, I really don't think you can do that." He said, "Get down to this damned place and help me pack my stuff." So Mother and I headed for the hospital. When we got there, he'd wheeled himself back to his room. Roy asked me to roll him outside. When we got outside, he said, "Damn it, I need to use the bathroom." What he'd needed all that time was someone to help him go to the bathroom. He had to have help to go, and I think he was too shy to ask a nurse.

The room he'd been in before had a bathroom door big enough for him to wheel his chair through and manage for himself. Where they'd moved him, the bathroom doors were about half the size and a wheel chair wouldn't fit through. Which meant Roy had to get somebody to get him out of the chair and onto the bathroom seat, then back into the wheelchair. It had to be tough, too, for someone who'd been able to step outside and take a leak by the corrals at night whenever he felt like it. He said, "I want to leave this damned place."

Doc Hill released Roy on a Sunday. He'd left a couple prescriptions for Roy at the City Drug, but it was closed when we went to pick him up. They opened up for us, though, and we got his pills and got him home. Mother asked Roy on the way back to the ranch, "Roy, wouldn't it be better for you to move into the guest room upstairs until you get to where you can get around better?" We all felt it would be better for him if he moved upstairs because the dining room was there, and Mother was just down the hall. No, he wasn't going to do it. That first night we got him into his room downstairs he didn't feel much like walking.

The next morning we took his breakfast down to him and asked him again, even offered to load him in the car and drive him around up behind the kitchen porch so he wouldn't have to climb the steps. "No, I've already figured out how to climb the front steps," he said. We were surprised. "What do you mean you figured out how to climb them? Those front steps are as steep as a mountain." "I can do it," he said. "You can help me." So he hobbled around to the foot of the steps with his walker, but the steps weren't wide enough for the walker; so, he grabbed ahold of the railing, stepped with his good leg and hoisted his bad one up like he was stepping on a horse. He had to stop three times and I could see he was hurting, but he was too damned stubborn to admit he couldn't do it. He finally made it. I brought him his walker up, and he got to his chair by the radio and eased down. "Knew I could do it," he said. About that time Mother's sister called and said Doc Hill had some written instructions for Roy. I told Mother I'd go on in and get them the next day.

When I got to Doc Hill's office, he had quite a list of do's and don'ts for Roy. I read it over and saw there was no mention of steps. I said, "Dr. Hill, should Roy climb steps?" "Absolutely not," he said, "not for three months at least." I said, "Well, he's already doing it." So he took the instructions back and wrote: *Do not climb stairs or steps until October first.* I got home and found Roy sitting on the front porch smoking a cigarette. I said, "Roy, Doc Hill told me you're not supposed to climb steps." He said, "Hell, I know that. He told me." I said, "Well, damnit, why'd you do it." He said, "To see if I could."

That night we refused to help him back down the steps. Time came for him to go to bed. I said, "Come on, Roy, we're going out back, and I'll pull the car around and drive you downstairs." He said, "Don't need to." I said, "Unless you can go down those steps by yourself, you do need to because we're not gonna help you." So he gave in and shuffled out the back door to the car.

Roy finally wore himself out after a week, but he was still too damned stubborn to admit he was wrong. Never did admit it, in fact. Finally one evening he said he thought he'd stay upstairs a night or two and rest. He said, "If you can bring my pillows up to me, I might sleep up here tonight." We brought his pillows up, and he reminded us again it wasn't a permanent move. It was always, "just until I get to feeling a little better." He never slept downstairs again. That was the summer of '75. It was January of '76 when they sold the ranch. So gradually over the next month we eased his things upstairs and the guest room stuff downstairs without ever making a point of it. The only time we took him downstairs was to shower because he couldn't get in and out of the upstairs tub. He'd said to Mother once when I wasn't there, "I think I'm gonna get in the tub," and she said, "That's fine, Roy, but who's gonna lift you out? I can't lift you." So he never did say anymore about it. After that she got Joe to help him downstairs for his shower.

He did use the walker we got for him his last year and a half, though. I think he used it because he was afraid he would run into something and fall again. And he knew if he did, he might not ever get up. He was almost blind, you know. In fact, the last several months he didn't use the walker to support himself at all. He just shoved it out in front of him to see if it hit anything. If it didn't, he put it down and took a step. That's how he got around. Every once in awhile he'd get a call, and he'd get up out of his chair and shuffle in and answer it without his walker. He knew where the phone was. Mother kept a high-backed chair for him to sit in by the phone because he had trouble getting up and out of low chairs. She kept certain paths he walked in the house clear of furniture, too. If guests came and moved a chair, she always moved it back.

Roy began losing sight in one eye right after Wade flipped

the pickup. Several years later when they operated on Roy's other eye for cataracts, they discovered a blood clot behind the eyeball he'd injured. The doctor said it was probably a result of the wreck. Mother took him to one or two doctors after Wade died, seeing if anything could be done for his eyes. They all agreed to leave him what sight he had in the eye because if anything went wrong when they tried to remove the clot, he would be blind. About the same time his hearing got worse, but he wouldn't admit that either. He finally gave in and bought a hearing aid for his glasses, then insisted the guy in El Paso who sold it to him had put it on the wrong ear. The man had put it in the strongest ear so Roy would at least have some hearing since he was virtually deaf in the other. But when you get good hearing in one ear and none in the other, it throws you off balance.

Roy went back and told the man again he wanted the hearing aid in his left ear because that was his worst ear. The hearing aid man insisted. Roy got mad. Then, just about a year before he turned ninety, after he was able to get up and around a bit with his walker, Roy tried a new hearing aid that I'd bought for myself in Odessa; the kind you could put in either ear. He decided it was better and said, "I want to go to your hearing aid man." He was convinced the ones in El Paso were wrong. Mother said okay, but Roy started stalling and we couldn't talk him into the drive to Odessa. I think he was afraid it might not help him. He hated to admit his hearing was that far gone, but as long as he just talked about it, there was no harm done. So he kept stalling. Then one day we were at the ranch by ourselves, and I said, "Roy, if you feel good in the morning, why don't you go with me to Odessa and let's see that hearing aid man." I must of caught him just right because he said, "All right, we just might do that."

The next morning after he got up I said, "You go ahead and shave and put on your good clothes. We're going to Odessa." I got him there and took him in and told the man

Roy wanted an aid in his weak ear and wouldn't settle for anything less. I said, "I know you'll want to strengthen what little hearing he's got, but that throws him off balance and makes him mad. Anyway," I said, "he doesn't hear well enough to make a hell of a lot of difference." The man said, "All right, I'll do whatever Mr. Reid wants." So Roy went in and said, "I want one just like his." He pointed to mine. So the man said, "Fine. We'll try that, Mr. Reid." And he got one and let him try it in his weak ear. Then he said, "Well, how is it, Mr. Reid?" Roy said, "Well, I think it's better." But the man said, "Before you leave now, let me try another one on you just to let you see which one you like best." He said, "If you don't want it, that's fine. We'll sell you this one." The man gave Roy another one to try in his good ear and, of course, it was better because it was stronger. Roy admitted he could hear a lot better with it. He asked, "What's the difference?" The man said, "It's just that one's a little stronger than the other and for your hearing problem, I think you need a little stronger one."

So Roy bought it. Usually he turned the volume up all the way. When he did, it made the damnedest racket. You could hear it squawk all over the house. I guess it helped him a little, though.

Before Roy and Mother sold the ranch there was some question over its minerals. The way you bought Texas land when Wade and Roy started was either dry grazing, watered—which meant you had a spring or some natural source of water on it—or mineral grazing, meaning you got the mineral rights, too. A lot of their land was originally classified as mineral grazing.

Anyhow, Wade and Roy bought most of their land from the state on patented fee-simple, forty-year notes at about a dollar fifty an acre; the whole idea being a rancher could pay the land off with what the land yielded. Wade also bought government bonds long before World War II's big bond drive. It was the only investment he trusted. The bonds, plus interest, helped pay off the land over the years, too. When Wade and Roy went to Austin to get their notes after they'd paid them off, they found state officials had re-examined a lot of state land during the Thirties and changed its designation without notifying the owners.

Wade and Roy never forgave the Texas Land Commissioner at the time because he wouldn't help them find out who was responsible for changing the classification. When they bought their state land, the title was supposed to be based on classification of the land at the time of their first payment. But when Wade's patents came in the mail after payoff, some of the classifications on their sections were different. I was at the ranch when he opened the patents and started reading them. Wade stopped and said, "This is a mistake. This classification is wrong." That's when they went to Austin and tried to dig into it. They found the original classification on the land missing and couldn't get to the bottom of it. Wade wondered just how much of the state's land classifications had been changed by politicians and lawyers without the original owners knowing it. When he saw that "crooked sonofabitchin' Land Commissioner and politicians" wouldn't help him, he went back to Fort Davis. It was never classified to his satisfaction before he died and before the ranch sold, which they had to sell according to the patents.

★   ★   ★

**From an interview with
Mrs. Dorothy Reid (1904-1990)**

Wade was such good help around the house. When I had company—and we sometimes had a lot of company during the latter years with deer season and all—I would rather have had Wade in the kitchen than anyone else I know. He'd cooked for them both for so long, and he always made the best biscuits. Help came and went, though, as Wade and Roy got older. We had one couple that worked at the ranch for awhile. They didn't have any kids and seemed like an ideal couple. We let them live in the little white house out back. Problem was, they almost broke all the furniture fighting with one another.

The man came over knocking on our window around midnight one night saying his wife had locked him out of the house. Wade told him to go back and everything would straighten itself out in the morning. But he kept saying, "It's my house and she's got me locked out." Meantime, she was at their back door yelling at me to "Call the Sheriff. Call the Sheriff." I just told her to go back to bed and stop that arguing. They did finally. Eventually they left.

Joe Alvarado, I guess, stayed longer than anyone. He quit right after Wade died. It just tore me up because he was such a good hand. He'd been with us four years, and he knew the cattle. He came back for awhile, but I don't think he knew how to take someone other than Wade bossing him. I might tell him one thing and Roy would tell him another. He just didn't know what to do without Wade around. Johnny Fitzgerald came out and helped us from time to time. Johnny always helped Wade and Roy when they got older, and they thought the world of him. He was there to help us make the gather when Roy sold the cattle. Roy and I stayed on the ranch two years after Wade died. We managed, but I was a wreck. Roy could hardly see. I would ask Roy how much feed to buy, and he would say, "Dot, you better buy so much." So I would order it and wouldn't have the receiver hung up good before he'd say, "You know, Dot, I don't think we need that much." Wade always took care of things like that. Then on Friday afternoon, a year after Wade died, Roy and I had been to town for something. I remember we'd had a real good time and had bought some cantaloupe from this man. Anyhow, we got home about five that afternoon. I went upstairs, needed my glasses, but couldn't find them. So I went back downstairs to look for them in the car. When I came back upstairs, I noticed Roy hadn't turned on the radio to get the news and baseball scores. I got worried then and went downstairs and found him lying on the floor in the dark room. This was like around five-thirty or so. He said, "Dot, help me up on the bed. I'm hurt." I told him I was afraid he'd broken something and that he shouldn't move. Well, there wasn't another soul on the ranch. We'd given our help the weekend off. So I got some pillows and put them under his head and told him I was going to call the Jeff Ranch.

Luckily, one of the Jeff hands answered the phone. I asked if he and Manuel would come help, that Roy had fallen. They came up, put him on some Army blankets, carried him to the backseat of the car, and packed pillows around him so I could drive him to town. It was around six when I started to town, and I remember the sun was right in my eyes. He was eighty-eight and had broken his hip. Roy always used the walker after that. That following Fall we had a big birthday party for him at the ranch on his eighty-ninth birthday. All of his family came, and they all sat around and ate cake and talked and drank coffee and punch. Shortly after this, Roy said, "Dot, I guess we better sell this ranch." I never could have sold it and wouldn't have asked Roy to if he hadn't brought it up. When Roy decided to sell the ranch, he asked me to call Bob McKnight. He said he'd rather sell it to Bob than anyone else if he wanted it. Bob said he'd just bought another ranch at the time, and that the mountain pastures were all he could use. I told him we didn't want to separate it, and that we didn't want a lot of people coming out to look at the ranch who couldn't buy it. Bob agreed and recommended a group of oilmen he knew could afford the place. We sold it to them. I wish I'd brought more things from the ranch. You know, all those old tools and things. They're selling them in antique shops these days. The people who bought the ranch didn't know what most of those funny looking tools were around Roy's shed, much less what they were used for. But I couldn't bring everything. I just couldn't. There was no way. Jack wanted me to save as much of the old stuff as I could. I tried. And there were pictures. A trunkful of pictures. I let Russell Jr. and Myrtle look through them to see if they could recognize anyone.

Wade Reid   Roy Reid

Circa 1942

Gathering cattle at the Reid's headquarters corrals.

Part III

As I Knew Them

The Cattlemen

21

Alpine High School always turned out early the last day in May. I would have my good-byes said, some work clothes stuffed in the cab of my old pickup, and be on the way to Wade's and Roy's as soon as I could slip away—through Fort Davis and north over Wild Rose Pass following Limpia Creek until it and the eleven miles of rough dirt road to their ranch turned east between the Barrilla Mountains and Horsethief Canyon. During earlier years the Reids had to cross Limpia twice to get home. Later, the county helped them cut a new road through the brush and rocks on the north side of the creek so they wouldn't have to wait out rises.

I always drove the old road the first day because it passed the Jeff Ranch headquarters where I'd spent time when I was young. I'd rattle across the dry creek and head east toward the Jeff's Rooney pasture. The color of the long, lava slopes climbing north and south beyond Limpia flats told me what kind of Spring they'd had. Past Barbara's Point I'd spot Horsethief Canyon slicing into the big mesa on my right. I'd explored the canyon once, crawling up its side to the mesa top where Melly Rodriguez told me his father and other vaqueros had roped and killed a grizzly in the late 1800's. Melly worked for the Reids, and his wife made the best Mexican food I ever ate.

There was a beautiful spring pool in Horsethief Canyon. It was blue and deep and stood in a big rock canajo scooped from years of flash floods pouring off slick canyon walls. You had to look sharp for rock rattlers around the spring, too. I killed my first there when I lowered myself for a drink one summer afternoon. Something caused me to look up and I saw it coiled in the shade of a boulder, not ten feet away. Later years, corporate deer hunters would discover the spring and leave it littered.

On past the Rooney Pasture, the oak and cottonwood

trees shading the Jeff's faded white headquarters buildings would come into view. The man in charge of the Jeff then was Pat Mulloy. His wife's father—John Killough—had been named by Mrs. Lee McCutcheon as executor of the Jeff Ranch when she died. Pat had brought his wife—Nellie Lee, or "Sug," as we called her—to the Davis Mountains from LaGrange when her health began to fail. Pat was a good businessman and had taken over the management of the ranch for Mr. Killough.

Several acres around the Jeff house were fenced to keep cattle and horses out. When you pulled into this area, you crossed a cattle guard. The main house, garden, windmill, cooling house, storehouse, and backyard bunkhouse sat behind a yard fence on the right. To leave, you circled a little dirt cul-de-sac with a cactus bed in the middle, passed a vehicle shed, another bunk house, and crossed the cattle guard again. Two more adobes behind the vehicle shed housed the families who worked year round at the Jeff. The barn and house corrals set about seventy yards northwest of the headquarters.

During earlier years, my father and I always ate a meal at the Jeff during deer season with Mr. Killough—who came from LaGrange for the hunt—and his guests. Everyone sat at the Jeff's long dining table with the old carbide lights flickering on the walls. Mr. Killough always ate a bowl of clabber, offering some to any who liked it. I never did. The Jeff usually kept two or three milk cows. Edna, a black lady who lived there, still cooked for them. She served a wonderful meal. After supper everyone retired to the Jeff's parlor for a cigar or cigarette and settled world affairs.

The parlor was a time capsule with its turn-of-the-century, high-back chairs and piano and rolltop desk—all genuine, all purchased by the McCutcheons. Everyone would sit by the fire and talk until early morning. I would usually wander through the rooms, each a livable museum. A huge mounted Longhorn head and a panther skin hung

196

above double doors with stained glass off the Jeff porch, beyond which lay bedrooms complete with large, genuine brass beds and legged bathtubs and dressing shields. The rest of the house consisted of the dining room, the kitchen, and a staples storeroom connected to the screened porch that wrapped itself around the east and south sides of the house.

A windmill sat alongside the house above a well Frank Heulster, Sr., had dug when he'd moved the stage station there from Barrilla Springs. It was only a few feet deep and had the purest, sweetest water I ever tasted. Overflow water pumped by the well's windmill flowed from the storage tank down a small pipe and into a waist-high trough about eight inches deep that ran three-quarters of the way around the inside wall of the adobe cooling house. Milk, vegetables, and other perishables were set in pans in the water to cool, and fresh beef was sometimes hung in the cooling house during early days. Milk was kept in big crocks until the cream rose. A towel was placed over the top of each crock to keep bugs out. A little overflow pipe at one end of the cooling trough drained excess water into a flower bed alongside the adobe where mint grew for summer tea. A second overflow pipe from the well's storage tank drained water into a fenced garden used to grow fresh vegetables, melons, and fruit for the ranch. Jeff hands took care of it and shared its produce.

Sometimes after the deer season meal, I'd step outside and wander about knowing it was too cold for rattlers, seeing if anyone lived in the backyard adobe usually occupied during the Forties by two brothers named Tom and Forest York. When I was a child, I sometimes slept out there if they had an empty bed. I liked to listen to them talk at nights. One of them couldn't read. The real thrill, though, was listening to the rattlers buzzing beneath the bunkhouse all night. They never could get them out, so they just left them to buzz and eat rats—right there beneath the bunk house. The cowboys clomping on the floor at night got them stirred up. Tom and Forest assured me the floors were tight and nothing could crawl up through them. I noticed they always checked their boots each morning, though. Anyhow, I'd go to sleep at night listening to those rattlers buzz. It got so I could pick up that sound no matter where I was—in the brush, the mountains, on a tabosa flat, at night. Once you've heard it, you never forget it.

Other times my father and mother would leave me at the Jeff, and I would nap on the porch on one of those big, black, overstuffed leather sleepers that, I suppose, would be worth a fortune today as an antique. It just sat out there, dusty, for the longest time. Some days, though, I wouldn't feel like a nap, and I would wander around the house or down to Limpia about a hundred yards west of the Jeff, poking around the smooth stones, smelling creek weed, seeing if I could find water. The creek would be dry unless there'd been a thundershower. Usually I could find a seep hole where living water—always just beneath the surface of Limpia—had worked its way out.

When we rode, they always set me on something gentle. I would tag along behind Pat and the Yorks and Manuel Garcia and the other Jeff hands, and we would ride the mountains together. I was too little to help much, but I loved the work and the country and always got a kick out of the riding with them. It was something only a handful of kids had the opportunity to do.

One year my father brought the Mulloys a registered collie we'd raised on our New Mexico farm. They named him Sonny; and since they didn't have children, they put in a lot of time with him. He grew big and followed Mr. Mulloy everywhere. Sometimes during the cool of an evening everyone would sit beneath a big oak in the Jeff's front yard. I would chase fireflies with a Mason jar and lid. The dog would run and jump and catch fireflies with me. He was smart and looked out for everyone. One day he got hold of some coyote bait in Fort Davis and died.

22

I'd leave the Jeff and drive north, then northeast, bouncing up the dirt road that wound its way around foothills until I reached the Reid cattle guard. It would rattle as I continued up the rough, winding road built through volcanic rock and arroyos sometimes graded by the county. Cartop-high white brush and catclaw lined the sides of the single-lane road. The desert blossoms always smelled sweet in May and reminded me of the fresh white brush honey the beekeeper left with the ranchers whenever he set his bees out.

The pickup's undercarriage would scrape against the center gravel as I'd bounce across gullies. Spring rains would sometimes washboard the road and there were no culverts in the dry gullies one had to cross to reach the ranch house, flash floods having long since swept them away in a foolish county experiment one year.

The jackrabbits darting across the road made me think of Reid relatives or friends from Los Angeles and other cities who came to plink at them each summer on minivacations, fascinated with Wade's and Roy's genuine hospitality.

Finally from the small hill I would see the two-level rock house in the distance, standing as it always had beneath the cottonwood at the base of the huge mesa. It looked like an oasis—was, I suppose, in many respects. To my knowledge, its doors were never locked. It just didn't occur to them that someone would turn off the highway and drive eleven miles of rough dirt road to steal from them. They'd never lived in the city. Here you could still enter a house for water, food, or help. The rule applied also to wetbacks traveling north through the searing heat in search of work. Often I would find a crudely scrawled IOU for a can of corn or Spam left by wets traveling through. Those were days before coyotes and drug runners.

The Reid's tin roof would sometimes have a new coat of

paint. Hailstorms destroyed a shingle roof and ranchers adopted the tin long ago to save money. A paint job lasted one, maybe two hailstorms. I'd seen hailstorms kill sheep and baby calves, and a rider caught in one had to huddle beneath his saddle and let his horse fend for himself.

The four-foot, red-rock fence still surrounded the house, enclosing some green patches of Bermuda grass, a few scattered flowers, and a fruit tree or two that looked the same size as when I'd left the summer before. The small, white three-room bunkhouse, a tin water storage tank, the generator storage shed, a garage, and an empty chicken coop sat out behind the main house. Usually several horses would be crowded around a graying latched corral gate near the barn.

They'd built the house just after Wade married the first time. Except for repairs made after the 1930 earthquake and some interior changes when Wade married again, it hadn't changed much. I usually slept in one of two ground level rooms they'd converted from a garage and storage area for summer visitors. Scorpions were not uncommon down there. You never crawled into bed without checking your sheets. Another night I'd killed a rattler as I started downstairs for bed. He was coiled at the base of the steps in the honeysuckle. I heard him buzz before I saw him. Rattlers were plentiful, and you never let one crawl away around the house. That was the rule. I'd seen them both dig around a pile of house trash, flushing one into the open to pound its head flat with rocks. We found a favorite colt standing at the corral gate one morning, its head bloated and swollen. Horses that survived a rattler's bite never forgot, and you had to have a deep seat if you happened to be riding one when a rattler buzzed.

Cans, bottles, burnable trash from the house were dumped in an old barrel out back of the ranch house and set afire. About once every three months we scooped what trash didn't burn into the back of the pickup and hauled it down to a deep arroyo below the house. Table scraps—any thing edible—were scraped into a little white-lidded metal pot that sat on the kitchen counter. When the pot was full, they took it out behind the trash barrel and pitched the scraps over an old chicken wire fence. A house covey of blue quail—twenty or thirty in good years—would come and scratch and eat.

The quail watered at the house, too. Wade and Roy had single faucets on the east and west sides of their house. The water pipe to both came from the small storage tank on the slope behind the house. The west faucet always dripped, so they'd set half of an old water trough float beneath to catch the drip. During dry spells, the quail would come to water at the dripping faucet just outside the kitchen door. Afterwards, they would wander up to the table scraps and pick through the coffee grounds and tomato rinds and onionskins. Wade and Roy got the biggest kick out of seeing the old mother quail bring her brood to water the first time.

Coon, fox, and ringtail hung around the house, too. Occasionally a pile of feathers would mark the spot where a quail hadn't been quick enough. One summer a roadrunner brought her two little ones into the yard everyday to catch lizards. Several swallows always built mud nests under the eaves of the house, and a family of mockingbirds nested in the cottonwood on the east side of the house each summer. Most of the cottonwood's branches were at eye level with the second floor porch, and you could watch the birds build their nest.

Wade and Roy never kept dogs or cats. Dogs boogered young horses, and cats ate quail and birds. They never had a rat or mouse problem, though, because bull snakes and racers hung around the house and barn. I jerked my saddle off the rack one morning and a bull snake hissed his way out from under it right between my legs. I stumbled over cake buckets and feed sacks and everything on that barn floor trying to get out of the way. It took ten minutes for my heart to quit pounding. Lord, I hated snakes. We didn't kill bull snakes or racers, though. Roy said the only dog he could ever remember having there was a little ratty-looking terrier someone had brought out and left. One morning Roy saddled a green horse, stepped aboard, and pulled out through the trap in back of the house. The dog followed and either barked at the horse or nipped at its heels—something—and the horse went to pitching and bawling. Roy finally got ahold of his horse, stepped off, and run the dog back to the house with rocks. Later he gave it away—or so he said.

Roy would usually be asleep on the front porch when I arrived. That's where he took his nap every afternoon, right there on an old, faded yard recliner propped at about a thirty degree angle, one arm tucked beneath his head, sound asleep while the afternoon breezes rattled the cottonwood leaves alongside the house, tugging at the tufts of gray on top of his balding head, his scuffed work boots sitting next to the recliner. He never wore socks during the week. He just powdered his feet and slipped them in his boots. When the mockingbirds in the cottonwood were trying to teach their young ones to fly, he'd always watch them a few minutes before he dozed off. The birds used the radio-aerial-line-wire he'd run from the tree across to the house.

The saddle horses hanging around the lots would usually have sweat stains on their backs from their morning's ride. Wade and Roy used a pickup and trailer then to get as close as they could to where they were going before backing their horses out and striking off up mountain trails they'd been riding for the last fifty years. The trailer saved their strength. They started napping in their sixties, working a hard half day until the sun was high and heating the desert. They would return to the house, have lunch, and nap for an hour or so. About midafternoon they would stir and go back to work.

Roy always pushed himself up on one elbow to see who was driving up. I would shake hands and he would ask how I was doing and if I'd finished another school year. Wade and Mrs. Reid—Aunt Dot as she was known to every-one—would be in the back bedroom resting, and I would step inside. Wade would emerge from their bedroom in his socks and Levis and T-shirt brief, hobbling along on his heels like he always did, having heard my tires crunching over rocks as I drove up. The front part of his feet were gnarled and lumped. I never understood how he walked at all. He'd ask me if I'd finished another school year. "Yes, and could he use somebody for the summer?" He would usually ask me how seventy dollars a month plus a cow and calf for the summer's work would be. I'd say that was fine; and he'd say, "Well, put your stuff in the extra room in the basement." Sometimes he'd ask me to go on down and start fixing flats. I would thank him, unload my truck, and start to work.

24

Flat fixing was a primitive job conducted in Roy's oven-hot tin tool shed that sat at one end of a car shed near the barn. It required the stem to be removed, tire tromped and busted loose with a pair of ancient tire tools worn silver-slick with use, dirty tube jerked from the tire, stem reinserted, a rusted Briggs and Stratton fired, and a frayed air hose connected to the tube's valve. If Roy helped, he always throttled the Briggs and Stratton until it wouldn't run any slower, lit a cigarette, and together we would watch the patch-covered tube jerk full.

When it was tight, I ran it around to the horse trough, pushed it quickly beneath the water, and marked the bubbles. It usually required two rotations to get them all. Satisfied, I returned, wiped the tube clean, let the sun dry it for a minute or two, deflated it again, and pasted slow-burn patches over the holes. Roy, meanwhile, would have seated a boot or two inside the tire where cactus thorn or rocks had punctured.

I'd stuff the tube inside the tire and around the rim, work the valve out, grab a couple bites with my tire tools, tromp the tire back onto the battered rim, and reconnect the air hose. The whole process usually took twenty minutes and was conducted in early afternoon when there wasn't a breath of air stirring. My shirt would be soaked with sweat by the time we finished. Roy's wouldn't. I think he was perfectly climatized.

Another after-lunch job was horseshoeing. I was trying to get a front hoof reasonably smooth one hot summer afternoon. Winded, I made a couple more passes across the hoof, eased the horse's leg down, pitched the rasp aside and staggered toward the water trough. Roy made it look easy, and I hadn't hesitated when he asked me if I thought I was ready to learn how to shoe horses. I dropped my hat beside the trough and dunked my head beneath the cool water. It must have been a hundred that day. I was watching a frog in the bottom of the trough when I heard him chuckle. I cocked my head and saw him standing beside me, surveying my sweat-logged clothes. He picked up the rasp and walked slowly to the horse, lifted its hoof and inspected my work. Placing the hoof between his knees, he worked on it a few seconds, ran his hand over the surface, lowered it, then proceeded to smooth another hoof, finally fitting and tacking both shoes. He did all this, it seemed, with a minimum of effort and without breaking a sweat. He was supposed to have been an old man.

Finally Wade would emerge from the house, and we'd start the afternoon's work—fixing windmills or fence or hunting pinkeyed cows they'd seen at waterings. We usually headed back in about sundown and ate a light supper. After supper I would go down to the barn and feed the horses. They would be standing at the barn gate, Wade's big bay among them. He was the smoothest riding horse I ever rode. Wade had trained him to a running walk. They would crowd behind me, pushing and nipping at one another as I swung the gate open and tied it back against the fence with a piece of rusty bailing wire. I would walk to the barn door, unlatch it, and feed the horses. The barn's dim interior always smelled of hay and cake cubes and cottonseed meal and leather. They kept their saddles sitting on racks inside the barn. Wade's had high swells, a deep, comfortable seat and fenders rubbed shiny black from hundreds of hours of use. Their chaps, always draped across the pommels, were torn and scratched from cactus and catclaw thorn as were their saddles' tapaderos. Roy rode an old, smooth-pommeled roping saddle. Their ropes were neatly coiled and hung from thin leather saddle horn straps. Boot-top leather pouches that once held brown jars of chloroform and cotton, and later EQ335 and Koral, were still tied behind their cantles. The government's screwworm eradication program would eventually render them useless. Wade and Roy said it and the PCA were the only good things the government ever did for the rancher. Because of the eradication program, they were able to get by with one hired hand and some occasional help for shipping and branding.

Shortly after the screwworm disappeared, Roy figured out a way to eliminate the need to gather and spray their cattle for horn flies and ticks during the summers—a hot, dusty, time-consuming operation that had to be done, else those seemingly harmless insects would gradually pull a yearling's weight down and cut into slim profits.

He got his idea from an advertisement in *The Cattleman* magazine. Rather than buy one of the contraptions though, he sewed himself a canvas tube, stuffed it with old rags, and saturated the tube with his own mixture of kerosene and tick poison. Then he had me set two long crossties deep near a mountain watering. Post-hole diggers were useless in the mountains, and it took me the better part of a morning to dig two holes. I chiseled away at solid rock with a crowbar and cleaned chippings from the hole with a half-pound coffee can. When we got the ties tamped, Roy strung the tube between them and spent an afternoon watching the cattle scratch their backs, adjusting the tube's slope so calves as well as bulls could get beneath it and work the poison into the hair along their backs. The idea worked, and they bought a tube for each watering. This, coupled with the elimination of the screwworm, enabled them to operate the ranch with the one hand until Wade's death.

Before the days of Roy's back scratcher and the pesticide bans, they sprayed their cattle with DDT to kill horn flies. One of my jobs was to load the sprayer off sawhorses onto the pickup bed and mix the DDT. I would back the pickup up to the heavy sprayer, get a bite with a crowbar between the truck bed and the sprayer's runners, and inch it forward until it was on the bed. Then I dumped in the DDT, poured a few buckets of water over it to get it dissolving, and filled the sprayer's tank. Finally I'd hook up with the horse trailer. We'd saddle and load the horses and go gather a pasture. When we had them penned, I would unhook from the trailer, back the truck up alongside the fence, help crowd the cattle into a small pen, and begin spraying. It was a hot, dirty, dusty job. Whoever sprayed walked among the cattle to make sure they were drenched with the DDT. Usually your chaps and Levis would be covered with manure and mud and dirt, and you'd smell like DDT. When you finished, you handed the hose through the fence to someone who wound it back onto the sprayer while the other person turned the cattle loose. Then you caught your horses, gathered another pasture, and repeated the process. Three weeks later you started again.

After my first day at the ranch, I'd sit with them awhile on the porch in the evening, then go downstairs and fall into bed. Even though I played football, I always got tired and sore the first few days I was there. Wade and Roy had worked hard all their lives and could put in days that wore out so-called athletes like myself.

They both stood about five eleven and carried around a hundred fifty pounds of lean, hard, knotty muscle—not the showcase weight lifter's muscle but the kind that just kept going—day in, day out. Wade never drank or smoked. Roy did and puffed at least two packs of ready-rolls—as he called them—a day for as long as I knew him. They never seemed to bother him. Both ate beef everyday for lunch and slept soundly.

Roy and I bunked in the two bedrooms downstairs where the old basement had been—me in the west room and he in the east. In the evenings he would come downstairs after the ten o'clock news and walk out aways from the house and pee, looking at the stars or watching a thunderhead blink in the distance. He'd return to his room, muttering how they "could use a little rain" while he undressed. Then he'd walk over to his small dresser where he kept his cigarettes and lighter and pocket watch and some arrowheads and buttons, empty his pockets, take out his false teeth, and go to bed. I never heard him toss or turn at night.

Roy began each day the same way, too. He'd rise before daylight and sit on the edge of the bed, talking to himself a minute and running his hand through what was left of his hair. Then he'd slip on his Levis, boots, and a fresh long-sleeved khaki shirt; stuffing a fresh pack of ready-rolls in the left pocket of his shirt. Finally, he'd put in his false teeth. After he got his teeth in, he'd leave the room and I'd hear the metal yard gate squeak open. He'd walk out aways from the house in the early morning darkness, pee, then clomp upstairs to make coffee—a ritual I never figured out. He used one of those old-timey tablespoons with the handle broken off. Two heaping spoonfuls and then about a half a spoonful and, as an afterthought, a third of a spoonful—then another afterthought and another fourth of a spoonful. That was it. I never could figure out why he just didn't put in three heaping spoonfuls, but that was the way he made coffee. Forever. Then he sat the coffeepot over a back burner on their butane stove, walked out to his old radio and high-back chair—arm elbows worn and thin—where he would sit down, light a morning smoke, and lean towards the radio, tuning it to pick up Bob Walsh's WBAP early morning livestock report out of Fort Worth. It always came in clear before sunup, but faded as the sun rose and the air heated and scrambled molecules. Eventually the static would fade Walsh out, and Roy would try to pick up the Pecos station for a little more news. When he got Pecos, he'd get up and walk back to the kitchen, observe his perking coffee a couple of minutes, reach back and lift the pot clear of the fire so the grounds could settle, then pour himself a cup.

Roy usually woke me up when he clomped upstairs. I'd dress, ease upstairs, sneak me a half teaspoon of sugar in my cup, and pour me some coffee. Then I'd go sit on the front porch and watch the sun come up, listening to the sound of a desert morning. I think those were the most peaceful moments of my life—on that front porch sipping coffee, listening to quail or an occasional coyote bark south of the house, watching first light creep across the desert brush, watching the cottontails still nibbling at green yard grass.

Sometimes the roadrunner that nested around the house would perch on the rock fence that surrounded the yard, watching for a lizard or snake. Usually an old cow would bellow in the flats; maybe a calf or bull would answer. Desert mornings are beautiful, and I count myself lucky to have observed them from time to time, quietly and by myself, uninterrupted, unfettered and unfiltered through camera or projector lens.

Wade, meanwhile, would have arisen, walked to the bathroom, shaved, and begun dressing. Every so often, Wade gave himself a shot in the morning. He was anemic and his body was without much digestive acid. He also took two or three drops of a special acid with water before each meal so his body could digest its food. Wade would come walking into the kitchen with a little tray on which sat his needles and medicine. He would take the alcohol and cotton swab his arm, stick the needle in, hook his syringe to the needle, give himself a shot, put his medicine up, and start breakfast.

Now we always ate the same thing for breakfast. In truth, there were times when I'd given anything for a mess of hot-cakes and sausage, but their breakfast was set and it never varied. You got two pieces of toast with two little pats of butter on each, a piece of bacon, one or two eggs, a small glass of orange juice and a bowl of oatmeal. If you could find some jelly around, you were welcome to it, but they never ate it. Roy also cooked the oats. Sometimes they were done and sometimes they weren't. It all depended. When they were half-done you just chewed them like a horse. Roy always put a lot of cream and sugar on his. It always fascinated me. He'd sprinkle three or four heaping spoonfuls of sugar on his small bowl of oats, cover it with half-and-half cream, and sit down and eat every bite. Neither he nor Wade ever gained an ounce in the thirty years or so I knew them. I was always having to fight my weight. I never did understand how they could eat like they did and not gain anything. I guess they'd worked so hard so long that no matter what they ate, they always burned it up during the day.

After breakfast, we'd walk down to the barn. If the horses were in the corral, we'd shut the gate and saddle up. If they weren't, I'd leave the house on foot, hunt them up in the little trap west of the house, and bring them in. They kept a few head to work from. Roy rode a tall black horse with stocking feet he called Bobby Socks; Wade rode the bay, Highball; and I rode a paint mare called Prissy that always threw a paint colt. She was from a mare called Maxine. She had a smooth gait and was powerful and good to ride.

They also had a horse called Mac that Wade brought in for me to ride when he thought I was old enough. Mac was broke, but would booger out from under you if you weren't careful, or if he caught you deadheading along. Truth is, I was worried the first morning I crawled on him. I was young and had no intention of being a bronc rider. Wade said, "Now this old horse hasn't been ridden in several years, and it's always best if you talk to 'em. Helps calm 'em down when they haven't been ridden." I spent the rest of the day talking to that horse before I finally figured out why Wade was chuckling to himself.

During the late Forties and early Fifties, Wade and Roy kept their two- and three-year-old horses in the trap east of the house. When everyone was saddled, we headed for the trap to gather and pen the horses right after breakfast. It got the colts used to penning so they wouldn't run through fences if riders suddenly appeared and crowded them.

Normally, the penning took us an hour or so; and it was great sport riding fast and hard, heading them for the corrals. Once penned, everyone turned their lathered horses loose, caught a fresh mount from the gather, and began the day's ride.

This routine was a carry-over from the Depression when they'd raised horses for the cavalry's remount stations. The cavalry furnished them with studs for their mares; usually big, solid-colored thoroughbred horses around seventeen hands. Bloodlines from these cavalry mounts were still evident in their horses. I always pictured Wade and the Army rep sitting atop the corral fence, culling the bog spavins and pigeon-toed.

Before they bought a horse trailer, we would leave the house every morning horseback for either the mountains or the flats. The thing I remembered about those rides was not so much the distance, but how thirsty I got. I never could get used to going without water and by midday, I'd be dry. We'd get to a windmill somewhere and I'd pray there would be enough wind to turn it so I could get a drink. If there wasn't any wind, I'd crawl off, go over and blow the moss off the top of the windmill tub, look for a fairly clear spot, stick my head in and drink. Sometimes I'd drink out of a cow track at dirt tanks. It's a wonder I didn't die of dysentery or stomach leeches or amoebas or something, but I didn't. Wade and Roy never stopped for water.

If we rode the mountains, we'd head west past the old stage stop and Barrilla Spring, through Jeff Ranch country, and back up the west side of Barrilla Canyon, on up past the Barrilla storage tank and Wood Canyon. One of us would drop down by the Old Lake and we'd come together at the Fonville, split, and one would work Rincon while the other rode the Camp Tub and Tub-On-Top. Later years we trailered around to the Fonville, Wade riding the clutch. He always drove when the three of us rode together. I could smell the clutch burning and would wait for Wade to take his foot off, but he never did. No one said anything. I always rode in the middle. We'd finally lurch out on top and unload Roy and Bobby Socks. Roy only rode Bobby with a tiny bit and single-strand rawhide bridle he'd made himself "special" for his horse. He'd mount and swing up towards Barrilla while Wade and I drove to the Fonville corrals where he'd stop. We'd pull our chaps out of the pickup bed, buckle them on, back our horses out, step aboard, and ride all the country north of the bluffs while Roy circled above us up through Wood Canyon. Any wormies we found we brought with us and penned and doctored them at the

Fonville. When we finished, we'd split up again. Roy would head for Rincon and Wade and I would head for the Camp Tub and Tub-On-Top. Any wormies on top we penned and doctored at the Tub-On-Top corrals, then we'd ride back into the Fonville, load the horses, and go eat.

It always fascinated me how Wade and Roy knew each cow they owned, where she grazed, and where she was apt to be found, even though they had no fences in their mountain pastures save those separating their land from the next ranch. Different cows kept to different parts of those mountains, calved in particular areas, and lived out their productive lives near certain waterings unless rains filled water holes or ran canyon creeks. They knew about where to find each cow, about where she would calve—and when—and how she would hide her calf. Before the screwworm eradication program, you had to find a baby calf the day after it was born or run the risk of losing it. Worms would eat its stomach out in three, four days. Roy would ride up on an old cow and could tell whether or not she'd just calved by the blood on her rear, and the way her bag looked. We would stop. The old cow would trot off a little ways to try and fool us. Roy would put his hand to his mouth and bleat like a baby calf. The old cow would turn and jog in the direction of the calf. Roy would get a little closer to the calf and the old cow would move closer and soon he would point to the tiny calf lying in the high grass or weeds. He would step off, take the worm medicine from the old boot top behind his saddle, walk to the calf and smear its navel with worm medicine. Then we would pen the mother, smear her rear end and hind legs with worm medicine, and let her go back to the calf.

Sometimes it was hard to find calves in the mountains. The country was rough and an old cow could hide one where you just couldn't find it. Other times you could smell a case of screwworms before you found it in heavy brush.

From a distance, Wade and Roy could tell by the way an animal acted whether or not it had worms. They'd stare at a

214

cluster of cattle a half mile across a deep canyon, then turn their horses in their direction and say, "That ol' yaller heifer's got worms." And when we'd get there, the yellow heifer would have worms. Occasionally we would find an old cow in the mountain pasture with a baby calf hanging partially out. When we did, we eased the cow into the nearest corral and, using one rope, would tie her horns to a fence post. Then Roy would walk his horse inside the corral and gently loop the calf, take a twist around the saddle horn, sit back in the saddle and slowly back his horse up until the calf came. Usually it sucked the cow's uterus out. To help cows that did this, Roy saved small half-pint whiskey bottles. He'd place the whiskey bottle inside the cow's uterus and push everything back inside, then take a couple stitches using a thin strand of rawhide and a tow sack needle. The bottle kept her womb from growing together and the rawhide kept the bottle in. We'd feed the cow and calf in the corral and watch them both for worms while she recovered. The rawhide simply rotted away and, if the cow didn't pass the whiskey bottle, we would remove it. All the cows we fixed like this healed fine and had another calf.

Roy's temper was legendary. Sometimes he would get mad and kick an old bull or cow. One day we were in a pen full of cattle trying to work some of them into a chute to "tick 'em." We were both hot, tired, and dirty.

Roy was pushing and shoving cattle into the chute. An old cow wouldn't get out of the way so he kicked her. The cow took a step, raised a hind leg and popped him right back on the thigh. He limped around and whined and cussed the cow for five minutes.

Roy made his own tick medicine, too. I think it was a combination of EQ335—a potent worm medicine—kerosene, oil, and something else. He claimed the kerosene and oil kept the medicine from washing out of the ears too soon. We used one of those big, long-spouted railroad oilcans with the handgrip and thumb pump to squirt the ears. You could walk down

215

the side of a chute and squirt every ear in it in a minute. One person would work the inside, then hand the squirter to the outside man. It was always my job to crawl the fence and work the outside. I would jog down a chute full of cattle, squirting tick medicine. When I finished, they would turn them out and fill the chute again. We could tick a lot of cattle fast like this.

I always got a kick out of being around Roy when we rode. If we were having trouble penning an old cow or yearling, he'd just unlimber his rope and take in after it. I, of course, would unlimber mine, one of which I'd bought in Mexico. When I dabbed it on an old cow one day, it popped like a piece of string. Roy chuckled about "me and my Mexico rope" the rest of the day.

One morning we were having trouble with a yearling that had crawled a fence. It kept running and cutting back at the pasture gate. Finally Roy shook his rope loose, wheeled his horse after the yearling, made a short run down the road, caught it around the neck and foreleg, and was dragging it back towards the gate before I had time to make a loop. He pulled the yearling through the gate. I got off, shut the gate, and jerked his rope off the steer. Roy was almost seventy at the time.

Roy could tell time by the sun, and taught me. Often we'd be riding along and he'd look at the sky and say, "Now, what time do you think it is?" And I'd squint and say, "Well, I think it's about ten thirty." And he'd say, "No, it's eleven forty-five," usually about an hour's difference from what I'd guessed. He'd pull out his old pocket watch and be maybe a minute or two off. He didn't live by time, but rather by the sun and seasons. I finally got to where I could tell time by the sun.

Roy showed me a pair of peregrine falcons hunting east of the ranch house one morning. They nested somewhere inaccessible in the big bluffs behind the house. He called them black hawks, the "kind that killed his dove 'n quail." To my knowledge, neither he nor Wade ever shot a quail or dove or hawk, though. Some days we would be riding and he would see a peregrine hunting or hear the cry, and he would rein up and say, "Now watch that old black hawk up there. In a minute it'll find something." And sure enough we would watch it make its dive, sometimes hitting its prey in a flurry of feathers. It would come away with a quail or dove or something and Roy would say, "Now that's why I don't like them old black hawks. They're always eating the quail."

Another morning Roy and I were easing along horseback through the Northside. We were heading for the English to look for some cattle when Roy pulled up, stepped off, picked up something, got back on his horse, examined it for a minute, then handed it to me. It was a beautiful arrowhead with agate in it. I gave it back to him. He stuck it in his shirt pocket, lit a cigarette, looked out over the burns and explained how a long time ago the place had been an Apache camp, and "that's why no grass grew there." I imagined the hogans, could hear the dogs bark and see a sentinel on the mesa, could hear the young boys laughing as they fought mock battles. Near us, also, was where the Plains Indians passed on their pillages into northern Mexico during the Comanche moon.

He showed me the Indian burns—round mounds ringed with burnt rock rising from the desert floor—on the North side flats. He explained this was where they fired their flint to make their arrowheads. There were flint chips and arrowheads everywhere. Some of the arrowheads in the Sul Ross collection came from Wade's and Roy's ranch.

Sometimes on Sunday, if I was caught up, I would either ride a horse or drive my old pickup down to the camp and spend hours poking around the burns, picking up flint awls, spearheads, and arrowheads. I found many, most of which I either lost or traded save for one tiny, deep-red bird head smaller than my thumbnail. It was so small I couldn't see how an Indian could have made it, but the chip marks were there. Later years, I found it with some stuff my grand-mother had saved for me. I started to put it back, but decided instead to take it to a jeweler and see if he could make a tie tack out of it, which he did. I took it home fully intending to use it, but for some reason, I never wore it. I keep it instead in one of those cuff link boxes men have tucked around wherever they live—keep dragging it out to look at it every year or so, to admire again its craftsmanship and size.

Fun faded quickly, though, and summers got hard fast—doctoring screwworms and pinkeye, spraying cattle, shoeing horses, checking water, digging postholes, repairing water gaps, fixing flats or windmills or corrals, and making sure none of the cattle had crawled a fence. If any of these things went wrong or got ahead of you, you had to work twice as hard to catch up. Cattle don't last long without water. Baby calves don't live long with a belly full of screwworms. You can't work a horse hard in the mountains without shoes. The cattle that crawled fences had to be found, checked for worms, and brought back. Every animal on Wade's and Roy's was important and represented potential income. There were no oil wells or lucrative mineral leases in the Davis Mountains. You either lived off—and paid your bills from—what your ranch produced or went broke. That simple.

This was one of the reasons we hoed cockleburs in an arroyo on the north side of their mountains. When the country got dry, cockleburs stayed green and cattle ate them. When they did, they died. So each summer when the cockleburs were big and green, we took our hoes up there and spent the day chopping them. It was a hot, thankless job.

One summer evening we were on our way in after chopping burrs all day and saw what we thought was dust in the evening twilight. But as it got darker, we saw the glow in the pasture. Lightning had struck dry grass in the tabosa flats east of the house during an afternoon thundershower.

We got to the house, loaded the pickup with tow sacks, an old barn broom or two, and a couple of barrels of water, then drove down and started fighting the fire. Two hands from neighboring ranches had seen the glow and ridden over to help us. We got it out before it got away.

When we returned from long morning rides and unsaddled, the horses would find a soft spot in the corrals and roll the white sweat stains off their backs. By the time they finished, I'd have a gallon coffee can full of dry cake scattered in their tin feed trough beneath the barn's overhang. If any yearlings were being fed at the house corrals, I'd scoop a sackful of cottonseed meal and cotton hulls and blackstrap molasses for them. It was a good, cheap feed before the hulls and molasses went up. I'd sling a tow sackful of the concoction over my shoulder, make my way up to the pen, and dump it out for them. Sometimes when Wade and Roy had fifteen or twenty yearlings at the house, I'd spend a half day on Sunday mixing a week's worth of the feed with a scoop on the barn floor. Coons loved the blackstrap molasses.

One afternoon Melly and I loaded up our fencing tools and drove into the Southside flats to build fence. You always dead manned the big corner post first, which meant digging a deep hole big enough to roll a huge boulder into to anchor the fence. It usually took both of us to roll the rock over the side. Then we'd wrap it a couple times with barbed wire, loop the wire around our anchor post a couple times, then back around the rock again, put a stick between the strands, and twist the slack out. We then filled and tromped the rock hole solid, twisted the anchor wires guitar tight, and started building fence; working on until late evening when the sun started down.

I measured those afternoons by the number of postholes I dug, usually no easy task. If you made two dozen a morning in the mountains, you were lucky. One afternoon—about three or four days after a decent rain—Melly and I hit a barren stretch on the Indian flats between the North- and Southside pastures. My diggers sunk to their head first rattle. Four punches and I had a hole. Something compelled me to see how many postholes I could dig and how far I could get ahead of Melly, who was tamping behind me. Sweating, I dug at the earth like a madman, jogging forward to the next spot. Finally I looked back down the row of mounds. Melly was just a speck.

Another afternoon I was patching the house corrals. It must have been a hundred ten that day. I picked up a burlap-wrapped water jug sitting in the shade of a corral post, took a deep swig, wiped my forehead, and surveyed my work. An old cow had splintered the fence early that morning while we crowded her onto a cattle truck headed for the auction barns in San Angelo. I set the jug down and headed for the tool shed to let Roy know I'd finished. He was making a metal gate out of discarded windmill pipe and chicken wire at the time, an intense project he fervently pursued each afternoon following his nap.

I heard him rummaging inside the shed, talking to himself while he searched for some primitive instrument. Moments later he stumbled into the hot Texas afternoon carrying a battered tin toolbox, knocking a fresh mud-dauber's nest off the door facing as he went. I squatted against a fence post and watched him scoot the pipe into position along the rock ground, knowing he wouldn't like it if I offered to help. Our conversation, as best as I can recall, went something like this:

"You git that fence fixed?"

"Yeah."

He began to bore a hole in the pipe using a hand drill and a dull metal bit I'd tried to get him to throw away. He swore the bit was good for several more years. I knew it would slip in a minute and he'd rap his knuckles on the edge of the pipe. I closed my eyes to keep the sweat out as it trickled down my forehead and heard the bit hit the ground. It was followed by a string of salty epitaphs. I figured Roy would either throw the bit or grab a rock and hit it.

He threw it. "I hope that sonofabitchin' bit rusts all to hell."

He surveyed his damaged hand, and I saw his knuckles were bleeding. I wiped the sweat from my eyes and got up to look for the bit.

It was lying among a pile of sun-purpled bottles in the bottom of the little arroyo below the house. When I returned, he had his hand wrapped with a dirty, kerosene-soaked rag and was working on the pipe again. He doctored all his scrapes and cuts with kerosene. I dropped the bit in the toolbox and squatted against my post.

"Damn, ain't it a hotun," he said to no one in particular. Pausing, he fished a cigarette out of his shirt, then tried to get his swollen hand inside the right front pocket of his Levis.

"Man's in a helluva fix when he can't even get his damn hand in his pocket..."

I pitched him my lighter. He lit his cigarette, tossed the lighter back, and sat down where he'd been working, smoking in silence. His face looked unusually red.

"You know," he finally said, "Man oughtn't have to work this hard when he gets to be seventy years old. If a man had any sense he'd get him an education and decent job somewheres, by God, where he wouldn't have to work like a shittin' idiot all his life."

He puffed on his cigarette. I knew he'd smoke it down to a nub. He never wasted anything—even tobacco—and he never threw anything away if he could find a use for it. The windmill pipe he was using to build the gate was at least thirty years old. I watched him smoke the cigarette down. He finally flipped the curling ashes off, studied the butt for a moment, then dropped it.

"Whew. Damn, ain't it a hotun?" he said, pushing himself slowly to his feet. He reached inside the toolbox for the bit.

Roy was as independent an individual as any I've known and seemed born to the cattle business. He kept his needs simple—a dry bed, something to eat, a dependable horse, enough rain to bring the grass, a decent shipment of calves in the Fall, his health so he could work, fresh air, the seasons. These things I know were a part of him—of them both, really—even though he never mentioned them.

I think Roy was gifted mechanically, too, and in doing things with his hands, even though he never had any formal training. He could braid eight, twelve, sixteen rawhide strands into beautiful quirts or hackamores, but only did it when he needed one. He carried a quirt on his saddle for years, but I seldom saw him use it. He also cut his own bridles from rawhide.

During earlier days he'd been known to ease into town and bend an elbow at a bar or two. One year they said he left to go to Balmorhea to get a barrel of motor oil for the ranch. A couple days later he and Bill Addison drove down the dirt road in front of the house in the jitney and stopped at the corral gate. Roy got out and opened the wooden gate. Bill Addison drove the old jitney through. Roy shut the gate behind him, set an empty whiskey bottle right in the middle of the road, climbed back in the jitney, and stayed gone for a couple more days. He seldom drank during his latter years, though.

Neither he nor Wade ever bought anything if they could make do. I think worm medicine, feed, DDT, groceries, and gas were about all they ever bought regularly. They drove their vehicles for years because Roy kept them running. He could take a pickup engine completely apart. I mean tear it down. Then he'd rebuild it, replacing worn parts as he went. He also kept an old pump motor going a couple miles east of the house. It pumped a one-inch pipe of water two miles back up to the small tin storage tank behind the ranch house. They'd laid the line from their east side well when the Miller spring at the house dried up.

Roy and I were driving to Headwater one morning in the pickup. As we crossed a rough arroyo, the transmission fell out. I walked the five miles back to the house, got his old car and tools, drove back to the canyon, picked him up and drove him into Alpine where he bought a new transmission. We loaded it in the trunk, drove back to Lockhausen Canyon, and changed that transmission before dark right there in the bottom of the arroyo.

Rain was crucial to Wade's and Roy's operation—something special—and if ever there was a genuine awe of nature by two men who lived by its confines, it was to watch them watch a good rain creeping across their country. Sometimes they would crawl into the pickup and drive to a hill or mesa where they could sit and watch a cloud as it began to form. The thunderheads always started in the northwest each morning. Some mornings when we left the house horseback, the sky would be so absolutely blue and clear you'd swear it would be a year before it rained. But about midmorning a little cloud about the size of a half-dollar would form in the northwest sky, then another and another and about midafternoon they would begin to come together and the thunderheads would form, generally moving east. You could hear the rain falling as it moved toward you across mesas and valleys, the big drops splattering on volcanic rock. Hard rains made a rushing sound; hail roared. Sometimes hail would creep across a section of the mountains and leave them winter-brown, stripping even the toughest mesquite of its branches and leaves. If they were horseback or in their pickup and saw a full arroyo, they would turn and go to its source to see if it had rained in their country. If it had, they would try to locate an unbroken rain gage on a fence post somewhere to find out how much. Rain was truly a thing of beauty to them. It never rained too hard or too much. They took it as it fell in any form, regardless.

They might cuss a washed out road or fence that flash-flood debris had swept away, but never the rain or its source.

Sometimes an afternoon thundershower would creep over the big mesa and down across the house and corrals, misting the inside of their screened porch where Roy napped on the old recliner. When it did, he would raise up, look, and mutter, "Ho boy, what a rain. Look athere." Then he would slip on his boots, walk to the back door of the house, and look out trying to see where all it was raining and the size of the cloud. Rain was their lifeline; their lifeblood. It was the thing that kept them and the ranch going. It grew grass. They had seen droughts and Depressions and ranchers selling out.

Rain was the key for anyone who depended on livestock for their profits in the Davis Mountains. It dominated their conversations when they got together—that and the price of cattle and feed. Most people cannot comprehend being so dependent on nature for your livelihood or having the kind of faith they did in the country during droughts and Depressions, much less being tough enough to withstand those years and still have the optimism to anticipate the good ones. People just aren't made that way anymore.

Rain was a time for new hope. It made the country smell new and clean, especially of an evening with a breeze blowing across the desert, carrying with it the lingering ozone from the lightning and the fragrance of catclaw and white brush, mingled with the smell of creosote. I tried many times describing it to my friends after I left the country. They usually laughed or stared at me. I finally stopped trying.

Early one summer morning after a hard shower had soaked the country the night before, I rose and dressed and stepped outside to look around, only to find clouds hanging below the bluffs in back of the house. I stood, feeling the wind and mist blowing against my face and realized suddenly I was chilly. It was the middle of summer and supposed to be hot. I returned and searched a storage chest until I found an old, tattered leather brush jacket. I noticed as we loaded our tools in the back of their old pickup, Wade and Roy were wearing jackets, too. We kept them on until mid-morning. It was unusual, especially when temperatures normally hit a hundred ten each day. Desert mountains are like that.

When the rains didn't come, summers got long and hot. I think the Fifties drought when their Headwater spring almost went dry was the worst while I was there. That's when they decided to drill a well rather than run the risk of the spring drying up and having two-thirds of their cattle out of water.

They started asking around and found there was a maverick driller named Pete who would take his rig anywhere he could put two wheels. We brought him to the ranch, snaked our way up Lockhausen Canyon, and showed him the Headwater spring. He nodded at a pretty good drill site, then showed us where the road would have to be widened, which arroyos would have to be filled in, and which corners were too sharp for his rig.

We worked steady and hard at the road for several days with crowbars and sledgehammers, carving enough space for him to maneuver. He finally worked his rig onto the dry creek bank opposite a high bluff, dropped his stabilizers, cabled up his mast, and began drilling that afternoon. Wade and Roy were impressed. When he drilled on into the night, they knew he was aware of the urgency. Each day when we made our way up to check on his progress, he would be sitting on an inverted ten-gallon can, smoking, his good fingers resting gently on the cable, net judging his drill's performance.

Pete was six feet and lean, said his wife had left him, and that he'd worked at several things throughout his life, not the least of which was making a commercial film or two. He told me he liked the country and its challenge, that he got a kick out of taking his rig where other drillers wouldn't go.

226

He said he was his own boss and relied on his own judgement and ingenuity to get the job done. At nights he tied a small tarp to the side of his drilling rig, propped up the other two corners with head-high sticks, sat a dirty cot up beneath, and went to sleep. Nearby, he had a small cookfire on which he kept a pot of strong coffee when he wasn't warming his beans.

The spot he'd chosen was about a hundred yards below the rugged Headwater spring. He drilled down about ten feet and hit solid rock, then spent the next few days chipping at the rock. Wade and Roy thought of moving him, but he said that rock couldn't go on forever. When he finally broke through, he hit an underground stream at about sixty-five feet. Wade and Roy stood spellbound, watching him bale water from his hole without making a dent in its level. I don't think there was anything either of them would have rather seen than the brimmed-filled dipper coming out of that hole. Pete was grinning, too.

He broke his rig down, followed us out of the canyon, and set up over the old Miller spring at the house.

While Pete was drilling at the house, Roy and I returned the following day to the canyon and dropped ten feet of well casing onto the solid rock. Wade checked the Headwater spring storage tank. He returned, stating it was dry except for a small trickle running into the bottom of the tank and directly into the line. Time became important. We lowered the pipe and sucker rod into the well, built a rock and cement platform for a new two-horse Briggs and Stratton, tied a pump and pulley wheel to the sucker rod, and fired the motor. A steady pipeful of water poured onto the ground. All we had to do was tie into the main line forty feet away.

I used the pick to work a hole around the main pipe, then started picking the pipeline bed toward the well while Wade and Roy cut and threaded the pipe for the tee. It was slow, hard work. There was no air in the bottom of the canyon, and I shed my shirt—already dark with sweat—as I dug.

Finally I reached the well. We tied into its pipe, laid a string out to the main line, coupled onto a checkvalve, tightened them all down, kicked in the motor, and found the main-line pressure kept the well's checkvalve closed, meaning we would have to run a pipe from the well up to the Headwater storage tank. And we would have to hurry because we had downline troughs going dry.

We returned early the next morning with a quartermile of pipe strapped to their old Chevy pickup, which we quickly laid to the storage tank after tying into the well. I jogged back down to the well, kicked the Briggs and Stratton in, and jogged back up to the storage tank. A steady stream of water throbbed from the pipe into the storage tank. They had water for the summer.

Pete was still dry at six hundred feet at the old Miller spring, and Wade shut him down. He collected his check, shook hands, and waved as he headed west over the dirt road through the flats. I never saw him again.

Air vents downline from Headwater were something that would have escaped the casual observer. They sprouted from among the rocks and mesquite every quarter mile or so. When dry weather hit and the spring weakened, air would get into the main line with the water through the bottom of the storage tank until it blocked water flow downstream, drying troughs. The only way to get water moving through the line again was to uncap an air vent. So we'd tie a small, rusted pipe wrench on our saddles when we rode the mountains. When we came to a vent between a dry and a full trough, we uncapped it. The vent would cough and gurgle and hiss like an oilfield gusher, finally shooting rusty water thirty or forty feet into the air. I was riding a boogery horse the first time I uncapped one, and had left him tied nearby to a bush. It took me a half day to find him.

Their big storage tank in the Barrilla Mountains held several thousand gallons, watered the eastern portion of their mountains, and would last several days if pressure couldn't get water to Barrilla or if the line washed out. They'd built a set of corrals around the Barrilla trough as well as other waterings throughout the mountains. Cattle got used to the corrals and weren't hard to pen when we gathered.

At Headwater they kept an old tin cup tied to the storage tank with bailing wire. If the tank was full when you rode up, you could dip yourself a drink. I always prayed for it to be full because I would be thirsty by the time we got there. Mostly, though, it stayed empty during dry years before Pete drilled the well; the water trickling in from the spring and out the bottom, sucking air into the main line.

There were a couple of pear trees at Headwater, too. I don't know who planted them, but near the end of each summer we would drive to the trees on a Sunday afternoon. Once there, it was my job to climb them and shake out what pears the coons hadn't eaten. These we took home for pear jelly. Remnants of an old chuck box sat among the rocks near the spring.

When dry weather forced Wade and Roy to cut back, they shipped their older cattle, along with any wild ones they could pick up during the gather. They had one wild cow that ran in the high country above Lockhausen. Her mother had been wild, too, they said; and it had taken them all day just to find her when she was born.

We spotted her one afternoon while putting out salt and saw she had a case of worms. The next morning we left the house about daybreak and circled into the mountains to doctor her, hoping we'd have time to check other cattle when we finished. We found her and got her started towards the corrals in Lockhausen Trap. We'd opened both the corral and trap gates when we left, knowing if we could get her inside the trap we could probably haze her into the corrals before she jumped a fence. Everyone had their ropes loose and loops shook out in case she made a break. Somehow we managed to get her inside the corral. Once inside no one dismounted because she was looking for something to hook. We forced her into the chute, slammed the gate, and slipped a fence post behind her. She had a bad case of worms. As we finished doctoring her, she began kicking and lunging against the old chute boards. Finally she splintered one side of the chute, came out over the top, and hit the middle of the corral, looking for trouble.

Roy happened to be standing in the corral with a bottle of worm medicine in his hand. He saw her coming and made a move for the fence—fast even for a man of seventy. He pulled himself up a couple of boards as the old cow slid to a halt beneath him, hooking at his legs. She was connecting about every other swipe, and I could hear her horns thwacking against his chaps. He started stomping her between the eyes with his bootheel, giving her a good cussing. Finally the cow shook her head, trotted around the corral looking for something else to charge, and spotted a low spot in the top of the old wooden fence. She circled the pen again, built up a head of steam, crashed over and through the low spot, and headed into the brush.

Roy stepped off the fence, picked up the lid of his screwworm jar, wiped it on his chaps, capped his jar, glanced once more in the wild cow's direction, and muttered, "Don't give a damn where you run to, you sonofabitch, 'long as you're around for shippin' time this Fall."

29

I always looked forward to Saturdays and a trip to town with Roy during my younger days. After breakfast, Roy would go back downstairs, shower, shave, slip on a clean shirt, his town trousers, some socks, and his good boots. Then he'd put a fresh pack of cigarettes in his pocket, take his town Stetson from its place in the closet, and clomp down to his 1940-something black two-door Plymouth that sat in the shed with a week's worth of dust on it and in it. He would slip into the front seat and back it out and up to their big gas tank that sat on a high metal frame near the cotton-wood. I would drop the hose from its perch, fill the car, and check the oil. It always needed oil; so, I would go down to his tool shed and pump a Folger's canful from their oil barrel, return, and pour it in. You just estimated about what a quart was, and you greased everything with a hand pump about once every other month if you remembered it. When we were ready, I would plop into the front seat with Roy; and we would head for town.

The ride to town was an adventure. I don't think either of them ever learned to drive a standard shift vehicle. They always left a boot on the clutch and seldom shifted gears on dirt roads until the engine got to whining good and loud. Once, when Roy and I were headed for town, he drove the eleven miles of dirt road in second gear—from a standing start. I made a silent bet he would drive all the way to Fort Davis in second, but he shifted into third when he hit the blacktop.

My father told me Wade and Roy had an old Model-T Ford during the early years. He said they were in this old jitney one morning, headed for the Fort Davis Mercantile for a load of salt. They'd just made it to the top of one of those hills in Limpia Canyon and started down the other side, gathering speed as they went, dust boiling up behind them. At the bottom of the hill the road crossed Limpia

Creek again. A carload of ladies was stuck in the muddy crossing. Roy saw them and reached to pull back on the hand brake—all the old jitneys had tire-type hand brakes—and nothing happened. He didn't have any brakes. Period. But he never said a word. He just kept both hands on the wheel, and my dad said the jitney just kept gaining speed down that hill. Wade was sitting by the door about to push his boots through the floorboard. Roy steered to the right of the car—by now the women had seen them coming and scattered—and hit the mud puddle so fast it didn't even slow the jitney down; spraying the ladies with mud. Roy roared on out the other side in the Model-T. When he finally got it slowed down, my dad said Roy muttered, "I believe there's somethin' wrong with the brakes on this thing." Wade said, "I was wonderin' when you'd find that out."

The reason Roy liked to go to town on Saturdays during the Fifties was that Alpine had a semipro baseball team—coached by Tom Chandler, who later coached at Texas A&M for several years—complete with a new ball park. They were called, originally enough, the Alpine Cowboys and had players named Cash and McDonald who would later make it in the majors. The park was beautiful, complete with a high, all-rock outfield fence and good, comfortable wood seats.

Roy had played a little baseball somewhere in the Panhandle around the turn of the century and was a great fan of the game. He always bought a season ticket. I only bought one when I went to the game with him. We always sat together. I mostly looked at the pretty college girls who came to watch the players while Roy studied the program and concentrated on the game and the plays. When the game was over, he would usually drop me off at a friend's and head for the American Legion Hall where he would have two or three beers.

Finished, he would crawl in his old Plymouth, pick me up, and we'd head back to the ranch. He had no air conditioner.

Usually we rode with the windows down. The night air was always good and clean and if it had rained, chilly. During the early years, high creek water sometimes held us up at the Limpia crossings. If it had rained hard that afternoon or evening near the observatory, the creek might be full, even though the road up to its edge would be bone-dry. Roy would stop and we'd sit there—judging the brown water boiling in front of us; knowing we had to cross it to get home; knowing if we drowned out in either crossing, we'd have to walk in. It wasn't that I minded the walking, but without a moon it was difficult to see where you were stepping; and rattlers were always out in the evenings when it was cool, especially after a rain.

Anyhow, if he thought he could make it, he would drive up the edge of the creek, ease his old Plymouth into low, and drop off into the muddy water. Sometimes I could feel the car slipping and moving with the powerful current. Sometimes water rushed across the floorboard of the car. I would lift my feet. Roy would be standing on the accelerator, gunning the motor. If we were lucky, we lurched our way through, slipping and spinning up the other side and out onto the dirt road beyond and on toward the Jeff.

Sometimes we'd pick up the gleam of a long, silver diamondback lying in the road. We would stop and kill it, watching where we stepped when we got out. I collected a cigar box full of rattles one summer. Later I traded them for a knife or something. I often wished I hadn't.

Anyhow, if we got to the second crossing and it was higher than the first, the ritual was to get out, take off your boots and socks, tuck them under your arm, and wade out into the creek a little at a time to check the crossing. It's a wonder one of us didn't drown. The water was always swift, and I could feel it tugging at my legs as we picked our way forward over sharp rocks. Our feet were always tender because you just didn't go barefooted in the Davis Mountains.

If the creek was crossable, we'd return and, with our boots off, try it in the car. Sometimes we'd drown out right there in the middle of the boiling creek in the middle of the night; Roy cussing and saying, "Well, I guess we're just gonna have to by God walk tonight." And so, with our boots under our arms, we would pick our way to the other side, wipe our feet off as best we could, force our boots on over wet socks, and walk the rest of the way to the house.

Or, if we got to the second crossing and it was obvious it was too deep and too dangerous to wade or attempt to cross, we simply turned the car off, stretched out as best we could, and went to sleep. We'd wake at the first light and the creek would be down or Wade would be on the other side with the pickup ready to help us cross. Always they came looking for one another if either failed to show up. When Limpia flooded, you could hear it from Wade's and Roy's front porch. It made a rushing, roaring sound as it tumbled rocks and debris along.

Roy finally traded his Plymouth off after the axle snapped on the way home one night. He'd pulled to the side of the road, found some bailing wire in his trunk, shored the axle with something, wired it, and made it back to town the following Monday to trade for a new one.

As I got older, they let me live in the white bunkhouse out back. It had a small, square cement porch that faced the barn and Limpia Creek to the south. Sometimes after supper I would take my chair and chewing tobacco out onto the porch and sit there in the twilight, listening to coyotes along Limpia or bullbats whumping past in the darkness. The horses would be clattering around the rocks in the corrals looking for cake cubes behind the feed trough.

After I got my driver's license—I got a special permit at fourteen so I could drive to school—I'd ease off by myself on Saturday afternoons in my old pickup and head into Alpine to spend some time with my girl. Whenever I did, I always stopped at Musquiz Creek on the way in.

Musquiz came out of a little mesa alongside the Fort Davis-Alpine road near an old stage stop. It ran freshwater year round and had several huge cottonwoods along the edge of a deep, cold, spring-fed pool about thirty yards off the road. The pool was out of sight from the road and was always crystal clear. You could see perch swimming ten or fifteen feet down. I would park my old pickup, crawl the fence, walk down to the pool, peel off my clothes, step onto the edge of a large tree root that grew along the bank, dive in, and swim in that ice-cold water for fifteen or twenty minutes. Finally I'd get out and sit on the root in the sun until I was dry. Then I'd slip my clothes on and head into Alpine.

After I dropped my girl off on Saturday night, I'd stop at a little all-night cafe on a hill west of Alpine for a piece of pie and a cup of coffee, all to the accompaniment of such melodic masters as Acuff, Tubbs, Heap, and Cash. Finished, I stuck my hat back on my head, paid my check, climbed into the pickup and started the fifty-mile drive back to the ranch.

I rode those nights with the windows down, the pickup bed rattling, my arm hung out the window, hat pushed back on my forehead, chugging along the deserted Alpine-Fort Davis road. The night air was always fresh. Every once in awhile I stuck my head out the window and yelled. No reason, really. And if I needed to pee, I stopped and did— could probably have stood there alongside the road until sunup, and no one would have come by. Usually I'd get back to the ranch around three in the morning, then spend the next day repairing water gaps or digging postholes or fixing flats, endless jobs all.

30

Wade and Roy eventually offered me the opportunity to stay and work the ranch with them, as they had my father. They were in their late fifties when my father got there just out of college. Being lean and tough from years and years of hard work, Wade and Roy just kept on working and finally my father saw the ranch wouldn't support them and his family too, so he parted friends and wound up with a small farm in New Mexico after the war.

I declined, too, knowing their offer was genuine, knowing all the while they were going to live to be a hundred, knowing they were where they were born to be and the place still might not support another family.

Thus it was I said my good-byes one Fall after several summers on their ranch, college-bound in search of the Great American Dream, following what I took to be progress toward some future nirvana, knowing full well the real money was Out There. We shook hands by the front gate. Wade smiled, sort of, and said, "Well, this ol' country'll still be here when you get back." I smiled, slapped him on the shoulder, and drove off into society's mainstream; adapting quickly to the latest dance and finding it fashionable to discuss my misfortune at having missed the first part of the rock era, stuck—as I'd shouted once after a stocking-footed bronc rolled me into the side of a corral—on that Godforsaken, rattlesnake-infested pile of rocks with two tireless old men intent on working me to death.

Laughter, another drink, graduation, job, jammed freeways, marriage, mortgage, family, city air and I found myself slipping away each year to visit the ranch for a day or two as he'd prophesied, glad to open a barbed-wire gate for them as they drove down to feed a bunch of heifers or to check the float on one of their mountain troughs. They'd inquire as to my family's health and allow as how I was getting too fat and that if I had a couple of months, they could do something about it. We would laugh about that. Late evening and I would putter around the saddle shed or barn, leaning against the graying corrals, recalling times when I had enough energy after a hard day's work to climb the game trail in back of the house and sit on the rim of that huge mesa overlooking the desert, watching a sunset, or some pickup twenty or thirty miles away sending up little spurts of dust into the twilight.

There were no more broncs or warriors or roundups or wild cattle. There remained only mountains and myths and fences and a handful of old ones like Wade and Roy. Even into the Fifties you could still work with an old one or two, or smirk at their funny walk or Sunday hats that looked like they'd just been taken out of the box and jammed on their heads—nothing like the meticulously steamed and curled and feathered and droop-shaped costume-crown that adorns the Southwest's pickup-driving, CM-listening, dance hall-stepping, boot-wearing subculture.

Subsequent years and I noticed, as I would pass through the country on a weekend, that the old ones had thinned or disappeared completely from the streets of those little West Texas towns. And it dawned on me one day I'd worked alongside two survivors of a world that would never again be; a world of soogans and canvas bedrolls and rocky ground and tired heads on saddle pillows, of starlit mornings and mesquite coals and scalding coffee and the rattle of chuck wagon pans, of range-killed beef tallow-fried and red beans and sourdough biscuits, of stiff ropes and stout broncs and the pop of saddle leather on crisp autumn mornings; of deft heelers and branding fires and running irons and rangy yearlings with unnotched ears, of strength-sapping rides and eighteen-hour days and bone-chilling downpours, of bootheels on lonely lineshack floors and the jingle of spurs and the whine of Manila around slick snubbing posts.

Theirs had been a tough world. And they were tough men. Another decade slipped by, and my grandmother called when Wade went into the hospital for the last time with pneumonia. She said, "Mac, you need to call him."

I promised her I would, knowing full well he was going to get up out of that hospital and go back to the ranch where he belonged.

A few days later my father called with the news. I never told my grandmother I didn't call. She'd known Wade wasn't going to make it. How, I don't know. They were both cut from the same mold, though. She'd come to Texas in a covered wagon.

I packed that evening for Wade's funeral and left my suburb with its city air and topless bars and twenty-four-hour hamburger joints, traveling Highway Ninety south to Del Rio before turning west towards the Davis Mountains, relaxing then as the cars thinned and the air grew drier and the bar ditch deer gave way to jackrabbits. I liked night travel; think, in some way, it reminded me of those late Saturday returns to their ranch when I was young and full of energy and heady with the lingering perfume of an evening date, times when I thought little of bills or weight or life insurance.

I crossed the Pecos River and pushed west towards Dryden for gas, a late cup of coffee at Sanderson and on towards Marathon until the mountains crept into view, silent cathedrals lying majestically in the Texas moonlight, unsullied, their peaks silhouetted by the occasional glow of a thunderhead hanging in the northwest sky behind them. I rolled the window down and cleansed my lungs, savoring the cool air and the fragrance; thinking of Wade and Roy.

They'd both had vision, as did many of the old ones who settled the rich, grama-covered mountains still considered by many as the best grazing land in Texas; settled it when Apache memories lingered in the Barrillas and Guadalupes and Chisos and Davis and Van Horn ranges. They'd told me of an Indian jogging a horse down in an exhibition near Pecos, Texas. I believed them. They never lied.

Still, it was the little things that kept coming back to me as I sat immobile on some exhaust-shrouded freeway, things like why you didn't load your range up during a good year or kill the bull snake hanging around the barn or kept a baby calf between you and its mother while you doctored it; things like why you didn't ride into a bank-full draw or use spurs on a good horse or throw your bailing wire away or found buffalo grama along the old Overland Route (stage horses carried the seeds in their manes and tails); things like how to pull a bronc into you when you mounted, tell time by the sun, plait a tie-down in your rope, work a pen of cattle, clamp a horseshoe nail, oil a windmill, appreciate a summer shower, and see if a pair of boots was well made (check the shank pegs).

Roy, they said, never recovered really the last time he broke his hip. He had to use a walker to get around. But when you're ninety years old and near blind and deaf, the walker probably helped him keep out of trouble. He'd gone into the hospital when it got so he could hardly walk. He wanted to see if they could fix his hip. They couldn't and said he was going to require care. Aunt Dot asked him what he wanted to do, and Roy said, "I'd rather stay in the hospital than a nursing home." So she had gone to the hospital administrator and negotiated a rate with him so Roy could stay in the hospital. That's where he spent the last nine months of life after ninety-some-odd years outside. He couldn't hear and was almost blind at the end.

They would take his hand and spell out in his palm the name of the person who was there to visit him. He would always acknowledge them and say hello, and thank them for coming by. Several times the nurses and doctors thought he was going to die when his blood pressure dropped and they would gather round, but something inside him refused to give up, and he would grab hold and come back again. This went on for about nine months while they spoon fed him tapioca and Jell-O and things he could chew easily. He had no teeth and had trouble using his false ones. The nurses helped him to the bathroom, bathed him regularly, and took care of him. He didn't give them any trouble. He hung on as long as he could.

Sometimes, if the sunlight was just right, he could see the outline of a tree outside his hospital window. If the wind blew hard, the tree would sway and Roy would look out and say, "Is the wind blowing? I think I see the tree moving." And the nurse would tell him it was. Finally one morning, two years after Wade died, he just didn't wake up. They called us all again to come.

After Roy's funeral, I drove out to the ranch for a last

look around. Their old house seemed quiet, peaceful. I left, then stopped for a last look at the Barrillas before I pulled onto the blacktop. I knew it would probably be the last time any of us would ever travel those eleven miles of dirt road to that ranch house. I noticed the slopes looked good. A breeze stirred the grass alongside the road as shadows covered the mountains, filling the canyons. Tufts of side oats and blue grama swayed gently beneath a long fence that disappeared into the distance, its posts hand-tamped and arrow-straight. Somewhere a calf bawled, and the deep, haunting cry of the bullbat mingled with the twilight.

I imagined Roy sitting on their porch, anticipating a shower as the evening breezes tugged at his gray hair, recalling some roundup or horse or moment when youthful energy surged through his hard frame, laboring alongside Wade through the desert summers and the Panhandle winters to keep their cattle alive and make their payments.

But they and those like them were all gone now, their land and lifeblood long since sold to developers or investors or lawyers—financial jackals all waiting for the old ones to fall.

I stared for several minutes, knowing the link had been severed. All that remained were memories, rare memories to be triggered by the creak of a windmill, the grip of a callused hand, the squeak of saddle leather; memories to recall for my sons when they were old enough to understand.

The End

Above: Copy Cat, a government remount stallion, was purchased by the Reid brothers during the late Thirties after the calvary discontinued its remount service. The Reids raised, broke, and sold horses to the calvary during the Depression to keep their ranch going. The government furnished stallions for the ranchers.

Below: A descendant from the Copy Cat bloodline three decades later (1971). The Reids kept mares from the Copy Cat bloodline to raise horses for ranch use. Child at right is Russell McAfee IV, great-great nephew of Florence "Happy" Reid, Wade Reid's first wife.

The Interviews

Pages

1-19   Roy Reid, 1886-1977. Corroborated with interviews from Wade Reid, 1888-1974.

20-28   Roy Reid, 1886-1977. Corroborated with interviews from Beau McCutcheon, Jr., 1904-1980.

28-31   *Italics: From an interview with West Texas historian Jack Scannell, Professor of History, Midland College, Midland, Texas. When journalist Barry Scobee came to the Davis Mountains to live about 1915, one of the first interviews he conducted was with Frank Heulster, Sr., operator of the Overland's Barrilla Mountain Station, and later the Toyahvale Mail Station. Scobee let Professor Scannell read the notes of his interview.*

32-33   Roy Reid, 1886-1977. Corroborated with interviews with C. K. Smith of Marfa, Texas, and Beau McCutcheon, Jr. 1904-1980.

33-41   Roy Reid, 1886-1977. Corroborated with intertiews with Wade Reid, 1888-1974, and Beau McCutcheon, Jr., 1904-1980.

41-49   Roy Reid, 1886-1977.

49-51   *Italics: Bob Reid, 1885-1976, oldest brother of the late Wade and Roy Reid.*

52-53   Roy Reid, 1886-1977

53-55   *Italics: Mrs. Lou Reid, Alpine, Texas, wife of the late Knox Reid, younger brother of Wade and Roy Reid.*

56-57   Roy Reid, 1886-1977.

57-63   *Italics: Bob Reid, 1885-1976.*

64-68   Roy Reid, 1886-1977.

68-69   *Italics: Myrtle Beights McAfee, 1892-1984, sister-in-law of Wade Reid's first wife, Florence McAfee Reid.*

70-71   Roy Reid, 1886-1977.

71-78   *Italics: Beau McCutcheon, Jr., 1904-1980, son of Beau McCutcheon, Sr.*

79-84   Roy Reid, 1886-1977

84-86   *Italics: Russell McAfee, Jr., 1920-1979, nephew of Florence Reid.*

88-96   Roy Reid, 1886-1977.

PART II

101-131   Russell McAfee, Jr. 1920-1979.

131-133   *Italics: Mrs. Dorothy Reid, 1904-1990, widow of Wade Reid, 1888-1974.*

134-153   Russell McAfee, Jr., 1920-1979.

153-157   *Italics: Mrs. Dorothy Reid, 1904-1990*

159-165   Jack Scannell, Midland, Texas.

165-166   *Italics: Mrs. Dorothy Reid, 1904-1990*

167-174   Jack Scannell, Midland, Texas.

175-178   *Italics: Mrs. Dorothy Reid, 1904-1990*

179-188   Jack Scannell, Midland, Texas.

188-191   *Italics: Mrs. Dorothy Reid, 1904-1990*

PART III

195-241   Author

The Cattlemen

Part IV

Historical pictures of early ranching in the northeastern Davis Mountains, circa 1880 to 1930. Except where names are indicated, the identities of the people in the pictures are unknown.

McCutcheon riders take a few minutes for lunch at the chuckwagon in the northeastern Davis Mountains. The McCutcheons had one of the largest herds in the Davis Mountains during the 1800's—more than 27,000 cattle by one count—and kept full crews working Spring and Fall. At left, a cowboy enjoys a plate of food at the wagon. The two women visiting the chuckwagon were a rarity in that women seldom went with the wagon. Note the Dutch ovens used for camp cooking and the ribs on the spit. Ribs were the quickest item to spoil from a freshly killed beef, and were always cooked first. Cowboys carved ribs off with their knives and ate them whenever they were hungry.

247

Assembling the gather. Davis Mountain cowboys normally gathered cattle in the morning and worked them in the afternoon or the following day if a large herd was gathered.

Working the cattle. Heelers drug calves to two men crews who stretched the calf while another man castrated, marked, dehorned, branded, and vaccinated the calf (after the Franklin vaccine became available).

Catching a mount. Above: Two Davis Mountain cowboys named Jim and Ben catch their mounts inside an early pole corral. Pictures were on post cards, a popular item at the turn of the century. At left: Foreman or roper has roped a horse from the remuda and is holding him while a cowboy slips a bridle on.

Top: A two-seat wagon with canopy normally used when traveling long distances. Note suitcase beneath the man's feet in the front seat. Bottom: Buckboards were used by Davis Mountain ranchers before the automobile was introduced.

These photographs were taken in front of the barn at the historic Jeff Ranch in the northeastern Davis Mountains. Man with dish towel around waist is Frank Heulster, Jeff Ranch cook. Wagons like this were used on ranches in the Davis Mountains at the turn of the Twentieth Century.

252

An early Davis Mountain cowboy washes his son alongside a mountain spring. Circa late 1800's.

Lineshack family and riders somewhere in the northeastern Davis Mountains. Circa late 1800's.

Early pictures of Davis Mountain women. Note side saddle below. Circa late 1800's, early 1900's.

Many early couples from the Davis Mountain ranching community were married in Fort Davis. Here a newly married couple emerges from what is thought to be the first Presbyterian Church in Fort Davis. Circa late 1800's, early 1900's.

Early couples in the Davis Mountains often rode and picnicked on Sundays, work permitting. Circa late 1800s.

The Cattlemen

A young boy, probably with his father and probably a McCutcheon family member or relative, draw water during a Fall afternoon near a lineshack somewhere in the northeastern Davis Mountains. Circa early 1900's.

Above: Young cowboy at far left is Roy Reid. Fourth from right is Wade Reid. Other cowboys pictured are unknown but probably were riders for the McCutcheon ranches located in the northeastern Davis Mountains. Below: Roy Reid, center, and Wade Reid at right. Identity of the other cowboy is unknown. Circa 1910-1915.

Above: The Reid's ranchhouse, rebuilt and finished with rock following the 1930 earthquake. Circa 1931 or 1932.
Below: The Reid Ranch headquarters as it appeared in 1971.

Index

Abilene, Texas, 33
Acuff, Roy, 235
Adair, John, (see also JA ranch), 5,7,8
Adams, Don, 102, 148
Addison (Bill and Maude), 80, 107, 116, 118, 119, 120, 147, 148, 223
Addison, L.W., 64
Aguja, Canyon, 23
Airedales, 50, 51
Albuquerque, New Mexico, 50
Alpine, Texas, 22, 27, 33, 37, 39, 41, 44, 45, 45, 47, 53, 64, 56, 66, 67, 69, 79, 89, 93, 97, 101, 117, 135, 148, 155, 165, 166, 181, 182, 195, 224, 232, 234, 235
Alpine Cowboys, 232
Alpine Drug Store, 149
Alpine High School, 195
Alvarado, Joe, 167, 189
Amarillo, Texas, 5, 6, 7, 13, 57, 92
American Herford Breeders Association, 146
American Legion, 141, 232
Angel (a horse), 132
Antelope, 8, 13
Apaches (see also Indians), 21, 29, 30, 31, 115, 136, 203, 224
Arizona, 40
Army, 30, 45, 47, 54, 82, 83, 84
Arrowheads, 217
Astros, 178
Aubrey (a roper), 66
Austin, Texas, 188

Balmorhea, Texas, 23, 40, 57, 62, 64, 65, 67, 73, 74, 84, 101, 105, 181, 223
Bankhead Highway, 101
Barbara's Point, 195
Barbed Wire, 8
Barrilla Canyon, 28, 45, 91, 107, 109, 115, 116, 120, 137, 213, 251
Barrilla Mountains, 28, 39, 40, 44, 59, 105, 109, 121, 137, 160, 195, 228, 238
Barrilla Pasture, 91, 109
Barrilla Stage Stop, 29, 30
Barrilla Springs, 28, 29, 45, 197, 213
Bears, Black (see also Grizzlies), 13, 51, 74, 75, 76
Beard(a man), 40
Beef, Canning, 103, 117, 118
Bell, Jimmie Tom, 88, 101, 134
Bell, Maggie Jo, 101
Bencomo
　Alfonso, 137
　Gregorea, 137
　Chone, 137
Berkley, Senator, 101
Bible, 6
Big Bend (see also Chisos Mountains, Rosillas Mountians, Devil's Canyon), 22, 37
Big Boy (a horse), 101, 134, 138
Big Bluff (country), 35

Black Grama, 101
Black Hawks (see also Peregrine Falcons) 216, 217
Blackleg (see also Franklin Vaccine), 62, 92, 101
Blizzards, 8, 11, 16
Bloomington, Illinois, 67, 69, 79, 80
Blowflies (see also Screwworms), 105
Blye, Pat, 37
Bobby Socks (a horse), 115, 124, 145, 158, 198, 199
Bobcat (see also Lynx), 50
Bonus (Land. See also Squatters), 39
Boy Scout Ranch, 25, 42
Brad, Texas, 6
Brewster County, 101
Briggs and Stratton (motors), 159, 205, 227, 228
Brisco County, Texas, 4
British Army (horse buyer), 89
Broncs (see also Chevy, Jiggs, Strawberry), 37, 38, 77, 78
Brownfield, Texas, 20
Buckboard, 251
Buffalo, 13
Buffalo grama, 239
Buffalo hunter, 13, 14
Bullbats, 234, 241
Bulldogging, 67
Bull snakes, 209, 201, 202
Bunchgrass, 50
Burnham, 35
Burros, 22, 23, 34, 50
Byrd, Tom, 16

Caldwell, Lee, 46
Camp, Doctor Jim, 41, 42
Camp Meeting, 142
Camp Tub, 107, 109, 115, 170, 213, 214
Candy (a paint horse), 132
Canning, 103, 118
Canyon, Texas 67, 69
Caprock, The, 5, 7
Carbide Gas (lights), 137, 196
Cargyle Draw, 20
Carlsbad Caverns, New Mexico, 59
Carr, Texas, 68, 69
Carrizo Creek, 30, 40, 95, 106
Carruthers (a roper) 66
Casey, Mr. and Mrs., 142
Casey, Velna 142
Cash (a baseball player), 232
Cash, Johnny, 221
Cavalry, 3, 82, 83, 123, 124, 212
Cavalry horses, 122, 123, 124, 212
Cayonosa, Texas, 67
Chandler, Tom, 232
Chevy (a bucking horse), 85, 86, 87
Chevy Coupe, 68, 261
Chickasay Bob (mares), 82
Chisos Mountains, 34, 35, 224

261

Chloroform (worm medicine), 112, 113, 206
Chuckwagon, 60, 247
Chuckwagon food, 58, 59, 247
Cigarette tax, 101
City Drug Store, 183
Civil War, 3, 4, 5, 29
Clarendon, Texas, 177
Cole Car, 260
Colorado City, Texas, 13
Columbine roses, 50
Comanche moon, 217
Comancheros, 15
Comanches, 6, 13, 21, 30, 217
Confederate Cavalry, 3
Connecticut, 131
Cook, Ranger Thalis, 32
Cooksey, Jim, 66
Cooksey, Pab, 66
Cooling house, 197
Coon, 116, 201, 220
Copy Cat (stud horse), 82, 123, 242
Cotter, Beth, 155
Cotter, Bill, 172
County Line, 68
Cougar (see also Mountain lion), 50
Cowans, 25
Cox, John, 90
Coyotes (an animal), 88, 116, 210, 234
Coyotes (transporters of illegals), 199
Crews (or Cruiz, a boxer), 65
Culp, Frank, 45
Cunningham, Milt, 58

Dallas, Texas, 10, 178
Dark Age (a horse), 132
Davis Mountains, 15, 21, 22, 26, 27, 40, 57, 58,
    74, 83, 95, 146, 176, 196, 219, 225, 233, 238,
    247, 248, 250, 252, 256, 257, 258, 268
DDT, 207, 208, 222
Deepwell, Texas, 147
Del Rio, Texas, 37, 238
Denver, Colorado, 10
Depression (The Great), 14, 24, 78, 79, 80, 81,
    88, 89, 122, 146, 147, 175, 212, 260
Detroit, 68
Devil's Canyon, 35
Dinwiddie, Jim, 45
Dominguez, Alfonso, 146
Dominguez, Fallis, 146
Dorealles (a horse), 124
Droughts, 11, 14, 20, 30, 40, 80, 90, 109, 176,
    224
Duncan, Jim and Rena, 142
Dunn, Nelson, 179
Dunn, Sam, 52, 179
Durham (cattle), 11
Dutch ovens, 50, 247

EQ335 (worm medicine), 206, 215
Earthquake, 88, 200
Eaton, Doctor, 159, 167
Eclipse (pasture) 62
Edna (a woman), 196
Electrolux (ice box), 102, 156
El Paso, Texas, 22, 37, 41, 49, 53, 74, 80, 144,
    175, 186
England, 5, 8, 131

English Blood Hound, 76
English (pasture), 28, 44, 116, 120, 132, 167, 169
Escondidas, 59
Espy, Clay, 74, 75
Espy, Joe, 18, 24, 74
Estes, Billy Sol, 145
Europe, 3
European parapets, 30
Evans, Worth, 144

Farmer, Texas, 6
Fatima (horse), 6
Fedral Reserve Banks, 12
Federal Reserve Board, 12
Feldman, Cal, 37
Ficklin, Ben, 28
Fitzgerald, Johnny, 132, 189
Fonville (Canyon), 42, 44, 45, 80, 90, 107, 108,
    109, 116, 120, 140, 170, 213, 214
Fonville, John, 44, 120
Fonville, Tub, 115
Ford "jitney" (see also Model A, C, K, T), 104,
    118, 231, 232, 260
Fort Davis, Texas, 18, 22, 24, 26, 28, 29, 32, 33,
    37, 39, 67, 71, 74, 101, 137, 141, 160, 167,
    188, 198, 231, 257, 268
Fort Davis-Alpine Road, 235
Fort Davis Bank, 24, 71
Fort Davis Merchantile (see also Union Mer-
chantile), 24, 32
Fort Davis-Toyahvale Road, 25, 32
Fort Reardon, Texas, 7
Fort Reno, Oklahoma, 122
Fort Stockton, Texas, 24, 26, 32, 38, 40, 49, 65,
    67
Fort Sumner, New Mexico, 49
Fort Worth, Texas, 4, 80, 82, 89, 210
Fort Worth-Kansas Railroad, 7
France, 5
Franklin Vaccine, 61, 91, 92, 249
Frazier Canyon, 23, 22
Frazier, Walt, 32, 33
French harp, 16
Fryer, Bill, 141
Frying Pan Ranch, 45, 58, 59
Fulton, 148

Gage, 36, 37, 39
Gage Ranch, 36, 37
Galveston, Texas, 29
Gann, George, 24
Garcia, Manuel, 190, 198
Garden Trap, 146
Gardner (a man), 9
Gato (a horse), 132, 167
Generator, 103-105
Gentry, Mrs., 148
German(s), 3, 72
Germany, 29, 94
Goat roping, 68
Goodnight, Charles, 5, 7, 13
Graef, Walter, 65
Graham, Texas, 6
Grama grass, 43, 238, 241
Grass fires, 22, 219
Grasshoppers, 14, 20
Green-broke horses, 128

Gray stud (a horse), 27
Grizzlies (see also Silvertip Bears), 46, 49, 50, 51, 195
Guadalupe Mountains, 239
Grouse, 13
Gusterol (a man), 47

Hawks (see also Peregrine Falcons), 216, 217
Hayter, Joe, 59, 148
Headwater, 44, 90, 108, 110, 111, 158, 224, 226, 228, 229
Headwater Springs, 108, 226, 227, 235
Heap (a singer), 235
Herfords, 11
Heulster, Frank, Jr., 28, 48, 136, 252
Heulster, Frank, Sr., 27, 28, 29, 30, 31, 197
Heulster, Fritz, 28
Heulster, Leo, 28
Highball (a horse), 123, 132, 212
Highland Herford Association, 146
Highway (80), 101
Highway 90 South, 238
Hill, Doctor, 173, 183, 184
Holland, Hotel, 54
Holstein (cows), 63
Homesteaders (Panhandle), 7
Hooltz (Brothers), 60
Hord, Clarence and Mildred, 148
Horn flies, 207
Horseshoeing, 205
Horse stealing (see also Horsethief Canyon), 33
Horsethief Canyon, 33, 72, 195
Hot Wells, Texas, 46, 56, 57
Houston, Texas, 32, 136, 178
Hovey, Texas, 56, 62, 64, 72, 80, 137, 138, 148
Huff, Lee, 26
Hutchinson, 6

Ikard (a man), 11
Ikens, Bill, 38
Ikey (a man), 64
Illinois, 4, 7, 67, 69
Indians (see also Apaches, Comanches), 6, 8, 13, 15, 21, 22, 29, 30, 31, 50, 136, 217, 238
Indian Springs, 29, 138, 147

JA Ranch, 5, 7, 8, 61
Jeff Davis County (see also Davis Mountains, Fort Davis), 101
Jeff Ranch, 21, 22, 24, 27, 28, 29, 30, 32, 39, 45, 48, 56, 70, 71, 80, 81, 82, 91, 92, 94, 109, 113, 122, 134, 135, 136, 137, 146, 176, 190, 195, 196, 197, 198, 199, 113, 252
Jigs (a horse), 128, 129, 130, 131, 132
John, Banker, 16, 17, 18
Jones, Bill, 138
Jones, Frank, 74
Jones, George (Asa), 66, 67

Kansas City, 47, 57, 138
Keesey, Whit, 24
Keesey and Company Store, 24
Kelly, Tyrone, 24
Kentucky, 4, 82
Killough, Annette, 136
Killough, John, 70, 71, 80, 135, 136, 137, 138, 146, 182

Killough, Lee, 70
Killough, Myrtle, 136
Killough, Nellie Lee (see also Nellie Lee Mulloy), 11
Kimball County, 39
King, Harold, 37
King Ranch, 120
Kingston, Bill, 32, 102
Kingston, Joe, 56
Kingston Ranch, 24
Koral (worm medicine), 93, 206
Kountz, Al, 61
Kress, Texas, 64

Land (leasing), 4-6, 23, 34
Land (patented), 20, 188
La Grange, Texas, 70, 71, 196
Lange, Kurt, 97, 154
Lee (a rodeo producer), 85, 86, 87
Lewis (a man), 26
Lightning (a horse), 170, 171
Limpia Canyon, 24, 28, 33, 37, 101, 142, 232, 233
Limpia Creek, 23, 24, 28, 30, 31, 32, 142, 148, 195, 198, 231, 233, 234
Limpia Hotel, 24, 141
Limpia Post Office, 32
Lockhausen Canyon (headwater), 40, 44, 81, 90, 104, 108, 109, 110, 111, 112, 113, 114, 120, 130, 131, 158, 165, 170, 172, 224, 225, 226, 228, 229
Lockhausen Flats, 93
Lockhausen Trap, 229
Longhorns, 5, 11, 196
Loraine, Texas, 68
Los Angeles, California, 199
Lubbock, Texas, 20, 52, 179,
Lynx, 50

Mac (a horse), 123, 212
Mackenzie (General), 13, 14
Mayfield, Dave, 68
Manuel (a roundup cook), 59, 60
Marathon, 33, 34, 238
Marfa, Texas, 22, 64, 93, 94, 144, 145, 161, 166, 171
Mary Lou (a paint horse), 125
Max (a trapper), 49, 50, 51,
Maxine (a paint horse), 125, 132, 212
McAfee, Agnes Pearl, 69
McAfee, Florence (Happy), 66, 69, 70, 88, 102, 135, 137, 148, 152
McAfee, Maggie, 69, 93
McAfee, Myrtle, 76, 77, 78, 191
McAfee, Russell, Jr., 67, 85, 86, 87, 101, 134, 191
McAfee, Russell, Sr., 68, 69
McAfee, Russell, IV, 242
McCamey, Texas, 70
McCutcheons, 21, 22, 23, 24, 25, 26, 31, 33, 45, 70, 71, 196, 247,258, 259
  Beau, Sr., 22-28, 32, 33, 39, 42, 44, 70, 71, 72, 74, 75, 76, 91, 92
  Beau, Jr., 71-78
  Bennett, 23, 24, 70, 80, 142
  Jeff, 21, 22, 42, 91, 146

263

index3

Jim, 23, 24, 40, 41, 42, 70, 95
Lee (Mrs.), 28, 48, 57, 71, 136, 168, 196
Mallie, 177
Marie, 70
William, 21, 22, 23, 42
Willis, 21, 22, 23, 25, 32, 45, 70, 142, 176, 177
McDonald (a baseball player), 232
McElroy, Jim, 56, 142
McIntyre's Store, 34
McKenzie (a young man), 49
McKnight, Bob, 94, 190
McKnights (family), 71
McSpadden, George and Diamond, 90, 161
Methodist Church, 70
Mexico, 10, 21, 30, 32, 34, 72, 96, 136, 216, 217
Mexican steers, 34
Meyer, Sal, 38
Midland, Texas, 26, 28, 182
Midland College, 28
Miles City (saddle), 93
Millan, Frank (see also German), 72
Miller (a man), 39, 40, 43, 44
Miller, Aubrey, 24
Miller, Keesey, 37
Miller, Ross, 33
Miller Spring, 41, 45, 70, 90, 121, 228
Miller, Walter, 24
Mission, Texas, 85
Mitchells (Joe and Mackie), 72, 146
Model A Ford, 106, 120, 140, 147
Model T, C, K, A (Ford), 260
Monahans, Texas, 20, 164
Money panics, 11, 16, 20
Mountain Lions (see also panther, cougar), 35, 36, 138, 196
M-System (grocery), 148
Mules, 33, 37, 61
Mulloy, Nellie Lee (see also Nellie Lee Killough), 71, 136, 196
Mulloy, Pat, 70, 71, 94, 196, 198
Murphey, Pat, 37
Murpheysville, Texas, 148
Musquiz Canyon, 33, 235
Musquiz Creek, 235
Mustangs, 8, 9, 75

New Mexico, 20, 45, 46, 49, 56, 58, 198, 236
Albuquerque, 50
Las Vegas, 46, 47
Put Mountains, 49
Rancho De Taos, 46, 49
Santa Fe, 49, 64
Taos, 47, 49
Nigger Baby (a horse), 138, 139
North (Union), 5
Norton, Charlie, 64

Oates, Charlie, 60, 76, 79
O'Dell (a man), 26
Odessa, Texas, 27, 38, 71, 186
Ohio, 14
Oklahoma, 84, 122, 170, 213
Old Lake, 90, 107, 108, 116, 170

Olive, Doc, 56
Overland (stage), 28, 239

Palo Duro Canyon, 5, 8, 13
Palomas Spring, 54
Panhandle, 4-9, 11, 15, 20, 21, 37, 38, 43, 45-47, 57, 61, 67, 82, 83, 96, 123, 155, 180, 232, 241
Panthers (see also cougar, mountain lions), 35, 36, 138, 196
Parker, Quanah, 6
Pecos, Texas, 20, 25, 26, 38, 41, 47, 48, 57, 59, 67, 101, 145, 162, 210, 238
Pecos County, 57
Pecos River, 40, 59, 144, 238
Permian Basin, 20
Peregrine (falcons), 216, 217
Pete (a driller), 226-229
Phantom Lake, 59
Pheasant, 13
Pine (a studhorse), 122, 123
Pistol(s) 35, 36, 74
Plymouth (car), 231, 233, 234
Polecats, 88
Postcard, 261, 267
Popham, Al, 57
Popham, Francis, 57, 58, 62, 120
Powell Ranch, 74
Presidio, County, 46
Price (land), 46
Prickley pear, 80, 81, 157
Prissy (a paint mare), 123, 132, 212
Production Credit Association (PCA), 90, 143, 144, 145, 146, 166, 177, 207
Presidio, Texas, 46
Put Mountains, 49
Pyote, Texas, 38

Quail, 13, 201
Quitaque Breaks, 10

Racer (snake), 201
Rain (importance of), 224, 225, 226
Rangers (baseball team), 178
Ranger (Felix Cook), 125
Ranger (Texas), 10, 11, 41
Rattlesnakes, 105, 139, 197, 198, 200, 233
Rawls, Bobby, 89
REA, 105
Redbone (hunting) hounds, 74, 76
Redding, L.C., 68
Reid
  Bob, 4, 15, 46, 49, 57, 58, 59, 60, 61, 62, 63, 66, 79, 155
  Dorothy (Mrs. Wade), 95, 131-133, 154-158, 175-178, 188-191, 203
  George, 4, 6, 15, 18, 20
  Grandma, 15
  Grandpa, 7, 13, 15
  Knox, 15, 47, 53, 152, 155, 182
  Lou, 53, 54, 55, 152, 155, 182
  Mama, 6, 7, 14, 16, 141, 155
  Roy, 3-242
  Sid, 4, 6, 15
  Ted, 15, 69

264

Tola, 15, 48
Wade, 3-242
Warner (Nig), 15, 155
Remount Service, 83, 124
Remuda, 37, 72, 250
Repine (a horse), 122
Revolution (Mexico), 72
Reynolds Brothers, 46
Riggs, Ann, 39
Riggs, Dick, 25, 39, 40, 41, 42, 59
Riggs, Monroe, 39, 41
Riggs, Raneck, 39
Riggs, Tom, 39
Rincon, The, 44, 107, 115, 213, 214
Ringtail, 201
Rio Grande, 49
Roadrunner, 201, 210
Rock Creek, 4, 18
Rodeos, 67, 85, 87
Rodeo Stock, 85
Rodgers, Frank, 40
Rodriguez, Melly, 172, 195, 220, 221
Rodriguez, Pablo, 88, 101, 102
Rooney Pasture, 127, 195
Roosevelt, Franklin D., 89, 90, 143, 144, 154
Rope Corral, 36, 72, 250
Rosillos Mountains, 34, 35
Ross, Roy, 48
Roy (a horse), 132
Roundup, 36, 61, 62, 71, 72, 92, 248, 249
Roundup Wagon, 72, 92, 247
Rowdy (a blood hound), 76
Rural Agriculture Credit Association (RACC),
   89, 144

Saddle horses (see also remuda), 58
Salt Lake, 40
San Angelo, Texas, 224
Sandia (The), 60
Santa Fe, New Mexico, 49, 64
Santa Fe country, 8
Santa Fe Railroad, 49, 64, 138
Santa Fe Ranch, 46, 49
Saragosa, 60, 62, 65
Saragosa Cattle Company, 40
Scannell, Jack, 28-31, 155, 156, 159-165,
   167-174, 179-188, 191
Scannell, Miles, 155
Schafter Lake, 20
School (one room) Building, 15, 16
Schulenberg, Texas, 82
Scotland, 5
Screwworms, 35, 112, 113, 114, 116, 206, 207,
   214, 215, 219, 229, 140
Scout Ranch, 42
Seminole, Texas, 20
Seven (7) Ranch, 25, 70, 91, 92
Seven (7) Springs Ranch, 25, 70
Sewell, Colonel, 29
Short (Ranch), 62
Sibley, Sid, 52
Sidegoats grama, 95, 241
Sidesaddle, 255
Silvertip grizzlies, 49, 50, 51
Silverton, Texas, 4, 15, 16, 18, 49
Slate (writing), 16

Slaughter, Colonel, 5
Smith, Terrell, 80
Snyder, Texas, 147
Solias "Sly" Cattle, Land, and Livestock
   Company, 46, 58
Son-of-a-gun stew, 59, 118
Sonny (a dog), 198
Sotol, 80, 147
South (Civil War), 5
Southern (Civil War) Lines, 3
Southern Pacific Railroad, 31, 182
Southside Bluff, 112
Spaniard Stock (horses), 8
Spanish American War, 11
Spanish Flu, 47
Spanish Peaks, 107, 115
Spot (a horse), 134
Spraying, 207, 208
Sproul, Mack, 74
Squatters, 15, 39, 46
Stagecoach, 30, 31
Stage horses, 239
Stage route, 28
Stage station, 115
Stallion (wild), 9
Stanley Steamer (car), 71, 74, 75, 76, 95
Star Mountain, 22, 24, 42, 142
Stark, Barney, 20, 35, 36, 37
Steel Dust (horses), 33
Strawberry (a horse), 127
Stroud, Jim, 34, 35, 36
Stuckler (a Deputy), 41
Sul Ross, 179, 217
Swallows, 201
Sweetwater, Texas, 47, 48, 64
Swine Flu, 49
Swisher County, Texas, 4

Taos, New Mexico, 46, 49
Tascosa, 57
Taylor, Texas, 23
Telegraph Line, 37, 52
Tennessee, 3, 82
Texas A and M, 118, 230
Texas and Southwestern Cattle Raisers
   Assoication, 146
Texas Land Commissioner, 188
Texas Pacific Railroad, 33
The Cattleman (Magazine), 207
Thoroughbred Horses, 82, 83
Ticks, 207
Tornillo Creek, 34
Toyah Creek, 40
Toyahvale, Texas, 24, 28, 37, 66, 101, 102
Tub-on-Top, 108, 109, 114, 115, 126, 170, 213,
   214
Tubbs, Ernest, 235
Tule Creek, 5, 8, 13
Tulia, Texas, 4, 47, 64, 82, 178

U-cattle, 62
U-country, 45
U-fence, 43, 108
Union (Civil War), 3
Union Merchantile (see Union Trading
   Company), 24

Union Trading Company, 24, 32
U-Ranch, 42, 43, 46, 57, 58, 59, 60, 61, 62, 63,
    107, 120
Uranium, 160

VH Ranch, 24
Valley View, Texas, 68
Van Horn Mountains, 238
Vermont, 131
Victoria, Texas, 21, 22
Volstead Act, 47
Vorhees (Major), 122

Wagons, 251, 252, 253, 254
Wallace, Judge, 57
Wall Street, 12
Walsh, Bob, 210
WBAP, 210
Weatherby, Judge, 33
West Texas State, 69
Wetbacks, 90, 109, 199
Whitetail deer, 75
White Steamer (car), 95
Wichita Falls, Texas, 14, 134
Wild cattle, 112, 229
Wild horses (see also Mustangs), 83
Wild (columbine) roses, 50
Wild Rose Pass, 142, 195
Williams, Ben, 148
Williams, R. C., 70, 140
Wilson, President, 11
Winchester (rifle), 10, 41
Winnsboro, Texas, 69
Wise County, Texas, 4, 6
Wolf, 50
Wood Canyon, 107, 109, 115, 213
Word (a young man), 69
Word (a young lady), 94
Word, Harry, 69
Word, C. T. Ranch, 15, 45, 58, 62
World War I, 49, 82
World War II, 127, 160, 187
Wright, Doc, 61, 62, 63, 135

XIT, 4, 61

Yellow House Canyon, 8
Yellow Tub, 109, 112, 115
York, Tom and Forest, 197, 198
Young County, Texas, 6

Zuck and Zule, 47